UNEXPECTED GRACE

A Journey of Love,
Loss, and Peace

Deborah Gilder

UNEXPECTED GRACE
A Journey of Love, Loss, and Peace

Book cover by Nathan Dasco

Author photograph by Jessica Lowman

ISBN: 978-0-9991067-0-9 (Print)
ISBN: 978-0-9991067-1-6 (Ebook)

Library of Congress Control Number: 2017913948

Printed in the United States of America by Deborah Gilder

Contents

Dedication

For Gregg

And all who walked this path with us and were touched by his joyous spirit.

~ 1 ~

The Other Beginning

I awake with a start. Something's not right. Am I dreaming? Crinkling my forehead, still drunk with sleep, I slit my eyes in the dark room and try to grasp what's wrong.

"Uhh!" *What's that?* I hear something, but I can't place it. "Uhhhh," I hear again.

Still in a fog, I hoist myself up on one elbow. Squinting, I roll over to look at Gregg. All I see is his indented pillow and ruffled blanket. Did he hear it too? Maybe he's checking it out.

"Gregg?" I call out tentatively, looking for reassurance. Silence.

"Gregg!" I say it louder this time. My heart quickens as I awake, trying to put the pieces together.

Another moan reverberates through the room.

"Where are you? Are you OK?"

"No," he mutters. I hear the agony in his voice.

I propel myself into a sitting position, instantly more alert, but my mind still full of cobwebs. What's wrong with him? As I stumble out of bed, different scenarios pop into my brain. Is he hurt? Sick? Did someone break in? I picture him lying on the ground, his head bloodied. What if someone is in the house? I freeze momentarily, glancing around the room for a makeshift weapon, but nothing looks useful.

Turning back toward the doorway, I decide to take my chances and peek around the corner into the bathroom to find a shape on the floor. There he is, barely visible in the dark, lying naked in a fetal position, clearly in pain. Flipping on the light, aware of the palpitations in my own chest, I stoop down next to him, put my hand on his shoulder, and then his forehead. His body is pale, his skin clammy, his face twisted with inner turmoil. "What's wrong?" I ask. "Are you sick?"

Grimacing, his hands balled up against his belly, he strains to answer, "My stomach is killing me." I vaguely become aware of the fecal smell in the bathroom and wonder if he fell off the commode or if he put himself on the floor. A towel bunched up next to him serves as neither pillow nor cover. While I'm caught in my thoughts, he interjects, "Can you help me back onto the toilet?"

I grab hold of him, and together we work our way up. He sits down and bends over, still holding his folded arms against his midsection.

"Do you feel like throwing up?" I ask, running my hand down his sweat-covered back, trying to assess the situation.

"I have major cramps." He can barely get the words out, rocking his body back and forth, trying to ease his discomfort.

"What did you eat tonight? Maybe something isn't agreeing with you, or you have food poisoning."

"I don't know," he says, scarcely able to talk, "but I feel like crap."

I continue to observe him critically, wondering what I can do to help him feel better, not sure if he just has the flu or some other intestinal something. He groans again, then suddenly sits upright, hands dropping to his lap, causing me to step back. Surprised at this abrupt change in demeanor, I find myself staring into his expressionless face, eyes open wide but unseeing. It's like he just flew out of his body.

My mind works feverishly to make sense of what just happened. The fog vanishes, and panic takes its place. "Gregg?" I call out anxiously.

"Gregg!" My hands are on his shoulders, shaking them. "Are you OK?" He is *not* OK!

"Gregg!" I yell louder with more urgency. He is totally unresponsive.

I shake his shoulders as hard as I dare. Still nothing. The look on his face totally unsettles me. He looks dead! There is absolutely nobody home. He was just talking to me a minute ago!

"Gregg!" I try one more time, feeling my adrenaline kick into full gear. *What do I do? What do I do?* I have to call for help! How can I get the phone and hold him at the same time? I have no choice. I will have to let go and hope he stays there.

Totally beside myself, I take his hand and hook it to the sink, yelling at him to hold on, that I will be right back. I fly around the corner, grab the phone, and am back faster than I knew possible. Amazingly, he is still upright and holding on. I dial 911 with a shaky hand, trying to remember all the rules of protocol and not be hysterical on the phone so that the dispatcher can understand me.

"Nine-one-one," the woman on the phone says. "What is your emergency?"

"I need an ambulance!" I say with forced calm. "Quickly! My husband is sitting on the toilet staring at me, and he is not responding to his name. He just has a blank look on his face!"

"Is he breathing?"

"I don't know!" I search his face for any sign of anything, afraid to let him go. "He's just looking right through me with his eyes open and there is nobody there!" I am aware of the tremors in my voice rising with each response, the phone slippery in my sweaty hand. *This can't be happening!*

"An ambulance is on the way, ma'am. If you have pets, please put them in another room, then unlock your front door and turn on the light."

"I'm afraid to let go of my husband. I don't want him to fall!"

"See if you can gently help him down onto the floor."

"OK, I'll try," I say, not sure how it's going to happen. "I'm going to put the phone down. Please don't go away!" I plead.

"I will be right here," she assures me.

I set the phone on the sink and somehow slide Gregg to the floor without dropping him completely. Once horizontal, he begins to stir. The siren wails in the distance.

"I hear the ambulance! I am going to hang up now," I tell the dispatcher.

I let Gregg know that I've called the ambulance, and help is on the way. He does not protest. "Wipe my ass," He grumbles. I am so grateful that he is among the living again, I'd be happy to kiss his ass. I grab his sweatpants, work them onto his legs, and tell him everything will be OK.

Looking up, I see our dog watching us from the end of the hall. Remembering what I am supposed to do, I jump up, run to unlock the front door, then quickly shepherd him into the back room, closing the door behind me. I return to Gregg. He is still prone and hurting, but at least he is conscious. Suddenly, there is a sharp knock on the door, then the sound of people entering. "Ambulance!" they yell.

"In here!" I shout.

First comes a man, followed by a woman, each dressed in a dark blue uniform, all business, carrying equipment bags.

"What happened?" the man asks, as he sets his bag on the floor and kneels beside Gregg, instantly starting his appraisal.

"I found him on the floor. He's been having severe abdominal pain. And then while he was sitting on the toilet, I thought I lost him. He just went blank and didn't respond to his name. I don't know what's wrong with him!" I float somewhere between objective observer and hysterical wife.

"Don't worry, ma'am. We'll take care of him," he says, lifting an eyelid and shining his flashlight into Gregg's pupil. The woman takes Gregg's blood pressure at the same time. I watch as their purple-gloved hands do their work.

Gregg cooperates—or at least doesn't resist. I am sure he probably just wants some relief. If it takes a trip to the hospital, then so be it. I don't know if he feels better, but I certainly do, having professionals here to help.

I step back as a third EMT rounds the corner with a gurney. The space available in the hallway is tight, but together, they all manage to maneuver Gregg onto it. Once he's on, they roll him toward the front door, stopping long enough for me to give him a quick kiss. "I'll be right behind you!" I assure him, squeezing his hand. He nods at me, and they wheel him to the ambulance.

Closing the door behind them, I lean back on it, letting go of the breath that I didn't know I was holding. My thoughts are still whirling. I can't get Gregg's empty face out of my mind. He obviously didn't die, but he was definitely not in his body either. What *was* that? Whatever happened, it scared the hell out of me.

I let my heart slow down a notch as I stand there a few minutes, then remember our dog, and go let him out of the back room, patting him on the head and telling him his dad will be OK. He stares at me as if trying to discern what important information I am imparting, probably wondering why he got shoved into the back room in the first place. No time to offer more comfort now. I throw on some clothes and head to the hospital.

~ 2 ~

Questions

The emergency room is awash with bright lights. Machines throughout the place bleat out at various pitches. A young doctor sits absorbed behind the large square counter in the middle of the room, staring at a computer, while a few nurses laugh in the far corner of the central workstation. Otherwise, all appears relatively quiet.

The smell of the ER overwhelms me, propelling me back to when I was dragged to the oral surgeon's office to get a tooth pulled as a child. I figured if I cried loud enough and long enough, my mother would call the whole thing off and take me home. It didn't work. Instead, I was subjected to the torture of a dreaded black rubber ether mask and told to breathe deep enough to make a whistle-inside sound. The whole experience left me feeling traumatized and toothless.

The girl behind the glass directs me to Room 5. I am eager to see Gregg, hoping that his pain has eased, or that they at least have given him some drugs. Although the immediate anxiety I felt at home has dissipated somewhat, there is still a wary anticipation roiling around in my stomach. I need someone to tell me what's wrong and to make sense of the scene on the toilet when I thought Gregg might have died. Most of all, I need someone to tell me that he will be OK.

Walking down the corridor, I can't help glimpsing at other patients lying in their beds. I wonder what misfortune brought them here. Did they break a leg? Slice off a finger? Have a heart attack? A nurse pops out of a room ahead and scurries past me toward another hallway, puke pan in hand.

I spot the number 5 and tentatively peek around the curtain, not sure what to expect. Relief washes over me when I see Gregg lying peacefully on the bed. His eyes are closed; he appears to be dozing. His body is covered in white blankets up to his neck with only his left arm visible, an IV stuck in his wrist and a thermometer squeezing his finger. His own personal set of beeping machines plays their syncopated tune beside the bed. He looks so content, I hate to disturb him, but I need to touch him and let him know I'm here.

"Hey Greggy," I say softly, coming alongside the railing, reaching for his hand.

His eyes open and he gives me a weak smile. "Hey, babe."

"Looks like they didn't waste any time hooking you up! How you feeling?"

"A little better, now that I've thrown up," he answers.

"You threw up, too? Ugh! Whatever cootie is in there has got to be out now between pooping and throwing up!" I joke, attempting to lighten the moment. "Did the doctor come in yet?"

"Nope, only nurses."

"Are you feeling sick still?"

"Not really. Just tired."

I begin to fuss over him before even taking off my coat, pushing the hair from his eyes and making sure he is snuggly and warm. It feels chilly in the room. As I fiddle with things, a nurse walks in to check the amount of fluid in the saline bag hanging beside the bed. She smiles at me, and I introduce myself and ask what's going on. She informs me that Gregg not only threw up, he threw up blood, a minor detail he forgot to mention. Maybe he didn't know. Apparently, they are still running tests, and the doctor will be in shortly to talk to us. She asks if we need anything. "I think we're good," I reply. She nods and walks out.

I turn my attention to Gregg, still pondering the blood. His face is pale. It's no wonder, I guess. You can't lose blood from two ends of your body and expect to look rosy. Otherwise, he looks as if he just woke up from a deep sleep. His glasses are on the bedside table, a sign he is not himself, as he likes to wear them at all times when awake.

"Guess we might not be heading to Niagara Falls this weekend with the gang," I say, changing the subject while continuing my silent scrutiny of his body and bearing.

"We'll see," he says, trying to rearrange his IV arm to a more comfortable position. The cord is tangled under the blanket, and I reach over to help him. "Once they figure out what is wrong with me and fix it, I will probably be out of here tomorrow." His unfailing optimism is in full swing.

"Maybe," I reply, unconvinced. "That would certainly be nice, but you'll probably be tired and weak, and you might not feel like driving all the way to New York to party all weekend."

"I already feel so much better than I did at home. I think I just needed to get whatever it was out of my system." Then he adds, "We don't have to decide now."

Nodding in agreement, I say, "Why don't you rest? I will be right here."

For as long as I have known Gregg, he has been a planner. He is always thinking of the next big adventure to go on, the next house to rent, the next vacation destination, the next cabin weekend, the next local gathering of friends and family. This coming weekend is no exception. A couple of friends mentioned they would like to go to Niagara Falls to gamble, and before you know it, Gregg had arranged a weekend with four or five other couples. There are rooms booked, dinner plans scheduled, and good times to be had by all.

I must admit that sometimes the plans get the best of me and I am not always on board 100 percent. If I don't override him occasionally, he would plan every minute of our lives away. Of course, I could choose not to go, which he would be fine with, but then I think whatever he has arranged really could be fun, and I don't want to miss out. So, after I pry myself out of my contrary mood and go, it usually is a blast. Gregg has his reputation as "social planner extraordinaire" intact, and I, once again, lose the opportunity to make my own plan or wait and see what spontaneous event might be fun at the last minute.

It's hard to not get caught up in Gregg's enthusiasm. He moves through life with an easy smile, a contagious laugh, and a very persuasive manner. The poster that says, "Some people ask why, I ask why not?" portrays him to a T. This weekend is no exception. Neither of us even gambles. We have already been to Niagara Falls, and it is now February, so the whole place will probably be frozen. But, as he sees it, any adventure with good friends is an adventure to be a part of.

I glance at the clock on the wall, big hand on the 12, small on the 3. 3:00 a.m. How long does it take to interpret tests anyway? It already seems like we've been here forever. I think of the blood again, not comforted. Hopefully, they are able to figure it out and decide what to do next.

My mind wanders to the past few months as I sit with one eye on Gregg and one on the curtain in case the doctor appears. He has had a persistent toothache; the dentist has been trying to decide if the pain is related to his sinus infection or something else and if the tooth needs to be pulled. Then, on top of that, his back began to hurt along with his stomach. And now this happens. For a guy who is almost never sick, Gregg seems to be having a health crisis.

I throw my coat over me as a makeshift blanket and try to find a way to sleep upright, never my forte, in the uncomfortable chair provided for guests. Finally, a doctor walks in and greets us. We both immediately come to attention. "Hi, I'm Dr. Bansick," he begins, shaking our hands, and then looks directly at Gregg. "Our preliminary findings seem to indicate that you have a bleeding ulcer, but we can't be absolutely sure until we look inside. We would like your permission to do an endoscopy.

It is a procedure where we insert a tube with a little camera on the end down your throat and into your stomach, so that we can see what it looks like. If there's an ulcer there, we'll be able to see it."

"Do I have to be put to sleep?" Gregg asks, scrutinizing the doctor.

"Yes, but it will be a light anesthesia. You won't be out long, just enough time to complete the process. It's a fairly common procedure, quite beneficial in helping with diagnosis. You might experience a little discomfort in your throat afterward from the tube, but that's about it."

Gregg and I look at each other. Neither of us comes up with an objection. Gregg shrugs. "It's OK with me if it will help you figure out what is going on."

Dr. Bansick nods. "OK, I'll get the ball rolling and the nurse will be in to get you in a little while. Any other questions?"

Gregg's seemingly dead face floats through my mind again. "When we were home, Gregg was sitting on the toilet and became totally unresponsive. If he wasn't sitting upright, I would have thought he was dead. What do you think that was?"

The doctor looks puzzled. "It could be a number of things, but perhaps he just fainted."

"But wouldn't he fall over with his eyes closed?"

"Were you holding him?"

"Part of the time."

"Well, the body can do strange things sometimes." That ends the topic for him, and he asks again, "Anything else?"

I shake my head *no*. Gregg does likewise. I'm not convinced of the doctor's fainting assessment, but I have no other explanations. Letting it go, I look back at Gregg. "An ulcer, Gregg boy."

His face is contemplative and he shakes his head slightly. "Well, we know I've had my share of indigestion over the years."

"Yeah, you have. You've gone through your quota of Tums and Brom-Seltzer, not to mention Coke—and beer," I add, kidding him.

He catches my drift, and the corner of his mouth tweaks.

"At least ulcers are common and treatable," I add. "You may have to adjust your diet a bit."

His eyes close again, signaling the end of the conversation and speculation. I sit back in my chair and try to close my own eyes once more, feeling slightly relieved.

At 5:00 a.m. we are still in a holding pattern. "Why don't you go home and get some rest, Deb? You look tired."

I raise my head from its resting place on my arm. "You sure?" I ask, tempted but not wanting to abandon him.

"It's been a long night, and there isn't anything you can do at the moment. I'm grateful you're here, but they'll be taking me off for the endoscopy any minute now."

"We can only hope," I retort. "Any minute has been going on for two hours."

I study his face, trying to discern the sincerity of his words. As if hearing my thoughts, he adds, "I'll be fine. I'm in good hands," and gives me a comforting smile.

"If you're sure you'll be OK," I say, offering him one last out.

"I will be."

Putting on my coat, I bend over and give him a kiss, then look into his long-lashed, green eyes. His face is relaxed and momentarily pain-free. "I love you, Gregg boy. I'll be back in a few hours."

"I love you, too, babe." He squeezes my hand and I look at him one last time before walking out.

* * *

The streets on the short ride home are still deserted at this early hour. I pass the signature sign of our town, "Sandstone Capital of the World," posted in front of our small but stately sandstone city hall, still aglow with night lights. It stands guard at the main five-point intersection and faces the two-block business area, which is filled with an overabundance of old-time and trendy bars along with a few restaurants, shops, offices, and a little movie theater around the corner. I have always been amazed that a town of twelve thousand can support so many drinking establishments. Nevertheless, it still has its charm with its Main Street USA designation.

At home, I start my bathwater and sit down to rest while it runs. Barring this past month, Gregg really has been blessed with good health. He has been in the hospital only one other time, for a kidney stone. They kept him for three days, waiting to catch the little bugger in a sieve. After the initial pain subsided, he was out of his bed, running around in his hospital gown, endearing himself to patients and staff alike. The stone was never found, so they finally had to let him go, probably because they had to get some work done. Ulcers are not uncommon, I decide. He'll be fine.

I turn off the water and ease myself into the tub, close my eyes, and let out a big sigh. As the heat penetrates my body, relaxing it one tense muscle at a time, I feel my forehead wrinkle and my eyes well up. In a matter of seconds, I am sobbing, realizing how scared I was; I just didn't have time to process it. Talk about shooting from a deep sleep into high alert! Gregg's face still haunts me, the way his eyes stared without seeing. How quickly life could have changed. Thank God I had my wits about me!

Once out of the tub, dressed, and feeling a little more human, I call my mom, knowing she'll console me as only a mother can do. I know she'll already be up; she's always slept only about four hours a night. "Hey, Mom, it's me."

"Hello, me. What's going on? It's a little early for you, isn't it? Are you at work?"

"No, I actually just got home from the hospital. It's been a big night." Before she can respond, I launch right into the story.

"Is he OK?" she asks incredulously when I'm done.

"I think so. The doctor said he thinks it might be a bleeding ulcer, but they want to do more tests to make sure."

"Oh, poor guy. But— it sounds like he will be fine. What about you?" she asks. "How are you doing?"

Once again my tears start to fall. "Well, I'm better than Gregg, but it was pretty scary. I didn't know what to do."

Her soothing, motherly voice kicks in. "It sounds like you did all you could. I'm sure the doctors know what they are doing and will take good care of him. Do you want me be with you?"

It hadn't occurred to me. I hate to have her drive an hour, now that the immediate crisis is over. "Nah, I'll be fine," I respond, probably not very convincingly. Why can't I just let her come and comfort me? My streak of independence waves like a flag in the wind. "I'll call you when I know more. I guess I had better let some other people know too. Thanks anyhow. It feels better just talking to you."

"I'm glad you called. Hang in there. You let me know if you need me to come up, and keep me posted," she says again, then adds, "I'm sure he'll be OK. And give Gregg my love."

Gretchen, our daughter, is away at college and Gregg's parents are in Florida for the winter. They will all want to know along with the rest of the family, but I make the executive decision to wait and call them when there is more information.

On Friday, the doctors say Gregg is free to go. They've done all of the tests that they wish to do, and the gastroenterologist will be in touch, along with his regular doctor.

In the car for the ride home, Gregg turns to me, "Let's pack up and go to Niagara Falls. We can still catch some of the weekend."

"Are you crazy? You just spent two nights in the hospital. Don't you think you should take it easy?"

"I feel fine" he says, clicking his seatbelt. "I'll be careful and watch what I eat. I won't even drink, Debbie. I will be a good boy." Debbie is the name he calls me when he is trying to butter me up. Most of the time he prefers Debb, with his own unique way of spelling my name.

Still protesting, I say, "We already told everyone we won't be there, and they cancelled our rooms."

"We can get the room back. It's a big place; there will be something else. Let's surprise everyone!"

It's hopeless. If I talk Gregg out of going, he'll give me his sad puppy look all weekend. With a sigh, I give in.

~ 3 ~

The News

The hotel desk clerk directs us upstairs to a private dining room where we find all of our friends enjoying a late supper around a large table. We have just appeared in the doorway when Eli, Gregg's best friend, happens to look up in the middle of a story. "Gregg and Deb are here!" he shouts, rising from his chair to greet us. A spontaneous round of applause breaks out.

Smiling, I glance at Gregg whose face looks like he just pulled off the perfect coup. He is in his element, grinning from ear to ear.

"How are you feeling?" Eli's wife, Kate, asks, her eyes wide with concern. "I thought you were in the hospital."

"He was!" I answer.

"I'm feeling fine. I've been sleeping for two days. I had to rest up so I could keep up with all you jokers."

"How did you break out?" another friend yells.

"After they inspected all my body parts inside and out, they couldn't find anything else to do so they kicked me out. I told them I had an important meeting that I had to attend, and people were waiting for me," he laughs. "You know they just can't keep a good man down!"

The bantering continues as others come to greet us with hugs.

I turn to Eli. "We do have the small problem of our room. Hopefully, there is one, since we cancelled it."

"Come on," he responds, putting his arms around both of us and walking us back through the door. "We'll get you one."

A room is resecured with the support of our good friend, who might be the only person I know more persuasive than Gregg. Even though the place is hopping and seems to be totally booked, they manage to find us a spot to sleep. It's not pretty, but it's a bed. I 'm very relieved, having driven all this way on a whim. Plus, I know Gregg is tired even though he rises to the occasion, as he always does. To him, there is no better medicine than being with friends.

He sticks to his word and is on his best behavior, even giving his cigarettes to another buddy, and swears he is done smoking for good. Over the years he has smoked sometimes more and sometimes less, even stopping totally for a few years. Now he smokes "only when I drink," he says, or about every weekend. The events of the past few days have, indeed, given him pause and the needed smack upside the head to make him stop and rethink a few of his usual habits.

We arrive home from Niagara on Monday, President's Day, to see Gretchen, our daughter, at the door to greet us.

"S'notty!" Gregg says, gleefully, as he hugs her, using the name he likes to call her from a time when she was little and kept responding to him with the phrase "No, it's not." "Good to have you home! Did you blow off your classes, or are you so smart you are ahead of everybody?"

Gretchen gives me knowing smirk as she hugs me too. "No, Dad. I told them you were sick, and you desperately needed me. They felt sorry for me and told me I could have some extra time to turn in my projects. Worked like a charm."

"Well, I'm glad you are learning something at college. Persuasion can be a useful tool," he replies, still smiling. "Uh oh, what's that on your shirt?" he says, pointing to an imaginary spot. She looks down, and he moves his finger straight up, clipping her on the end of her nose. "Gotcha!" he laughs.

Gretchen smacks him on the arm. "Stop! I can't believe I actually fell for that again! I must be out of practice. College is dulling my mind."

He carries our suitcases to the bedroom before coming back to tell us he is going to shovel the neighbor's driveway from the record snowfall we've been having. He doesn't appear any worse for the wear after the hospital stay or the big weekend. I figure he knows how much energy he has. Besides, our neighbors are elderly, and he enjoys doing what he can to give them a hand.

Gretchen sits back as one of our cats jumps up beside her. "I hope Dad takes it easy. You know how he's always going at a hundred miles an hour," she says, stroking the cat's back as it starts a contented purr.

"Yeah, I know. I'm sure he'd be happy to put it all behind him, though this definitely got his attention. He was pretty careful this weekend and did his best not to go overboard. Nobody really did, thank God, which made it easier. Maybe we are all just getting old," I add, wistfully. "I guess we'll just have to keep after him a bit to slow down. It is hard to curb his enthusiasm, as you know."

I look at my daughter, seeing not only the little girl she used to be, but also the young woman she is becoming. She is on the taller side, slender from regular workouts, dressed in her usual workout attire, and currently sporting hair darker than her natural blonde. It's pulled back into the messy knot that she wears most of the time. Living away from home has been good for her. She seems more self-possessed and confident. When you are an only child, you live your life in a fishbowl, no matter whether your parents try to keep it from happening or not.

"It's great you were able to squeeze out a few days at home, my kid. I'm glad to see you." My heart warms just saying the words. Her presence seems like the return of a missing piece of our equation, the three of us, our family unit, together again. When something affects one of us, it affects us all.

Soon I hear the door open and feet stomping. "Man, it's cold out there!" Gregg says, rubbing his hands together to generate some heat. Before he can sit down the phone rings. Moments later, he's back. "That was the secretary from our family doctor. They want me to come in as soon as possible."

My stomach drops at the news. How often does the doctor's office call you rather than the other way around? We *were* told that the doctor would be in touch—but the phone call still puts us all on guard just a little bit, though no one dares mention it. "Want me to go with you?" I ask.

"Nah, you two stay here and visit. I will see what he wants and let you know when I get back." If he's wary, he's not showing it. I decide to follow suit and think positive.

"All right. We will probably be right here in the same place." But I'm already uneasy.

He's back in an hour. He sits on the couch beside Gretchen, rests his elbows on his knees, and looks at the floor. "Well—I have good news and bad news." Before we can comment, he looks straight at me and says, "The bad news is that I have stomach cancer."

I hear myself suck in a small breath of air as my heart skips a beat. The look on his face tells me he is serious. My shoulders drop though I try my best not to show too much emotion. I know he must be in shock and I don't want to scare him any more than he already might be. "What's the good news?" I ask, my voice tentative.

"It's only the size of a quarter."

I pause to absorb what I just heard, then burst forth with questions. "What does that mean? Does the doctor have a plan? What else did he say?" I'm sorry I didn't listen to my intuition and go with him. I should have just gone; I should have asked these questions of the doctor myself. My reputation as a questioner precedes me. I am always more inquisitive than Gregg in most any situation, let alone this one. Besides, once you hear news like that, your mind tends to stop processing other information as you take in what you have just heard.

"He wants me to talk to a surgeon. He feels there is a good chance that, due to the size, it can be removed."

"Does he know a surgeon?"

"He referred me to the one who works at the local hospital."

"When are you supposed to see him? Did he already make an appointment?"

"Yes, we scheduled it for this Friday."

Cancer. The dreaded C word. How can my healthy and happy husband possibly have cancer? It is unfathomable to me. Cancer has reared its ugly head in and around my life enough already. My father passed away from leukemia a few years earlier. My two stepbrothers each died from colon and brain cancers respectively at ages thirty and forty a few years before that. I had had my own bout with thyroid cancer when Gretchen was just two years old. Mine was the success story: here I am over twenty years later and going strong.

Perhaps that is what will happen with Gregg, I think to myself. If I can be cured, why can't he? Modern medicine has come a long way, and many more cancers are at least treatable. People continue to live their lives and get on with it. They just stay vigilant and on top of their symptoms. Nobody wants to be cut open if it's not necessary, but if it would mean the cancer would go away, it would be worth it.

"What are you thinking, Greggy?" I ask, observing him, not able to read his face.

"I guess I'm still trying to take it in," he replies, staring blankly at the floor again. Our cat is now weaving in and out of his legs. He reaches down to give a quick pet and then, with a sigh, leans back against the couch. The cat leaps up and lands on his lap. "I had a feeling that the call would not necessarily be good news."

Still processing the news myself, I try to keep perspective. "There's a lot we don't know. You can't freak out until you get more facts and see exactly what is involved and what the surgery entails. We need more information, and we should probably think of some questions to ask before we meet with the surgeon."

I can see the wheels turning in his head, still trying to grasp the reality of the news. I am, too, even though I hear myself prattle on.

"Wow! Cancer," he says, absently staring at his fingers, as if trying to see if they now look different to him.

Gretchen has scooted to the edge of the couch, taking in every word. She's been unusually quiet, but now reaches over and gives Gregg a hug. "You'll be OK, Dad. You are strong, and you have always been healthy. This is probably just a little bump in the road. It sounds like surgery will take care of it, and you will go on your merry way." Her tone and face offer encouragement, but I'm not sure she believes her own words.

"Maybe, kid" he says, giving her an appreciative smile along with a pat on her leg. "I sure hope so. All the things that have been going wrong in my body this past month must have been leading up to this."

I walk over and encircle him from the other side. "Yeah, your body *has* been giving you fits lately. I guess it could all be related. But you've always had a strong constitution—that should count for something."

*　*　*

We meet with the surgeon, Dr. Andrews, on Friday. He has a nice, rather gentle manner, and we discover as we get acquainted that we have some mutual friends. Then he's all business, the buttons on his white jacket straining against his girth, as he explains the surgery: he'll remove a chunk of Gregg's stomach and some of his esophagus since the cancer is located where the two connect. He will then resect Gregg's esophagus to his stomach. He speaks confidently and knowledgeably, making it sound like cutting out the cancerous section will not be that difficult.

My mind stays in that unemotional, clinical place while I try to picture what he is saying. I conjure up a procedure akin to fixing a leaky pipe. Cut it apart, take out the rusty sections, put it back together, and off you go. I don't want to think about any fallout in the process. It really never even enters my mind. It is just something that must be done to eradicate the problem, so there is no time to hem and haw. Very cut and dried, no pun intended.

We both listen intently, not wanting to miss anything, but also trying to think of and ask the questions necessary to make us comfortable with the procedure. I glance at Gregg, who looks straight at the doctor. It's hard to decipher what he must be thinking.

"What about eating?" I ask, turning back to the doctor.

He looks at me, then shifts his eyes over and addresses Gregg. "You will still be able to eat orally, but your diet may be limited for a while until the surgery heals. Your stomach will be smaller, so you will not be able to ingest as much food at a time."

"How long will I be in the hospital?" Gregg wants to know.

"Probably about a week to ten days. You'll need to be off work for about six weeks all together." That's another indication of how serious of a situation this is.

"What happens after that? Will there be any follow-up treatment?" I ask, trying to think ahead.

"We'll have to see how things go. Once we actually know what we are dealing with, we'll have a better idea. At this point, there's a good chance the cancer can be removed through surgery. You'll be referred to an oncologist as a matter of routine."

Ugh! I don't even want to think about chemotherapy. I had radiation in the form of radioactive iodine back in the day. All it amounted to was a teaspoon of liquid, one time only, and three days of quarantine in the hospital while my radioactive self became non-radioactive. It was painless, but I wasn't thrilled to have to put it into my body. I was fairly young and trusted in the powers that be at the time, my dad being one of them. He was my direct link to the medical world, even though his specialty was ob-gyn. He worked at the same hospital and knew the doctors involved. He would have investigated the entire process before letting me go through any of it. Unfortunately, he's gone now, so we have only ourselves to rely on at the moment and the advice we're getting from those currently in the know.

When I quiz Dr. Andrews about the quality of care at the local hospital and his confidence in his team and the doctors there, he assures us that he trusts them completely and that they are competent in what they do. He himself has done several stomach surgeries, so this is not his first rodeo. The thought crosses my mind that we should probably ask about a second opinion, but he seems so sure and matter-of-fact about what needs to be done that he allays my fears, and I guess Gregg's, too, since he doesn't say anything. So we don't ask.

"So, will the surgery be Monday?" I ask. This is Friday, and I am pretty sure they don't work on the weekends.

The doctor gives us a little "humph" sound. "Things don't happen that fast," he says. Other people also need his care, and it takes some maneuvering to secure the operating room and line things up. It will probably be in a few weeks.

A few weeks! Is he nuts? Don't we want to do this as soon as possible? If the cancer is the size of a quarter now, what will it be like in a few weeks? Why isn't Gregg protesting? But when I look over at him, he seems satisfied. Or maybe he's just numb. He's already standing and reaching out to shake hands and thank the doctor, who tells us we will get a call soon letting us know the details.

*   *   *

"I think I'll write a letter to our friends and family, letting them know what is going on," Gregg says to me a day or so later. Now that he has digested the news a little bit, he says he needs all the help he can get. "I know everyone will send some positive vibes my way if I ask, and maybe, even if I don't. I want to do whatever I can to ensure that all goes well with the surgery."

He has no doubt about this. To him, this is how the world works and what we are supposed to do for each other in times of need. It's what he would do for anyone else without question. He has always espoused the idea that it's better to take action yourself than to wait for things to happen when, then, your only choice is *re*action.

"Sounds like a good idea," I agree. "You're important to a lot of people who care what happens to you. Besides, it doesn't take much time on their part. I'm all for setting up the conditions and scenario for your surgery in the best way possible!"

People have already offered to come up to help prepare for the surgery and manage the recovery afterward: his oldest sister, Maddie; my sister, Lila; our friend and another of Gregg's best friends, Vic, from North Carolina. It is amazing how people are quick to surround, protect and support you when adversity rears its ugly head.

If anyone deserves the love, it is Gregg. He has always gone out of his way to connect with people by writing notes, arranging get-togethers, and doing nice things for them even before they ask, if they ever do. He is rather old-fashioned in that he would much rather write notes than talk on the phone. People love to get "fun" mail as much as he likes to write, so it all works. Most of us care about others, but we don't always take the time or make the effort to stay in touch. But Gregg has been the glue that has kept our friends together. They know it and have said so on a number of occasions.

The two weeks before the surgery go both too fast and not fast enough. The whole prospect of what's to come is unsettling, and we both want it to go away. Even though the doctor made it sound fairly routine, there is no doubt that this is major surgery, and it could open a Pandora's box of other issues. I'm glad we have a little time to process the situation, talk with people, ruminate, and try to gain a perspective that we can both live with.

Needing a break from our worries of health and medical issues, we put our border collie, Wiley, into the car and head to a local metro park to walk and soak in some nature. It's a chilly February day, but the sky is blue and the sun's rays shine through the trees, giving us a false sense of warmth. The trail is muddy from melting snow, and we have to dodge some big puddles. Wiley trots along carefree, his tail wagging, sniffing whatever captures his attention. Gregg has trained him so well, we rarely use a leash; he is just happy to be where we are and stays close.

There is something about being surrounded by trees that has always drawn me in. It's like I have friends all around wherever I look, many older and wiser that have weathered many a storm, watching over and protecting me, setting an example. It is a safe haven that offers a welcome respite and clears my head.

"Let's sit on that log for a few minutes," I say to Gregg, pointing to one lying squarely in the sun.

We step over branches and manage to find a comfortable position and sit down. The tree bark is damp and rough. I close my eyes, aiming my face toward the sky, letting the sun's warmth envelop me. The air teases my nostrils with the smells of damp earth and mud, a false harbinger of a spring still several weeks away. Birds trill in the distance; either they've managed to survive in this climate all winter, or they're the early birds back from afar. Sitting in silence, I am easily transported to wherever I imagine myself to be, the beach, the mountains, floating in a hammock somewhere. "It's nice to be outside doing what we normally do!" Gregg offers, as he picks up a stick and tosses it into the trees beyond the dog. "It's a beautiful day."

He watches as Wiley races after it, his favorite game, and soon returns, dropping it at Gregg's feet. Gregg and I are quiet, immersed in our own thoughts. Eventually, I put my arm around him, drawing him close. "Tough times, huh, Gregg boy?"

He kicks at a branch a few times to try and move it out of the way. "Yeah, but here we are," he replies. "They say God only gives you what you can handle. I guess I must be tougher than I feel sometimes."

"I don't suppose we understand how tough we really are until we're faced with something like this. Maybe that is why we go through stuff. So we know. I don't think that when I went through my cancer, I ever thought I was going to die. And here I am. Maybe that's the key."

"Maybe," he responds, pensive, and then adds, "It was so strange being at the basketball game the other night and having Ken tell me he was sorry to hear I was sick. I am not used to people looking at me with pity. I'm not even used to being sick! It made me uncomfortable. I didn't know what to say or how to react. Somehow it made it all the more real to me." His face sags with anxiety and doubt as he picks up the stick and throws it again.

I turn his face to me. "You know we are a team, don't you, Greggy? No matter what's ahead, I will be right here with you every step of the way. You don't have to do this alone. We will figure it out together."

He nods almost imperceptibly, returning my gaze. "I know, babe. I wish neither of us had to do this. It probably won't be much fun for you either."

He puts his arm around me and hugs me to him as I rest my head on his shoulder. "We can do it," I say with resolve. "It will all be OK. You'll see."

~ 4 ~

One Less Part

Mom takes a chair in the waiting room while I walk back with Gregg to get him ready for surgery. It's Fat Tuesday; all the doctors and nurses are adorned with colorful and shiny Mardi Gras beads. This lightheartedness belies the weight bowing our shoulders. I watch while Gregg is prepped as the nurses, the anesthesiologist, and the doctors take their respective turns introducing themselves and explaining what will take place.

Always up for a party, Gregg appears somewhat delighted at the atmosphere, though I sense his underlying apprehension. He smiles and talks to everyone, reiterating how he feels great and has never been sick a day in his life. Perhaps it is his weak attempt at escaping his fate, hoping someone will say, "Oops, Mr. Gilder, our mistake. If that's the case, why don't you jump up and go on home now. Sorry to have bothered you." I get the impression they don't usually encounter such boisterous patients on the way to the operating room.

Too soon, the nurses tell us they're ready to take him to surgery. I grab hold of his hand. "I will be right here waiting when you come out, Gregg boy," I say. I want to tell him not to be scared and that he will be fine, but somehow, I can't get the words out. Instead, I gaze into his uncertain eyes, hoping he is soaking up the silent courage I'm sending. He raises his brows in resignation as if to say, "Here I go." "You know I love you!" I add, reassuringly, with a small smile. Maybe it will help him feel at ease.

He smiles back at me. "I love you, too, babe."

I give his hand a "you can do this" squeeze, then nod to the nurses who start to move the bed. "See you soon!" I yell to the back of his head as he rolls toward the double doors at the end of the hall. *God bless you, Greggy, and everyone who will be working with you today. May their brains be clear, their hands steady, the surgery minimal, but effective. May the light of God surround you.* Mom is in the waiting area, reading the book that she hauls around with her whenever she has time to fill. I have a book also but am not in the frame of mind to read, at least not yet. I'm thinking of how vulnerable Gregg looked. Is it because men are used to being in charge, telling others what to do, rather than having to trust that someone else might know what is best for them? When they are down and out, they instantly revert to little boys. Of course, that sends my motherly instincts into a rage, and I want to put up a protective shield around them. If I could make it all better, I would.

"So it begins," I say to Mom.

She lays her hand on top of mine. "I know you're worried, but you have to trust that the doctors know what they're doing, and that Gregg will be fine."

My stomach is in knots. We have hours to kill, but concentrating on a book does not sound appealing. Instead, I ask Mom if she wants some tea. She says yes, and I am happy to go find it. I dawdle as much as possible, roaming the halls, checking out the gift shop, chatting with the sales clerks.

When I return with tea, I'm still not in the mood to read, so I resort to people watching. My foot bounces furiously around at the end of my crossed leg. I used to rock myself to sleep at night, and I suppose this is the daytime version of soothing myself.

The whole time, I'm praying that all is going well, and all of the cancer is being removed. I surround those involved in white light, even calling in angels and healers from the other side. My mind fills with pictures of Gregg healthy and back to his old self. That's the way I know him.

That's the way I want him to be. That's the way *he* wants to be! Could it really be that simple? A little cut here and there and back to normal? Of course it could! *Anything is possible*, I remind myself.

After a couple of hours, I hear my name. My stomach leaps. I wave, in case the lady thinks I'm not here. Hurrying over, I feel my heart bump hard against my chest. "Your husband is fine—out of surgery and in recovery. The doctor will give you a full report shortly." She smiles comfortingly.

"Thanks," I say.

Returning to my seat, I see that Mom has already packed up her stuff. Her eyebrows are raised expectantly. "Well?" she says.

"False alarm, but he's OK and out of surgery," I say. I feel some relief, but I still want to hear the doctor say they got it all.

Another fifteen minutes has gone by when I hear my name again. *This is it*. "Time to go," I say to Mom, hurrying to gather up the rest of our things.

The doctor meets us in a small conference room. All my senses are on full alert, trying to assess his demeanor before he even speaks. "The surgery went well," he says. "I had to remove about 60 percent of Gregg's stomach and also some of his esophagus." *Yikes, 60 percent!* I didn't think they would have to remove so much.

As if reading my mind, the doctor continues, "We did an immediate biopsy and the margins of his esophagus weren't quite clean, so I had to remove a little more than I originally thought to ensure that we got all of the cancer. It was beginning to attach itself to his spleen, so I also removed that, which is an organ that you really don't need. I checked the liver several times and could not find any sign of cancer there." *Thank God for that!* I thought. Some unidentified spots had shown up in his liver on the CAT scan. The doctor had said they can sometimes just be fatty deposits, but they need to eyeball it to be sure.

"Do you think you got all of the cancer out?" I am on the edge of my chair, hoping against hope that he says what I want to hear.

"I feel as confident as I can. We will have to wait and see what the further lab results tell us."

Mom remains quiet on the couch, listening while I pummel him with more questions about what to expect in recovery, Gregg's ability to eat and so forth. He patiently answers them one by one. When I can think of nothing else to ask, we sit in silence for a few minutes while everything sinks in. There may still be some glitches, but overall, I am relieved. He made it through.

And then, just like that, I feel myself start to come undone, eyes watering. The doctor takes the lull as his sign to go and stands up. I stand at the same time and impulsively move to give him a hug, tears now running down my face. "Thank you for everything," I say.

A little surprised, he responds with "You're welcome," and hugs me back. "We'll talk again when I check on Gregg in the next few days. I will be able to tell you more once the test results come back." He looks at me kindly and walks out.

Mom gets up and hugs me. "It sounds like a good report and that he did the best he could," she says encouragingly. Her eyes are also watery, though she is adept at keeping her cool. I know it has been hard on her too. Gregg is like a son to her, and she has always had my back. As we hold each other, I not sure who is comforting who, but I am happy she is here.

I call Gretchen and Gregg's parents and tell them what the doctor told me. Then Mom and I find the empty room where Gregg will spend his next few weeks. Eli is wandering the hall, wondering if he is in the right place; he says he wants to be here when Gregg gets back. I am touched. I know they love each other dearly, having been best friends since childhood.

Soon Gregg is delivered to the room. He is groggy, but happy to see our smiling faces. I am aghast at all the tubes and bags hanging from everywhere. The seriousness of the surgery is staring me in the face, unsettling me. *Oh Greggy, what have they done?* It looks like they have turned him inside out and then back again.

We surround his bed and tell him he looks like crap, but at the same time we are thrilled he is OK. "Thanks!" he offers, eyes half-mast with a smirk barely visible on his face.

"Are you in a lot of pain?" I ask, leaning over so he can hear me better.

"Not really. They have me drugged up pretty good." He shifts his head to see me more directly. "Some little old lady shaved off all my pubic hair!" he shares, very put out. *Really?* That is the first thing that comes out of his mouth? I let out a giggle.

"I'm sure she took her time!" Eli chimes in. "It's not every day she gets to see a stud like you."

I'm happy to see he is his old self despite the trauma of the past several hours. "You'd best rest," I say. "Now that we have seen the whites of your eyes and know that you're alive, we can all relax." I smile, my hand on his forehead. "Go to sleep and we'll see you again in a little while."

His eyes close before we even move away from the bed.

~ 5 ~

One More Step

The next few days creep along. I struggle to entertain myself in the hospital room while Gregg spends much of his time asleep. Air is trapped painfully inside him and isn't dissipating quickly. I can only watch as he squirms to find a more desirable position. I would gladly, tenderly rub his stomach, but there are still too many attachments everywhere to make it productive. Just as the pain begins to subside from the air, he develops an allergic reaction to the antibiotics and begins to itch all over. There is nothing to do but switch medicines and wait for improvement.

It doesn't take long before I become his personal nurse and advocate for whatever ails him. I track monitors, report beep irregularities, watch the color of the liquid in his drain bags, help change the sheets. The hospital staff does their best but cannot be everywhere at once. I don't mind as it gives me something to do.

At one point a nursing assistant comes in and massages Gregg's legs and feet. It is the most gentle and genuine measure of care anyone has shown thus far, the true mark of someone who has a natural gift of healing and connection. My heart melts, and we both express to her how grateful we are.

Gregg brightens for short periods as a steady stream of visitors filters in to see how he's doing. He always perks up, amazing me. People really are his medicine. They leave knowing he has been through a lot, but also feeling reassured that all is as good as it can be and that he will be well very soon.

* * *

In down time at home, I do my yoga and then sit quietly or write in my journal. I need to contemplate all that has transpired and continually adjust my perspective. I will not be of any use if I fall apart. And, to be honest, I don't feel on the verge of that, thank God.

I'm looking forward to seeing my sister, Lila, who flies in in a few days. I have always deferred to her as the older sister, the taller, smarter, and more together one. I was the social one. Though we tried to distance ourselves from each other growing up, as the years have passed, our true friendship has emerged. She has the pragmatism of my father and an interest in science. I know that she will ask the tough questions and talk us off a ledge at the same time, if necessary.

*   *   *

On the fourth day, the doctor finally visits. I wondered why it was taking so long, but told myself that he was giving Gregg time to get past his initial recovery period. He pulls a chair closer to the bed and sits.

"I have the lab reports from the surgery," he begins, looking from one of us to the other. "The cancer cells are what we call aggressive in nature, meaning not that they multiply quickly, but rather they are shaped like tentacles reaching out as opposed to being round. Unfortunately, even though I went back and took a greater section of the esophagus, the margins on the upper section were not clean. Because of this, we have to assume that the cancer is on the move and may have traveled through the bloodstream." Disappointment overtakes me, and my heart sinks as I register what he is saying. "We did take some lymph nodes during the surgery, however, and they are all clear."

I look at Gregg. He is also dispirited, but says nothing, perhaps just waiting for the other shoe to drop.

"That does not sound like good news," I say, still hoping he will tell us there is nothing to worry about. "Does that mean you have to go back in a cut out some more?"

"No. I cut as much as I felt I could without interfering with the organs above it. It is not necessarily bad news; it just means that we have to treat it more aggressively than we originally thought."

"As in chemo?" I ask.

"That will be up to the oncologist. It may involve chemo and/or radiation," he replies. "There is a good chance that we can eliminate any remaining cancer that might still be present, but we do need to do the treatment. If the cancer is still there, it's microscopic and would be next to impossible to detect. The follow-up treatment will, hopefully, knock out any stray cells that might be floating around."

That, at least, sounds positive. He wonders if we have more questions, but we can't come up with any. The first thing to do, he says, is recover from the operation. Then we can discuss the rest. He moves around the bed, lifting sheets to check the incisions, perusing the color of the liquid in the bags to see if the bleeding has stopped. Apparently, when the color becomes clearer, they will be able to start removing some of the hanging debris around his body.

Gregg, forever cordial, shakes his hand and tells him thanks for all he has done and that he knows he did his best. The doctor smiles a little sadly and nods. I can tell he wishes the news were better.

"Well, that wasn't exactly what we were hoping to hear," I say after the doctor walks out. I'm seated on a chair by his bed, my arms across the side rail near his head, my chin resting on my hands. I need to be as much in his space as possible, as if my strength will support and lighten the weight of this unwanted news. He is slumped against his pillow.

"No," he says succinctly. He frowns and stares at his wiggling toes as they make little tents under the covers. "I guess God isn't done with me yet, but the doctor's right, first I have to heal from the surgery. With luck, that will be sooner rather than later." He leans forward, attempting to sit more upright, and I grab his arm to help. "Can you rearrange my pillows a little? My back is getting tired."

Fluffing the two pillows while he waits patiently, I try to put a positive spin on things. "If whatever is left is practically impossible to see, it would seem that chemo would knock out whatever might be lurking around in your blood. He made it sound like it was more preventative than an actual treatment. So, that's good."

"I hope so." I see fatigue overtake his troubled features. "Let's just take it one step at a time."

"It's all we can do, Greggy," I answer.

He relaxes with a sigh against his new backdrop. I lean over and give him a quick kiss on the lips. Closing his eyes again, he is lost in his own world.

I had recently been thinking how our days had become routine. We had fallen into a rut of doing the same thing: get up, go to work, come home, eat dinner, watch TV, go to bed, and then do it all again. Now I rue the day it crossed my mind.

My love for Gregg has only grown over time. We have always been a good match and have managed to create a relationship that we both have reveled in. You could even say that we have thrived as a couple, with mostly equal amounts of give and take. He is strong-willed but endearing. I am grounded and practical. At various times, he has been my challenge, my frustration, and my teacher, but always, always, my best friend and my heart. We seem to understand each other at the deepest level.

I lay my head back on the chair and close my eyes. I remember when we had youth on our side; so much of life was yet to come. It was all new, and we lived each day with abandon, daring the world to get in our way. We treated our bodies and our health with little regard and expected that we would always snap back with a resilience we never even questioned. We just trusted that everything would right itself in due time, and off we would go again.

~ 6 ~

Forever For Now

The first time I laid eyes on Gregg, I was amazed. Not because it was love at first sight, but because of the fact that he existed at all. I had never seen him before and could not fathom where he came from or why he was sitting across from me in the speech clinic. Did I just not notice him? Was he new to the campus? I was already a senior at Ohio University, majoring in speech/language pathology. My final three years of classes had pretty much all taken place in the speech department, so you'd think I would have run into him at some point. I knew of only three males who were undergrads, and he was not one of them. Yet here he was, large as life.

"Hi! I'm Gregg," he said enthusiastically, extending his hand to me with a big grin on his face. He was dressed in nearly electric blue pants and a white pullover synthetic shirt, his other hand holding a couple of text-books against his side.

I smiled back and took his hand. "I'm Deb. Nice to meet you. It looks like we've been assigned to the same client this quarter. This is Kathy," I said, pointing to the girl standing beside me, who also happened to be my sorority sister. We didn't hang out much, but I knew her to be lots of fun. "She'll be with us too." Kathy reached out her hand and greeted him as well.

The clinic was set up so that there would be one senior and two juniors assigned to each case. I was the senior, and it was my last quarter of school before graduating. Somehow, when assignments were doled out fall and winter quarters, I fell off somebody's radar and hadn't had a client all year. I hadn't bothered to rectify the situation, happy to have less work and pull one over on the department. This time, however, it seemed I couldn't escape, which was fine—I knew I needed the practice.

"I've got the case history here," I said, holding up the file. "How about we go sit down somewhere so we can talk about it and decide what we're going to do."

We found seats at the end of the hall. I opened the file and gave each of them a part of it to read. Our client's situation seemed pretty cut and dried, a six-year-old boy with a variety of articulation errors, the main one being a lisp. We decided where we would start and how the therapy would evolve. It didn't appear to be a complicated case, just a matter of coming up with some fun activities to get him to practice saying sounds the proper way.

While we talked, I was surreptitiously checking out Gregg. He seemed quite friendly and relaxed, kidding around with both of us immediately, showing off an inviting smile full of even, white teeth. His straight brown hair hung over his ears, touching his shoulders, slightly longer in the back. He stood a little taller than me with a slim, rather muscular build. What caught my eye, perhaps more than anything else, were his glasses and the peculiar way they sat on his face. They were tinted wire rims, bent back at an odd angle on the bottoms, so that they rested on his cheeks. I wondered if they were intentionally designed that way, or if maybe they made him see better. Either way, his looks and manner were generally appealing.

"How about I begin the therapy the first few times, then you guys can take turns with me?" I proposed, closing the file, and resting it on my lap.

"Works for me. Do you want the first rotation, Kathy?" Gregg asked, eyeing her with a hopeful look on his face.

"Sure," Kathy responded agreeably. "Then you can take the week after, then back to Deb."

"Sounds like a deal!" I stood up and collected the rest of my things. "I think he's scheduled for 3:00 on Tuesdays. Should be fun," I added, injecting a little humor with an exaggerated smile. "I've got to get to my anatomy class. See you next week."

Right from the start, Gregg was easy to be around. His demeanor was always upbeat, and he seemed to enjoy talking to me and making jokes. Apparently, I was hilarious, as he often let loose a wonderful, rather wild laugh that couldn't help but make me smile in return. It was fun to banter with him, and he didn't seem to take offense.

"So, I'm surprised that I haven't seen you here before this," I prodded, as we walked beside each other down the hallway after our first therapy session. Kathy had already taken off. "Have you always been in this department? There aren't many males around, in case you haven't noticed."

"Oh, I've noticed!" he responded lightly. "It's the reason I decided it would be a good major for me."

Did he just say that? I looked at him to see if he was serious. His face was unreadable. "You're kidding, right?"

He chuckled, turning toward me. "Well, one of the reasons anyhow. I've been here since last year. I started out in psychology, but my grades weren't the best. A lady I was dating was a speech major and kept talking about how interesting it was, so I decided to switch. Being surrounded by all these women was icing on the cake."

"Well, I'm glad to know it wasn't *only* the women," I teased, as we turned the corner. He made it easy to kid with him. "I'm surprised that you haven't been in any of my classes."

"I don't spend any more time here than necessary. Besides, I'm a year behind you. Remember?"

"Oh yeah," I said, amused. "And I don't spend much time here either. Obviously, neither one of us could be classified as overzealous." I smiled to myself, thinking that at least we had that in common.

We reached the room with our mailboxes where our supervisors left weekly evaluations of our therapy. I read mine: my work had been deemed satisfactory with the only suggestion being to strive for more repetitions from our client.

"Did you ace it?" Gregg asked.

"Of course!" I bragged airily, hoping to impress him. "Did you expect less?"

"Nah, I thought you did great." He lingered, watching me as I stashed away the evaluation, then said, "I better get going. I'll see you next week!"

Walking together after each session became a regular event. Our conversations flowed easily as we got to know a little more about each other. Kathy rarely hung around, so it became just the two of us.

Whenever we came face to face with one of our professors, he would call them by their first name. It seemed beyond familiar to me and something I would never have felt comfortable doing. In my world, it was an unspoken no-no. But none of them seemed to mind. I could see that he had ingratiated himself by using his charms on them as well and was probably able to get away with doing even less than the average speech major because they liked him. The more I got to know him, the more I realized it wasn't manipulative as much as just who he was. It most likely never occurred to him *not* to call them by their first names.

After a few weeks, Kathy took her turn at being the clinician and Gregg was to be in charge the next time. When we all showed up at the clinic the ensuing week, I reminded him that he was up. He looked at me with an innocent face and said he didn't know it was his turn. *Seriously?* I was pretty sure that he was full of shit, but it was hard to be mad at him. I really had no choice—the client was there and the professors were waiting—so I took over. He just gave me a mischievous smile and took a seat in the corner. I could sense his eyes on me; I was getting the feeling that he was more interested in watching *me* than the therapy, which made me self-conscious. I might have even blushed, had I been the blushing kind.

That day, as we made our way once again to the mailboxes, I turned to him with a knowing look and said, "Tell me you really didn't remember it was your turn for therapy today."

"I like watching you," he said, grinning back at me, looking to see my reaction. Was he flirting with me? "After all, you are the senior here, and you have much to teach me. I'm still learning."

It seemed an appropriate time for a snappy comeback, but instead, I found myself rather tongue-tied, taken a little off-guard by his response. "Whatever," I replied, nonplussed. "You'll have another chance soon enough. Like next week!"

"Ha!" He cackled, reaching over to put his hand on my shoulder, guiding me first through the doorway to the mailboxes.

We were still talking when a girl I had never seen came in and asked him if he was ready to go. He turned to her and nodded. Returning his gaze to me, he said, "I'll see you Tuesday. Don't worry, I'll be prepared!" He grinned at me, and they left. I didn't know who the girl was, but they seemed to know each other well and I assumed maybe they were a pair. I had no claim on Gregg, and in fact, I was just getting to know him, so it really didn't faze me.

As the weeks went by, we continued to enjoy each other's company. He invited me to go camping with some friends one weekend. I politely declined, thinking that as nice as he was and even though it might be fun, I didn't really know him that well or any of his friends for that matter. I wasn't about to get stuck on some backwoods southern Ohio hill with a bunch of people I didn't know in case it didn't work out.

Besides, I still didn't know his situation or whether he had a girlfriend. If he did, he was certainly being pretty forward with me. I enjoyed our weekly conversations and figured he was a big boy, and he knew what he was doing.

The end of the quarter drew to a close with finals week. I was typing away on a big report, almost at the end, when I heard a knock at the door. I'd already turned down a chance to go out with my roommate and her boyfriend, and another to go out with other girls from the speech department. I opened the door and was extremely surprised to see Gregg and his friend, Denny, standing there. It seemed to be a banner night of invitations. How many times could I say no?

I invited them in. Gregg had never been to my apartment before. In fact, I was a little amazed he actually found it. Four of us lived above a jewelry store on the main street of town. We were right in the middle of everything, but being on the third floor, it was also relatively quiet. You just had to find the right street entrance and walk up a jillion stairs to get in either the front way or from the back ally.

I offered them wine, and we made polite conversation. Meeting in the speech building was one thing, but having Gregg here in my apartment seemed a step closer to something, though I wasn't sure what.

Suddenly, I became very self-conscious that I wasn't wearing a bra, not that it was anything out of the ordinary. It was the early 1970s, the age of anti-war protests, hippies, free love, and drugs. There were boobs on every corner. When God passed out breasts, he didn't forget me. But I usually kept them under wraps a little more, and Gregg had really only seen me looking halfway professional in the clinic. This was the other me, the at-home me. Maybe it was the way he subtly glanced at me that made me feel kind of naked. I didn't want to make a big deal about it and go change in the middle of their visit. So, I tried to play it cool, like it was the most natural thing in the world, although I was totally aware that it wasn't. Had I not been attracted to him in the first place, it probably wouldn't have mattered.

We enjoyed ourselves in this new atmosphere away from school. Gregg and I seemed to have a whole litany of topics to talk about, and after a while, I think Denny began to feel like the outsider.

From that time on, Gregg came by the apartment every day. I learned that he and the girl I had seen, Denise, had been together since high school. She had transferred to OU to be with him, and she was the speech major he had told me about. Their relationship was on the skids, and they were in the process of calling it quits and moving on. I could tell he cared about her, but their romance had run its course.

We continued sharing the story of our lives, learning more and more about our families, our interests, and our aspirations. Mostly, we made each other laugh. When I thought about Gregg, he did not fit the mold that I had pictured for myself. He wasn't tall or dark, but he was hand-some to me and certainly endearing. He just had charisma that was hard to resist. I found myself looking forward to our time together to the exclusion of other people. We couldn't seem to get enough of each other's company or stop talking; there seemed so much we wanted to tell each other. He was becoming my best friend—and maybe more.

Unfortunately, there were only a few days left to be together. I would soon be moving home to northern Ohio and leaving OU behind for-ever. Even though I would be a college graduate with a speech degree, it had been my aspiration since eighth grade to become an airline steward-ess. It seemed to combine my even earlier desires to be a waitress and a nurse with the natural wanderlust that rumbled inside me. I figured being a stewardess would knock all those out in one fell swoop. So, rather than scoping out speech jobs like I should, I got applications to work for the airlines. I was following the path that I had laid out for myself long ago, never questioning if circumstances were now differ-ent, or if I might have changed my mind.

Gregg and I decided to keep in touch. His family's home was about an hour northwest of mine, closer to Lake Erie. I had only been home for a couple of nights when I received a phone call from him. He was headed home and made a point of passing through my hometown. He wanted to stop by but needed directions to my parents' house.

Twenty minutes later there he was, in the pastel turquoise 1958 Rambler he had inherited from his grandmother. It was packed to the gills with his college stuff. He wore only burgundy cutoffs, no shirt, no shoes, along with a four-inch wide leather armband below his left shoulder containing his cigarettes. His black cat, Farley, had been riding on his lap the whole way.

The look on my father's face was anything but inviting as he stood on our front door step watching Gregg climb out of the car. He had never been overly friendly to any of the boys who showed an interest in me or had been over to visit for whatever reason. I guess he felt like he had to come off as a badass to intimidate them in case they wanted to take advantage of me. It was always embarrassing, and my mom usually tried to make up for him by becoming even more welcoming.

Gregg, amazingly, seemed unfazed by my father's face or his attitude. He walked right up to my parents and shook their hands as I introduced him. He was his usual friendly self, putting on no airs, treating everyone with the same openness that flowed so naturally from him. I had seen how he quickly put people at ease, a testament to his strength of character and his view of others as equals.

After a beer and an hour's conversation, Gregg headed back to the Rambler. My dad was polite but remained leery and watchful. He spent the visit sizing Gregg up and trying to judge just how close we were. My dad believed that clothes make the man and took great pains to dress well himself. It was evident that Gregg was not dressed to impress, no shirt, no shoes. Strike one.

* * *

Over the summer, Gregg worked at a local foundry near his hometown. We talked by phone almost every day and got together as often as we could on the weekends. I was still pursuing the airlines, but I was beginning to have second thoughts, wondering if that was really the path I wanted. So as not to close any doors, I also looked for speech jobs around the area. With Gregg still in the picture and my attention more focused in his direction, he was becoming a factor in my decisions.

One evening, we went to the drive-in movies near his home. Instead of watching the movie or steaming up the windows, we talked. The conversation led to just what did we think was happening here, how serious were we, and where was it leading? These were questions I had not asked myself, as they somehow scared me. I knew by then that I really cared for him and absolutely loved being with him. Could I make a commitment? Did I love him? I hesitated to label it. If I actually was in love with him, what did it mean? Would we eventually end up married? Yikes! I had just never let my thoughts go that far.

Gregg, on the other hand, seemed as sure and confident as ever. He knew his feelings. We talked about all my insecurities, my parents' not-so-great marriage, and a bunch of other "what if's". Each time, he responded earnestly with his natural common sense and managed to convince me that I should think positive, and that, together, we could conquer anything.

I did a lot of pondering the next day and felt the need to reiterate our conversation in a poem. It had always been a way for me to express the thoughts that I sometimes couldn't convey face to face.

I haven't stopped thinking all day long of the talk we had last night,
It really made me happy, as it brought some thoughts to light,

Of something that had admittedly been on my mind throughout,
The entire time we have dated and it was causing a little doubt.

The subject was commitment in a roundabout sort of way,
A topic that I've always refrained from until just yesterday.

Forever is a long, long time, much too far to tell,
If people will change or a relationship will last that now is going so well.

On the other hand, not forever can bring about a very bad start,
End something that's hardly begun and cause two people to part.

The fact that you made me realize this, means so much to me,
The attitude with which one looks at life influences it more than he may see.

The positive way of looking at things, I know I am capable of,
It just takes someone like you to help me with a little bit of love.

We ended the night with a beautiful thought, one which my feelings will allow,
That thought was to think in terms of forever, forever that is, for now.

I titled it "Forever for Now," wrote it in a card, and sent it to Gregg. It was my way of saying, "OK, you got me, warts and all. I surrender myself to you and trust that we will work together to keep our relationship going strong."

Needless to say, I gave my airline applications to another friend and ended up taking a speech job with a small school district in Southern Ohio, not far from Athens, so I could still see Gregg while he finished up his last year of school.

~ 7 ~

Unconditional Love

In 1973, I suited up for my first job as a professional speech pathologist. I would be the only therapist in the entire county. Since it was a
huge area, I had to divide the year into nine-week chunks and alternate
travel between the northern half and then the southern half. Though
it was doable, it resulted in fewer speech services than was desirable.
Sadly, the school districts were poor and that was the best they could
offer. It was a challenge that I somehow managed, even though I was
stretched pretty thin.

As it turned out, my second year, right after Gregg graduated, the
county decided that they should split the districts and hire a second
speech therapist. We secretly applauded their decision, and Gregg got
the job. Lucky for him, he had connections!

We had decided early on that, if we could live together successfully,
then maybe we would think about marriage. We found an apartment
conveniently located in the county seat between the two school districts. We moved in, dressed up our little space, making it as homey as
possible given our meager assets, acquired a few cats, went to our jobs,
and got on with life.

It was fun to be in that next phase of life, even having so little. My self-
respect would not have let me ask for help. Doing so has never been
easy for me, even with my family. My father was very much about mind-
ing our own business. He professed that our problems were our own to
be dealt with. It was better not to be beholden to anyone if you could
help it. I guess I took it to heart. When I graduated college, he made it

very clear to me that he would not be paying any further bills of mine. I knew he meant it, and even if he didn't, I was ornery enough that I knew I would not ask. I would take care of myself. I was fortunate that he had supported me thus far. I am sure it contributed to my sense of independence and wanting to handle my own issues and solve my own problems.

Besides that, I had my mother as a role model my whole life. She has always been a survivor in the sense that she couldn't depend on my dad to be around when she wanted or needed him. Sometime when my sister and I were young, their marriage went sour. Though she longed for his love and support, she never felt like she got it, at least in the way she wanted. I knew it made her sad. Rather than falling apart, she compensated by making a life for us and for herself without his help. If she had only herself to count on, then she could not be disappointed.

On a visit home one weekend, my father cornered me. I had not sought out my parents' approval for what I was doing. Living "in sin" was still not greatly accepted, but it was becoming more common.

"So, what's the plan?" he asked from his seat on the couch. He was dressed casually in plaid golf pants with a perfectly matched, solid-colored shirt and color-coordinated socks. Never one to slump in his seat, he always took great pains to arrange his sharply-creased pants so as not to bag out the knees. He leaned forward, elbows resting on his thighs to let me know he was serious. I was on the floor in my cutoffs, leaning against the armchair.

"What do you mean, what's the plan?" I asked.

"Well, you and Gregg seem to have made the decision to live together. I was just wondering what was next."

I squirmed a little at the directness of his question. "Do you mean, have I thought about it?"

"Yes, you seem to have jumped in with both feet. I just wonder if you know what you are doing." His tone was both critical and tender at the same time.

"I think so. Believe it or not, I did not do this lightly. I knew it was a big step." I stopped short of saying, "that you wouldn't necessarily approve of." I had already flown the nest, though not for long, and was emancipated, supporting myself and out of his immediate control. Besides, deep down, I knew that he couldn't be too judgmental. His own decisions and marriage did not make him the best role model.

"Do you love him?"

"I feel like I do," I said, trying to verify the words even in my own head. "I'm not really sure I have a complete idea about what love is exactly. But I do know that we seem to fit together well, and we have a great time with each other. Do I know if he's the one? If you asked me today, I would say yes, but how do you know he'll be the one forever?"

Why did I have such a hard time saying that I loved him? My parents thought that they loved each other and look where it got them. I was too pragmatic just to be swept off my feet, so I kept trying to make sense of it in my mind by asking myself: Would I miss him if he were gone? What if I never saw him again? Is there anything about him I can't deal with? I would miss him and be very sad if I never saw him again. There were things about his personality that were different from mine, but none that annoyed me that much. Rather, I found him curious and interesting.

I looked up from my feet, where my eyes had absently been resting, back to my dad. He was watching me, still scrutinizing my demeanor. "I just don't want you to make a mistake that you'll regret later," he responded. "Living together is like being married without the paperwork." He knew that I was on birth control, so that wasn't the issue. Most girls talk to their mothers about sex, but not in this family with an ob-gyn father. I think he just wanted to make sure that I hadn't acted on a whim and settled for less than what I should.

"I appreciate your concern, Dad. This isn't something that your generation really did. You and Mom haven't had the best marriage, and I guess I agreed to this because I don't want to make a mistake. I want to be sure that we can be together all the time and still be happy and content with each other. We actually talked beforehand and agreed that, if we could make it a year, then we would get married."

He seemed placated with this statement, taking it in and weighing it in his mind. Then he said to me more gently, "You know I haven't always done things the best way, and I want better for you. There are a lot of big decisions in life, and this is one of them. You know I care about Gregg, but I am more interested in you. I don't want you to be hurt; I want you to be happy."

"I know. But you have to trust me, that I believe I am doing what's best for me. Maybe it's because you and Mom haven't always been on the same page. I just want to be as sure as I can be." I gave him a weak smile, a silent thank you for his caring about me.

Soon our small apartment began to feel cramped, and Gregg came across an old farmhouse for rent in the northern part of the county. It would mean a longer drive for me, but it really was a prettier area, in the Appalachian foothills. It had been an old Christmas tree farm at one point, and the house sat back on a hill about a quarter mile from the main road. There was a good-sized fresh water pond in front surrounded by many rows of pine trees. The idea of living more of a country life excited both of us.

Country living was fun for me. I was a city girl, or more accurately, a suburbanite. I reveled in wandering the property and living off the land. We found a rototiller in one of the barns and plowed up our first vegetable garden. The driveway was lined with apple trees, making it easy to pick fresh apples that I made into pies.

Gregg figured out how to build a floating dock with a couple of fifty-gallon drums and some wood, where we would sit with the cats beside us, drink tea or wine, and ponder our lives. Taj, our cat, had had kittens at our previous abode, multiplying our charges to four, along with a collie mix, who had shown up at our door. Not sure we needed a dog, we named him Exit, hoping he might go back to his real home, but he was happy to stay with us.

We had no doubts about a life together by then. We informed our parents that we had chosen July 12 of that summer to be married, so we best get things rolling because we wanted to still have time for a honeymoon before the school year began again.

The wedding took place on a patio outside the carriage house of an old mansion in my hometown. We enlisted a bluegrass band that regularly played at a bar in Kent and proceeded to have a hoedown.

Our "honeymoon" consisted of a three-week trek to the West Coast and back in a 1965 Chevy panel van that Gregg had worked diligently to transform inside and out. He had painted the outside shades of dark and light green with a gold lace stencil around the middle. It was unique, to be sure. The inside was hung with green shag carpeting 360 degrees around and privacy curtains. He installed a nice sound system, a vanity with a sink, and large cushions that could be used as either a couch or a bed.

We traveled to the Northwest, through the Badlands, Glacier National Park, Seattle, and all the way down the coast to San Diego, Tijuana, and back through Nevada and Denver.

We also experienced one of the worst times of our entire marriage during that first week of "wedded bliss." We were snippy with each other and constantly bickering about this or that. Was it the fact that we were now "tied" to each other for life? Maybe the thought gave both of us pause. I must admit there were moments when I wondered if we had made a mistake. It was so unusual for us to not get along. I looked at the ring on my finger and told myself that this, too, would pass. At least my heart told me so, even if my mind was being stubborn. Maybe we were just tired from all of the stress of the past few months.

As week number two rolled around, our moods began to even out and we regained our usual rhythm. We laughed often and got a kick out of exploring so many different places together. Though it was interesting to have met new people along the way, we still never lacked for conversation between the two of us.

Back in Ohio, after losing running water at our current residence with no assistance from our landlord, we moved into a different farmhouse where we cared for sixty head of beef cattle in exchange for reduced rent. It was a beautiful place with a unique round barn, the crowning glory of the property. The art of feeding cows was both challenging and invigorating, making us feel like genuine farmers. Our days flowed from one to the next, neither of us needing more than each other. It was in this setting I came to a realization of something that will always hold a special place in my heart.

One summer day, I was absently washing dishes, listening to the leaves rustle outside the open window above the sink, musing about our lives, when it dawned on me in a way it never had before, that Gregg loved me. The thought came unbidden and out of the blue. I could feel my heart swell, my eyes well up almost immediately as I took in the moment. He could have chosen anyone. There were a million women in the world, yet amazingly, he had singled me out from among them, just me and nobody else.

In that same instant, an awareness washed over me that I am not sure I ever really grasped up until then, that if he loved me, I must actually be *lovable*. It was personally profound and somehow filled me with a solace that I can't even describe. There was a void inside that I had never consciously acknowledged as lacking in my character, though I must have carried it with me for a long time. And now it was a void no longer. In a heartbeat, my own self-doubt and self-protection vanished, like the final petal of a flower opening to reveal the perfection inside. His unfailing, unconditional, generous offering of his spirit to me had finally penetrated my soul and wrapped itself around me in a warm and joyous embrace. It didn't matter that I wasn't perfect. He loved all the parts of me, not just the parts that I deemed he should. Whatever I brought to the table was what made me who I am and beautiful in his eyes. Even to this day, that knowledge makes me feel safe and protected and confident in my being and what I have to offer the world.

I wiped the tears from my cheeks and, reveling in my new and enlightened state, stood gazing through the glass as a butterfly danced in and around the branches of a hydrangea bush in full bloom. Whatever else might happen in my life after that, I knew something inside me had irrevocably changed forever. I finally grasped the power of unconditional love, a love that allows our true being to shine forth, the love that is the essence of who we all are inside, the piece of us that is connected not only to each other, but also to the source that we call God. It filled me up.

~ 8 ~

Is It Possible?

I had been waiting a long time for an understanding of love like the one Gregg provided me with, though I'd done some homework along the way, questioning the mysteries of life and wondering about God. When I was about thirteen, for instance, my mother's friend Margaret invited us over for a party that featured a tea-leaves reading. I didn't know there was such a thing, and it intrigued me. I never had my fortune told before. Being a teenager, my head was filled with dreams of boyfriends and what I would be when I grew up. Perhaps she would set me straight once and for all.

The night of the event, Mom and I joined a small group of women in Margaret's family room. She had brewed the tea and poured us each a cup to drink as we munched tasty little niblets. The tea-leaves reader chatted with us for a bit, then retired to a table in the adjacent screened porch. The rest of us sipped from our teacups, careful not to swallow the leaves that floated in the hot water, which was tricky. Then one by one as we finished, each person joined her on the porch for an individual reading.

When it was my turn, I carried in my cup with its blob of wet leaves at the bottom, handed it to her, and took my seat. She looked like any other mom, no turban or bejeweled hands like the fortunetellers on television. Her eyes focused on the cup, and she began to talk. She told me about myself, what I was good at, some things I was currently doing, and connections to a few people I knew. Much of what she said was accurate; other comments were questionable or about things that supposedly hadn't happened yet. It was impressive.

When she was done, I took the cup and looked again at the bottom, wondering if I missed something. Nope, just the same blob of wet leaves, no particular shape or sign to give me any clue about anything. Yet the process was fascinating and gave me something to ponder. I determined I would pay attention in the days ahead to see if what she said came true.

All the women shared their experiences and openly wondered if the tea-leaves lady really could "know" about us, and if so, how? Was she reading our minds? What if she really *could* zero in on every thought in our heads? We came to no conclusions, but everyone got a kick out of it, deemed the party a success, and went home with new things to think about.

In high school, another friend passed along a book, an ostensibly true story about a minister who had begun to wonder about life after death as a result of counseling many families and performing many funerals during his years of preaching. Parishioners often shared stories about inexplicable events that happened after their loved one had died, leading them to believe that Grandma or whoever was communicating with them. The experiences gave them the feeling that the person who passed on was still around watching over them offering comfort. It stirred the reverend's own curiosity. Was it really possible to get in touch with those left behind? Or did they just disappear from our lives never to be heard from again?

In his old age, the minister became ill and told his son that, if there *was* any way to contact him after he died, he would. The story detailed his death and how the son began to find things amiss in his house afterward, such as pictures on the ground, objects moved to a different spot not far from where they had been, and a pile pennies knocked over that the son had deliberately left stacked high. There were no other plausible explanations for the events, and his son reached the conclusion that his father was, indeed, communicating with him. *I* certainly couldn't explain away the details in the book. It resonated with me as sincere and credible.

These two events played an integral part in refocusing my spiritual views of life from traditional religious dogma toward more metaphysical thinking. The whole idea of living only one life and ending up in heaven or hell never sat well with me—that you get one shot and it's over. It leaves so many things unexplained, such as why people are born disabled, why babies die, or why some people are extremely intelligent and others are not. If what we call God is truly loving and merciful and you get one chance at life, then shouldn't we all start with equal opportunities on the same playing field? The inequities don't make sense. However, the idea of living more than one life on earth does. At least you can learn from your mistakes and do better the next time around.

Another aspect of my perspective that began to change was my view of the Almighty. Most monotheistic religions nix the idea that we, as humans, could have what we call God within us. It is sacrilegious and blasphemous to think so. Instead, the message is that we are separate, us here, Him there. In an effort to provide rules for living together peacefully and monitoring our behavior, they preach about the watchful eye of a God who not only loves, but also punishes, and at the same time, gives the church leaders the power to direct our lives as though they are the only ones who might have God's ear. It creates an atmosphere of conditional love and competition.

The information I read contradicted this and led me in another direction. That is, we are all formed from the essence of God, a chip off the old block. Even the Bible says we are made in His image. We are extensions of God, not separate. We are then left to contemplate the ramifications of having God within us and all the creative potential that goes with it. If our true nature is only pure love, then each of us must take responsibility for our lives and realize that the reason things go awry is a reflection of our own conduct and decisions we make as opposed to being dealt a raw deal when we were born. We all have the capability to act and perceive the world from that perfect place within, the place of unconditional love.

~ 9 ~

Alternatives

Finally, the first of the tubes comes out! It's the catheter—hurray! Gregg takes a pee and a little poop under his own steam and we celebrate and laugh about how all modesty flies out the window in the hospital. Good humor prevails!

A few more days pass, and his appetite begins to return. He needs to go twenty-four hours with no hookup to his stomach drain before he can try some food. His mood has perked up a little, and he seems to have been able to find a perspective he can live with at the moment. He is more matter-of-fact about his situation, and since he has mentioned how uncomfortable it is, I know he will really be happy when he can get the tube out of his nose.

I'm back doing my job as a preschool speech therapist while Gregg recovers, but I visit daily. The hospital is literally on my way home. A week or so after surgery, I phone Gregg before going to work to check in and see how he's doing. Any little tidbit of good news seems like a mountain of it. My heart drops when he says hello. "It's been a really shitty night," he says, despair audible in his voice.

"What happened?" I'm not sure I want to know.

"For some reason, I was in a major amount of pain and could not get comfortable. After rolling around forever, I finally rang the nurse and she doubled my pain meds, but it didn't help much. Besides that, my ass hurts from these hemorrhoids. They bled when I tried to use the bathroom. Now my shoulder is hurting, and my head is aching."

What can I do but listen and reiterate for the umpteenth time that everything will be OK soon? I feel so helpless that I can't even go visit at lunch. My stomach is in knots again, and I don't want to see any doctors. They are becoming the harbingers of bad news. And anyway, why can't they, the supposed healers, fix this?

Despite my trepidation, when I finally visit after school, I look down the hallway in the direction of his room and see him walking toward me. I blink. Is it really him? But there's no mistaking his robe, a black, red, and green hand-me-down number from my dad that Gregg rarely wears at home, but is a vast improvement from the lovely, open-air, butt-showing hospital gown. A smile plasters itself to my face, my droopy spirits immediately transported from the gutter to the sky!

"Greggy!" I shout. "What are you doing?" I turn my amble into a trot. He grins ear to ear as he reaches out to me. I wrap my arms around him and can hardly believe this is happening. We stand entwined, transported to a place we have sorely missed.

"They unhooked me and I couldn't wait to get out of bed and move! I feel like I just got out of jail!"

"You sounded so miserable this morning, I didn't even know what to say to you. I guess you never know what's right around the corner!" I'm still squeezing him. It feels like forever since we hugged, there were so many tubes everywhere. It is as if I can finally give him the comfort I have wanted to give him from the start but couldn't. Or maybe, I'm getting the consolation that I didn't realize I missed. All I know is that I don't want to let go. This is what feels right and familiar. This is where I belong, wrapped in his arms.

"After last night, I feel like I have been reborn!" He's holding onto me as much as I am to him. I nod, breathing in his warmth mixed with the familiar scent of his skin.

I pull back a little to see his face. "Do you want to keep walking a little more or are you tired?"

"Let's see if we can make it to the end of the hall and back." I help him move the IV pole to one side and put my arm around his waist. He puts his arm on my shoulder and off we go. The nurses see us and smile. His joy is infectious.

He tells me he is off the pain pump and hopes Tylenol with Codeine will be enough to keep his pain in check. After the previous night, I wonder. Returning, we sit on his bed as he attempts to eat his first meal of juice, Jell-O, broth, and tea. I watch him tentatively, hoping against hope that it all goes down with no problems. It does, and later we both cry a little in relief about the whole thing.

"You know Deb, I really feel like a new man. Something happened today. I can't explain it, but something has shifted." He's back in bed, under the covers, but sitting upright.

"This last week has been probably the hardest of your life, with lots of ups and downs," I say to him. "It probably felt like more downs," I add on second thought. Sitting on the edge of the bed, I rest my hand on his leg. "But here you are! You've made it through the toughest part. When you get so low like that, it certainly magnifies the highs. I'm just so relieved and happy to see you feeling better!"

He shakes his head in acknowledgment, but there's an introspective look on his face. I assume his feeling of "rebirth" is because he is free of all of the encumbrances of the past week, but now, seeing him, I realize that maybe it's more. I'm not sure he could express it to me even if I asked, so I don't. I'm just happy he has found something positive to gain from this experience.

Ten days after surgery, Gregg is released to come home. He is absolutely ecstatic to be outside and breathing fresh air. We take a short walk with our dog, holding onto each other and walking slowly, enjoying the beautiful day, and thanking God we have arrived at this point.

Later in the afternoon, we drive to the local arboretum with his parents, Ron and Claire, who decided to come home early from Florida; Gregg's sister, Maddie, who arrived from Connecticut a few days after my sister left; and his brother, John, to take in nature. The sun shines down upon on us and there is gratitude in the air. Life is good.

* * *

That evening, doing some research on the internet, I learn that Gregg's type of stomach cancer cannot be cured, just treated, as it went through the stomach wall, and I immediately decide not to share it with him. He's barely recovered from the surgery. My shoulders drop, and I feel dispirited and sad. Any illusions we had of being free from this ordeal are most likely unfounded. But then I think, at least the option of continual treatment could keep Gregg alive. His uncle has been living with lymphoma for twenty-one years. The road might not be desirable or easy, but at least, it *is* a road.

Leaning back in my chair in the basement, I rest my head on the headrest and close my eyes, my brow furled. Are we up for this? We have always been interested in the ambiguities of life and have pursued an active search for answers off and on for many years. It feels like we have a good foundation and perspective. But are you ever just totally sure of what you think you know about the world? Our current options seem to be staring us in the face. They are on the table, daring us to find out.

* * *

When the surgeon, in our very first conversation with him, alluded to the fact that Gregg would have to make some adjustments to his eating patterns, we didn't understand the full ramifications of what he was saying. We were so concerned with removing the cancerous tissue, we figured we would deal with the rest later. Now, as I sit watching him eat, it is clear it will be a long and arduous process.

The incisions and sutures from the surgery have almost healed, but learning which foods to ingest and how much of each to eat is a crap shoot. Every wrong move results in major stomach cramps and pain. Just what he needs on top of everything he has already been through!

I try to pay attention to what works and what doesn't because it is all I can do. Gregg is not savvy when it comes to analyzing his food. His inclination is to go for whatever appeals to him rather than pick and choose.

Our subsequent requests for help land us nowhere other than an offer of encouragement to aim toward a healthy diet as opposed to junk food or sweets. No kidding! The hospital didn't even manage that with food trays full of pudding, Jell-O, and ice cream. Where's the nutritional value there? The word is that everyone's system varies, and we just have to work our way through trial and error to see what goes down and what upsets his system. It frustrates us both, but I tell myself that maybe this part is only temporary and will work itself out in time. Perhaps that's why no one shows much concern. Still, it doesn't feel right.

As we later come to realize, though each doctor has his or her own expertise, no one is responsible for coordinating all of the aspects of a single patient's care; there's no case manager who can see the whole picture as opposed to just the individual parts. Consequently, it is becoming painfully obvious to us that the patient and/or caregiver must become his or her own advocate.

That sounds like a good idea until you realize that you have no clue where to begin. The patient is often down and out without the energy to do research, which leaves everything up to the caregiver, if there is one. It sounds silly, but it is kind of a catch-22. You have to ask the right questions to become knowledgeable about what you need, but then you have to be knowledgeable about what you need to ask the right questions.

So, we do our best and begin to have conversations with a number of friends who offer their support and point us in couple different directions. First, we try a chiropractor, whose caring demeanor and knowledge of her practice inspires confidence. She combines an interest in Chinese medicine with a holistic approach to healing. Her helpful suggestions include the importance of hydration along with avoiding foods harder to digest, such as glutens and sugars, and adding enzymes and stress-relieving activities. To complement that, we find a naturopath who lives in rural Ohio and looks like an Amish Santa Claus. His manner is warm and self-assured. He tells us that one of the main reasons people get sick is due to a variety of parasites that live in our bodies and insists that he knows exactly which parasite is responsible for Gregg's cancer. He shows us pictures and diagrams. He has some regret that Gregg has already been through the surgery as he feels that traditional medicine is overly invasive, thereby complicating an already complicated situation.

It all sounds a bit hokey at first, but he speaks with authority and is convincing in his explanations. As he talks, I am reminded of finding tiny bugs in my spice jars if left too long. Where do they come from and how do they get in there? Are the tiny eggs just hanging around waiting to hatch? Once I poured what was a box of perfectly fresh Cheerios into a bowl with milk and then got interrupted and couldn't eat them right away. When I returned, there were little black bugs floating in the milk! Had I eaten them when I was supposed to, they would have traveled down my throat with the rest of the cereal unbeknownst to me. So, who's to say he is not on the right track? I don't believe that traditional medicine holds all the answers. When you are given a diagnosis of a potentially terminal illness like cancer, keeping an open mind about all possibilities is imperative. We are looking for solutions. No rock need be left unturned.

I'm chagrined hearing that maybe Gregg shouldn't have had the surgery. Did we move too fast? Both of us have always embraced holistic thinking when it comes to health, not that we've always practiced what we preached. Maybe we should not have been so quick to take the word of the first doctor who came our way. It is a dilemma that pulls me in both directions, being the daughter of a physician, yet still feeling there is a much bigger picture here.

"Now that I am generally healed from the surgery," Gregg says, "I'm scheduled to begin chemo and radiation. What are your thoughts on that? Do you think I should go through with it?"

The doctor faces Gregg, leaning forward in his chair, elbows on the armrests, hands loosely folded in front of him. With genuine concern he responds, "I can't tell you what to do. I can only say that if it were me, I would not put that into my body." He then proceeds to explain what the drugs do, and how radiation affects the body.

Gregg listens intently with a serious, troubled look on his face. I got a dose of radioactive iodine after having my thyroid removed and was told that a body could only take so much radiation before it becomes hazardous and actually creates cancer. Ever since, I have limited the number of dental x-rays I get a year, which may not help much, but it makes me feel better.

We leave with a bagful of medicines. It's been another visit full of thought-provoking information, leaving us feeling muddled about which path we should follow. Knowing more does not always make things clearer.

The idea of naturopathic medicine seems like the way God intended it to be originally, using plants and herbs that grow naturally and are not extracted to be ten times the potency, only to cause a multitude of side effects. But does that mean excluding traditional medicine or including it? The term "holistic" would seem to encompass all forms of healing. Can we do both? Will they be counterproductive?

Every conversation seems to bring something new to consider. Options and perspectives are piling up. We want to make the right choice, but that assumes that there is a "right" choice to be made. Dragging our feet and waiting for the light bulb to go on will most likely result in waiting forever. There seems to be no right or wrong, only the path we choose. Will either path extend Gregg's life? How do we know? And how much control do we really have, anyhow? In the end, it seems all we can do is trust ourselves to make the moves one by one and see what happens next.

~ 10 ~

Onward

Six weeks after Gregg's surgery, we have our first appointment with the oncologist. Neither of us is excited to be meeting him, however nice he might be. It's like being forced into a mud puddle we would prefer to avoid, especially after our conversation with the naturopath. But, we also don't know what to expect. Perhaps he won't even recommend treatment.

The pleasantness of our surroundings as we walk in the front door surprises me. The foyer is well appointed with beautiful art work, interesting lighting, and nice couches and chairs in soothing colors of muted gold and more vibrant blue. Large, striking fish swim in a few large tanks. Whoever designed the space knew what they were doing. It has a decidedly inviting feel.

"This place is pretty nice!" I proclaim, taking it all in. Letting go of Gregg's hand, I point to an area on our left. "Look, Gregg boy, they have a mind/body/spirit area. What do you suppose is in there? Maybe we'll have time to check it out before we leave," I offer, desperately hoping that it cancels my preconceived notions about what's in store. I'm grateful for any little ray of light I can add to my plus column.

Gregg is already looking that way, his face calm and unreadable. I hate to keep asking how he feels or what he's thinking. We both have our own apprehensions we keep to ourselves. "Yeah, it looks like maybe they might have some interesting things," he says.

The receptionist tells us it will be a little while and yes, feel free to roam around. I glance out a wall of windows to see a nicely landscaped patio with large garden sculptures, a labyrinth, birdhouses, and wind chimes. I resist the impulse to wander through it, figuring we should wait until after we meet with the doctor. It appears someone has put in a great deal of time to create a place where people might find solace.

Everyone seems so cheerful. They smile, they laugh and kid around. They greet each other with happiness; not just the ones who work here, but also the ones who are ill, along with their caretakers. *How can they be happy when they are getting chemo drugs and radiation shot into their bodies?* I wonder. I'm sure many of them are sick and probably feel awful. Are they choosing to be lighthearted in an effort to keep their heads above water? Are they just naturally pleasant people who are grateful to be here at all? Maybe, it is for the benefit of others, as if to say, "It's not so bad." It contradicts my expectations. But then again, maybe it is more a reflection of *my own* mood. Gregg and I are just starting this phase of the journey, and we are not as far down the road. Perhaps they know something we don't.

We find seats, then chat and read a few magazines. After sifting through all the reading material on my lap and then some, I glance at the clock. "I can't imagine what is taking so long," I say to Gregg. "We've been here two hours already."

He puts down the book he is looking at and glances at the clock to confirm my observation. "Maybe they forgot us."

When I ask the receptionist, she smiles and explains, patiently and gently, that the doctor likes to give everyone their due time and sometimes gets backed up. "I'm sure it won't be much longer," she adds in a voice probably intended to be comforting, but it just sounds patronizing to me. I'm guessing she has had to give this speech more than once. "Can I get you something to drink? Coffee, water?"

"No thanks," I say, probably snippier than necessary. It seems important for her to know that I am not happy.

Returning to my seat, I tell Gregg what she said. It's hard not to be annoyed. "I don't know how they can justify making people wait so long, especially sick people. It really just strikes me as rude and does nothing to lesson our anxiety. Everyone wants their time, but perhaps they should work on more efficient scheduling or hire a few more doctors to keep the pace going."

"It's OK, Deb. I'd rather have a doctor who will spend some time with me than one who shoves me out in five minutes. We'll just have to suck it up and wait our turn."

"Humph," I grunt, not assuaged. I don't get why he seems so complacent, though it's probably easy to put off what might be bad news. "I still find it irritating. Hope it's not like this every time. I think I need to walk around."

We make our way to the mind/body/spirit area, figuring someone will track us down. The room is filled with a variety of curios, music, meditation CDs, and lots of inspirational reading, everything that might be helpful in looking inward and upward to find peace with one's circumstances. I'm Impressed: this finally seems to be a spot that encompasses what is necessary in working to heal people. It is not just about the science of disease; it is about treating all the aspects of a person including their spirits and attitude. Maybe something in here will help *my* attitude!

Finally, we hear the nurse call Gregg's name. It's been nearly three hours since our arrival.

Dr. Escobar walks in the examining room and warmly introduces himself, shaking our hands. He is a smallish man with dark skin and features, perhaps Filipino. He's in no hurry, talking to Gregg and wanting to get his take on things to fully understand the situation. The hospital reports are in his hands, and he glances at them as they talk.

Based on the records and what Gregg has told him, he informs us that it would be best if Gregg receives six weeks of radiation in conjunction with three rounds of chemo. Since the cancer is microscopic at best, the radiation will aim for the point where it was last identified within his body, and the chemo will be preventative, in case there is any floating around in his bloodstream. He then refers us to the radiology department around the corner in the same building to gain further information on the plan of action. Gregg thanks him, and we move to our next stop.

As soon as the radiologist walks in, I feel a sense of unease. Something about him bothers me, but I can't quite put my finger on it. Maybe it's the sinister look of his features. His eyes are beady, and his skin is pockmarked. *Get it together, Deb.* My preconceived ideas seem to be coloring everything that I encounter here. At any rate, he is the doctor in this department and since they all work together, we push through the conversation.

He says Gregg will have a little tattoo where the machine will point each time. I don't like the sound of it, picturing a permanent mark on him that will forever be a reminder of this awful phase of his life. Who wants to relive it every time you look in the mirror? I glance over at Gregg, expecting him to react, but his look is nondescript, taking it all in without protest, much to my dismay. Maybe he really doesn't care, having no tattoos already. I imagine he feels there are bigger things to be concerned about, like life and death. But I continue to voice my displeasure, and they assure me it will be small.

They take him to a room in the back of the office to mark the spot. When I see it, it's literally the size of a pinhead, like a tiny freckle. OK, so I overreacted. A week later, the official radiation treatments begin. It seems harmless enough and does not interfere with us getting on with the business of living. But further in, it starts to take a toll as the effects compound each week. Gregg's energy gradually seeps from his body, making him more tired, though he stays positive with no complaints, and makes the most of his days.

Then the moment comes when he is due to receive his first chemo treatment. Once he is comfortably seated, they hook him up to an IV and pump him full of fluids before he actually gets the chemo drugs. My stomach is a mixture of anxiety, regret, and resignation.

We sit and look at each other but neither voices our feelings. Gregg is crossing a threshold of sorts, a point of no return. Not only is it poison that we attempt to view as helpful and medicinal, but we don't know what the repercussions will be later, especially in conjunction with the radiation. We hold hands, quietly praying to God once again that this is a good move, weakly embracing faith rather than reservations and take one more step down the road.

~ 11 ~

Routines

Most days we rise from bed knowing that there are things we must do and places to go in order to get on with living. The world doesn't stop just because someone becomes sick. I still need to fulfill my work obligations. Gregg has missed more days than he would like from school, but amazingly, he's been keeping up with his usual jobs around the house. When he does falter, either they don't get done, or I do them. It doesn't bother me. I know he is doing his best and needs his energy to get better.

None of us can honestly say what we might do or how we would cope with a serious illness until we actually experience it. So, because I really don't know what *I* would do and because we are all different, watching Gregg has been both instructive and captivating.

He goes about it in his own way, the way he does everything in life, by trying to orchestrate every aspect he can. He notes all activities on a big calendar in the bedroom, listing doctor's appointments, visitors, and most importantly, weekends away. This gives him something to look forward to and helps him feel his life is going along in a somewhat normal fashion. Of course, we both know it's not.

He thanks God daily for the connection he has to all of the people in his life. Cards, letters, gifts, poems of inspiration, talismans, and books arrive regularly. Gratitude flows from him and he makes a point of carving out time every day to respond to each person individually in a card.

Sometimes it's been a surprise who has stepped up and offered kind words and encouragement, especially folks he is just acquainted with and even some whom he's never met, such as a woman from a nearby church who sends him weekly cards to let him know someone is thinking about him. It deeply touches us both.

I watch him do his routines each morning and wonder at his discipline and dedication. He rarely deviates if he's at home. I suppose they offer structure that helps him control a situation in which he feels somewhat helpless. The routines vary depending on the specific day of the week and may include doing yoga, meditation, reading the Bible, or throwing the I Ching, a Chinese study of seeing how in tune you are with the rhythms of the universe. But without fail, his activities always include writing. He has done this for many years, even prior to getting cancer, though he has upped it a notch since then.

Though his job has been waiting in the wings, Gregg is finding that he's tired and not sure he can keep up with the daily rigors of running a middle school classroom. He is currently teaching technology education in a nearby school district, which is ironic because he was not very technologically savvy when he applied for it. In fact, he rather avoided it, and we were a little surprised that he was chosen as the candidate, though his name and reputation may have preceded him. He knows a lot of people. Even though the opportunity was a bit of a learning curve at first, all had faith he would be successful, and he has been. In his words, 'Even if you're a very, very good dinosaur, you are still extinct. I need to move into the twenty-first century and learn to embrace technology."

The people at this school have been nothing but kind and accommodating, almost unusually so, considering he really hasn't been on their staff that long. The superintendent tells Gregg to do whatever he has to do to get well. He has plenty of sick days that he can use, which makes us both happy. Of course, I know he would rather be working. He loves the kids and enjoys his interactions with them, while they have always been drawn to him like a magnet. He has a knack for connecting with them and leads by example. But he's just too ill.

I, on the other hand, work most days unless we have a doctor's appointment. Friends have offered to help in a variety of ways, including driving with Gregg to treatments. He can drive, but it is better if someone else does in case of any complications. Besides, he loves the camaraderie that comes with hanging out with his friends for a day, and it really does keep his spirits up. And I love that I don't have to keep taking time off. I never thought that I would want to escape to my job, but it has been a soft place to land. It also gives me some feeling of normalcy and gets my mind out of my problems and into other concerns that are a little more removed.

My good friends at school have been a godsend in guiding me to keeping my head on straight. They are patient listeners who help me to gain perspective and keep me laughing. I have not always socialized with people I work with, and it feels neither random nor a coincidence that they are with me at this difficult time in my life. It's as if the universe made sure I had extra support, knowing I would need it. I am so grateful that they are with me on this journey, and they have become very dear to me.

I write in my journal when I can. Friends and family cannot be on standby every second, and they often don't know what to say anyhow when I need to vent, though their hearts are open. Writing helps me to express and define what often isn't even clear to me until I write it down. When I go back and reread what I have written, I often see myself as an outsider would. It offers me an observational perspective that helps me monitor what is going on within me. I can see the train of my thoughts along with an inner knowing or wisdom that flows through the words which often, unexpectedly, comforts me.

So far, I seem to have been able to focus on the tasks at hand and keep a lid on things. People know me as being upbeat and levelheaded, and I'm usually content to be that person. I really don't feel like I am working too hard at it. It comes naturally and seems to be who I am. Maybe I've just had a lot of practice.

I actually did toil at squashing my feelings about my parents when I was younger. I wanted to be "unaffected" by their problems back then. I told myself that I didn't care. I pretty much perfected it. But I would like to think that I have realized the error of my ways and have worked through some of that; I have consciously tried to let my feelings out when I feel them. I just don't always do it in front of people. I am sure that the process is incomplete and that this encounter is taking me to task. Gregg has helped immeasurably by loving and supporting me, no matter what.

I certainly do bear his hurt now, no hiding from that. There is always an underlying feeling of helplessness. I continually adjust my perspective about how to be loving wife, nurse, watchdog, cheerleader, confidante, advocate, fellow adventurer, or anything else that calls my name or that Gregg seems to need. It is exhausting at times, but I wouldn't have it any other way. I am acutely aware that this is Gregg's journey and that I am here to be by his side. I can't walk in his shoes; I can only walk in mine.

Though I don't know the bigger picture, I am confident there is one. How can there not be? He depends on me to be comforting and sane. And I depend on him to live his life as normally as possible. Neither one is a stretch for us. It is what we do. Are we both hiding our feelings? At the moment, it doesn't feel like it. It just feels like us getting on with it the best we can.

*   *   *

My Journal:

Gregg had an interesting experience last night. He threw up and was feeling bad but dealing with it. He fell asleep, and he started twitching and mumbling unintelligibly in his sleep. I said something to him and he said, "The Lord just gave me a big hug, right on my stomach," and then he fell back to sleep. Today he remembered the sensation of hands and a head on his stomach and felt the pressure of it. After-wards, he felt fine and was able to sleep. "Divine intervention," he said. Wow! He certainly has been closer to the Lord than ever before. I'd like to think of it as a divine and lasting healing, and I pray that he is fine and will continue to be.

Thank you for sunshine today and spring flower smells and mallard ducks in the pond and catnip in the garden for the kitties and for the cat enjoying the garden.

Thank you for friends and love and family and support.

Thank you for daughters who are loving but frustrated.

Thank you for Gregg's good days

Thank you for being with us always.

~ 12 ~

Reflections

Usually by the time summer rolls around, we're in the midst of vacation plans, plotting who to visit and when. Of course, there are always house and garden projects to sink our teeth into, besides. This is when it's especially nice to be in education, even though people like to give us a hard time about having summers off. Never ones to let grass grow beneath our feet, we've always taken full advantage of the opportunity to go.

This year, however, things look a little different. We originally planned to visit friends in Texas, but with Gregg's treatment schedule and his overall health, we both think it's wise to stay closer to home. Affirming that we've been fortunate to do many things in the past, this doesn't seem too big a sacrifice, though to be honest, we would prefer to carry on as usual. However, we know that choosing life and good health are the first and most important priorities.

So, with this decision made, Gregg decides that he needs a project. He has always had some sort of old car that he has purchased, painted, got running, and driven for the heck of it. It is something that connects him to both his childhood and his father—plus he loves to do it. A few of the cars and trucks have been desirable, like the 1948 pickup with Betty Grable stamped on the ceiling or the 1958 Nash Metropolitan; others, like an old Marlin or a nondescript Datsun, Gregg has been attracted to for reasons that I cannot explain. He's quirky that way. He likes having something different from what most people would choose. The "cool" factor doesn't matter. The funny thing is that because Gregg thinks it is cool, and most people like Gregg, the vehicle somehow gains prestige. At the very least, people just smile and shake their heads. It is his hobby and I am just along for the ride, literally, although I have on occasion helped him design and redo the interiors.

"Hey, Deb! Guess what I found?" Gregg walks toward me with the newspaper in his hand. I'm engrossed in a movie on television with our cat on my lap, my fingers absently scratching its neck.

"Don't tell me," I say, half-heartedly, without turning my attention to him, "another new truck."

"Better than that. There's a guy who has an old Lyman for sale. He wants $2,500, the same price I want for my car!"

"What's an old Lyman?" I ask, changing positions as our cat jumps down, trying to keep my eyes and at least one ear attuned to my show.

"A boat!" he exclaims. He stands right beside me, paper in hand, partially blocking my view. Realizing that he is going to keep talking, I reluctantly mute the television and look at him, trying to appear interested, although my body language is probably more than transparent. His face shines brightly with delight, as if he has discovered a buried treasure.

"A boat! What do you know about boats? You don't even like to swim. And you get seasick every time you've ever fished. I'm pretty sure we don't need a boat," I say, dismissively, turning back to the TV.

"I don't know. We live right next to one of the largest lakes in the country," he says. "It would be fun to be able to go out for some sunset cruises whenever we feel like it. We wouldn't have to rely on being asked. Maybe we could even water ski!"

I can't believe he's really serious. Cars are one thing, but boats? He is still standing there with the paper, looking at me, waiting for me to join in his enthusiasm. Of course, he knows I take some convincing.

"You wouldn't only need the boat—you'd need a trailer and a truck to pull it." I'm trying to discourage him, but it backfires and sounds as if I'm really considering it.

"It must be sitting on something now, and it wouldn't take much to put a tow package on our SUV. Let's go over and look at it. The guy lives right here in town. Maybe he'll trade me."

"What makes you think he wants a car? He's trying to get rid of something, not gain something."

"Come on, Deb. What can it hurt? I need a project to keep me busy if I am going to sit around here all summer. It will give me something to do. Eli will help me. He knows more about boats than I do."

He continues to stand there, a pleading smile on his face. Now that he has played the "What will I do with myself now that I'm stuck here?" card, I feel myself softening. Plus, I have always had a hard time saying no to him. Grabbing the remote to click off the television, I let out a little sigh and get up off the couch, not the least convinced, but allowing myself to be drawn in by Gregg's sob story.

The man is excited to show us the boat. He explains in detail what he's done to it, what it still needs, and assures us that the motor runs and that it won't take much to make it water-worthy. We wouldn't know if it was or it wasn't, so we are forced to take his word for it, trying to learn as he talks.

Gregg turns on the charm, works his magic and against all odds, makes the trade. I can't believe the seller fell for it. I am sure he was a little flummoxed that he really didn't come out ahead, but instead became the proud owner of an old car. But he agreed to the trade and now we own a boat.

Eli agrees to be a partner in this endeavor. He and Gregg look over the boat, which is twenty-two feet long and designed to handle large waves. They figure out what exactly it needs so it doesn't sink into Lake Erie.

They look over the body first, as they would a car, and decide that it needs to be cleaned, sanded, and sealed. They rig up giant hooks to the roof of our carport, put straps underneath the boat and pull the trailer out. The boat hangs from the rafters where work can take place.

We all take turns doing one job or another, including Ron, Gregg's father, who is often a part of Gregg's projects. He also knows nothing about boats, but he might be able to have some input on any issues with the engine, and they all just enjoy having their "boy time."

Gretchen pitches in, too, since she is home for the summer, happy to spend more time with her dad. She has been somewhat removed from the day-to-day happenings being away at college, although she has always been in touch by phone and supported us in her own way. It is difficult to see a parent in a vulnerable state. Gregg has been a guiding force in her life in so many ways. He has always supported her, encouraged her, and cleared the path for her, so that she can be the person she is destined to be. Like his dad before him, he has also taken the time to get to know her friends and connect with them as well. She does not often let her guard down around us, but tends to direct her energies towards the dramas in her own life. Her friends at school have been there for her, and Gregg and I are both grateful that she can lean on them if she wants to.

During the boat transformation, Gregg finishes his final two chemo treatments and his own continued personal transformation. He is doing OK most days. His weight has dropped because eating is still often touch and go, as are his energy levels, but he is enjoying the boat and spending time with his buddy, Eli, just like so many times before.

It always lifts my spirits to see him happy and getting on with his life. I am not sure I could do the same, but his desire to live surpasses anything else. He is determined to get over this bump in the road and let his spirit shine brightly. We do not talk about the fact that his life could be short, although we both are very aware. It lingers just over the horizon out of sight. Instead, we choose to take each day as it comes and make the best of whatever it entails with Gregg leading the way.

Nina, his sister in Denver, has often been in touch with him by phone and letters, sharing words of wisdom and encouragement. For most of the time I have known her, she has been on her own journey through life as a single woman. She has traveled, been in the Peace Corps, and lived in fun places like Hawaii and Colorado. Her path has not always been easy, but she often manages to land on her feet and find a support system to help her get through. She, in turn, has always appreciated the importance of community and how we are all here to help one another.

As with many of us, her beliefs have also evolved through the years. She has pursued Native American philosophies along with other types of wisdom. Her little notes of encouragement and perspective to both Gregg and me have sometimes taken me by surprise. It is not that I didn't think she was capable of these actions; it's just that the circumstances of life have never before shown me this side of her. I have come to see her in a whole new light, and I think Gregg has too. After he had his surgery, she began referring to him as Half-Stomach Warrior. It has taken on a special meaning and gives him an extra dose of courage.

One night she calls to see how he is holding up and to share stories about what she has been doing. Afterward, he tells me that the one thing that struck him most from the conversation, the thing that he takes to heart, is that he needs to rest, relax, recuperate, and reflect during this healing part of his life. In other words, consciously taking time to exist in a state of being as opposed to a state of doing. Not only is he male, but he also comes from a family of doers, so it is difficult for him to just "be." It's easier to keep busy. Then you don't really have to sit down and be alone with yourself. It's not just about doing things like meditating—it's about being your authentic self.

He tells me that in church on Sunday, the minister spoke about the importance of a name. As he was contemplating the message, it came to him that he should christen the boat "Grace." It seemed the perfect marriage of his thinking at the moment, the boat representing a form of rest and relaxation and a state of grace he aspires to.

Gretchen and I both agree that it is fitting, and we paint it on the back of the boat.

The day finally comes when we are ready for the maiden voyage. I snap a few pictures of the boys in their boat, arms around each other, smiling. We ease it into the water at a local marina, and all give a little cheer when no leaks appear. All systems are go. Eli takes the helm. I stand beside him with Gregg sitting in the rear, leaning back and beaming with the sun on his face. I can see from his smile that he is ecstatic, happy to finally see his little project come to fruition. We only want to take it out for a short ride to see how it works and if there is anything else we need to do.

Another boat down the way is moving out ahead of us and by the time we wind our way through the waterways toward the main entrance to the lake, the same boat is heading back in. The man waves and says there are some high rollers out on the lake. We smile and thank him for the report. I have no idea what that means, but it seems like it was enough for them to return.

"Maybe we should turn around," I say to Eli, as he maneuvers us under a bridge. "Those guys didn't stay out long."

"It's pretty tight to turn here. We'll just go out past the pier and circle around." He sounds confident, so I don't think any more about it. I can see the opening to the lake, and there aren't even any whitecaps on the water. It's a beautiful, blue-sky day. I turn back to look at Gregg—he is oblivious, just enjoying the ride, wind in his almost nonexistent hair, baseball cap in his hand to keep it from blowing away. The breeze is warm and the air smells of lake water, damp earth, and algae, along with an occasional dead fish aroma when a carcass floats by.

Eli expertly guides the boat past the rocky pier and out into the lake. You can immediately feel the waves lifting and rocking the boat, and though they are not breaking, it is obvious they are rumbling beneath us. My heart beats a little faster as I realize what the man meant by "rollers."

The boat moves out and slowly circles around to reenter the marina. But just as we are about to head back, we glide past the opening and continue the loop. I think to myself that Eli must just be testing her out a little bit more since we are already here, so I try to enjoy the ride, figuring he knows what he is doing. He, at least, has had some experience skippering boats before.

After about the third circle, I am feeling uneasy, thinking that we can test out the boat some other time. We are rocking and rolling like crazy. A strong wind is blowing, negating what looks like a perfectly calm day, and we can hardly hear ourselves think, let alone converse. The waves are definitely messing with our equilibrium.

"Let's go back in!" I yell to Eli, who can barely hear me over the noise. "These waves are crazy." He keeps his eyes aimed forward, intent on what he is doing, which seems to be keeping us spiraling in the same direction.

"I've been trying to, but the boat will only turn one way. I can't get it to go any other direction," he shouts, a note of panic in his voice. It is becoming more evident to me by the second that we are rapidly moving into an even more precarious situation.

Gregg sits forward on his seat, bracing himself as we bounce around in every direction. He tends toward seasickness even on the best of days, and I wonder if he feels queasy. His eyes are on us though he cannot hear what we are saying. In answer to his unasked question, I bellow at the top of my voice, "Eli says the boat won't turn!"

"Maybe it's the rudder lock." He swivels around and leans over the back of the boat to check the motor, which totally freaks me out. We are rocking so much that if I let go, I know I will fall. And now here is Gregg, barely holding onto anything. He weighs considerably less than he did at the outset of his illness. It wouldn't take much to flip him out of the boat, and of course, none of us thought to put on life jackets. I am not even sure we have any on board yet, since it was to be just a short ride. Obviously, we aren't the sailors we should be, and here we are in a very perilous circumstance. What were we thinking?

The waves continue to edge the boat toward the rocks in the throes of its endless circles. I envision us all splattered against them. I can see the dock not far away, but there is no one visible who might even be aware that we are in distress. Eli is still ineffectively attempting to guide the boat, and I am just trying to stay upright. If I thought I could be useful, I would help Gregg, but at this point, I might be more of a hindrance. Whatever he is up to, it doesn't seem to make any difference.

"Be careful, Gregg! We don't need you tossed out of the boat," I yell, as he is still hanging over the back. I wonder what we are going to do and how we will escape this situation—or even *if* we will. In a panic, I send out a silent prayer for help: *Please God, help us out of this mess safely!* I know Eli is doing the same.

After about the sixth rotation, in utter amazement, we miraculously begin to head in the right direction and make our way past the rocks and back into the safety of the marina. *Thank you, God!* I think as I unhinge my fingers from the frame of the window. Eli slows the boat to nearly an idle just inside the pier so that we can all take a minute and breathe. There is no hiding the stunned looks on our faces as relief washes over each of us, along with the awareness that we could easily have died.

"That was scary!" I say to Eli, finally plopping down on the passenger chair.

"You're telling me! I kept trying to aim us back, but the boat had a mind of its own. The steering wheel just kept spinning and doing nothing." He takes off his hat and runs his hand back over his head before putting it back on. He looks back to where Gregg is wiping his arms off with a towel he found. "Are you OK, Gregg?"

"Yeah." He steadies himself and makes his way to the front where we are. "I was pushing to turn the motor manually, but it wasn't budging. I wonder what the deal was?"

"I don't know, but thank God you didn't fall out. That would have really been a problem!" I say, turning to look at the dock, still not a soul around. Where were they? What would we have done if we didn't get back in? Were we the only witnesses to our debacle? "I guess we learned one big lesson. Lifejackets are onboard for a reason. I can't believe we didn't think to wear them. We could have been shit out of luck." They both nod in agreement.

Later, once we get the boat situated back on its trailer, Gregg makes his way to the boathouse to use the facilities. I glance at Eli, who looks worse for wear, his brows furrowed in thought on the other side of the boat.

"Are you OK?" I ask, walking around to join him, wondering what's on his mind.

He shrugs and says, "The whole time we were out there circling, all I could think of was what would have happened if the boat hit the rocks and my buddy, Gregg, had to swim and try to survive. He's so much weaker than he was. He could've died." An edge of guilt sharpens his words. He stares out at the water, the sadness evident in his face. I know he's not only thinking about our most recent experience, but the future as well, a possibility that ever lurks around the corner.

I put my hand on his shoulder in an effort to soothe him. "Well, thank God we didn't have to find out. Somehow you managed to get us back safely. It certainly wasn't your fault. Apparently, the boat still has problems."

He looks at me, but the air of remorse sticks with him.

"That nearly scared the shit out of me!" We look up to see Gregg ambling back, and the moment passes.

"I guess it's a good thing we made it back to the bathroom!" I retort, my nose curled up. "That would not have been pretty. Then we would've been happy to push you in for a swim." We laugh and get in the car.

"Well, it wasn't the maiden voyage I was planning on, but I'm glad it turned out OK," Gregg says thoughtfully, as Eli starts up the truck. "Looks like we still have some work to do, big guy." Later, we find out that the steering wheel pin, which is connected to the steering wheel, came loose, and part of it had broken off. It really made no sense that we finally got turned around and were able to get the boat back in past the pier to where the water was calm, but it happened just the same. It was a brush with death that had us begging for mercy. It certainly got our attention.

Reflecting on the whole experience in the days following, all the metaphors for life strike me. Rough waters, no control, prayers for help, a miraculous turn of events, being guided to safety and most of all, a state of grace for which the boat was so aptly named.

I feel there is a lesson here. Is it as obvious as it seemed? Divine intervention? God will always get us out of rough waters if only we ask? I want to believe that it's that easy: say a prayer, and all will be well. The trouble is, I'm not sure it will be. Maybe what is well in God's eyes is not what's well in mine.

~ 13 ~

Ups and Downs

I watch the little house finch swoop into my view, landing on a wind-swept branch of the bush outside our big picture window in the living room. It rides the bouncing branch, tilting its head this way and that, taking in its surroundings. Looking directly into the window, it contemplates its own reflection in the glass. Unimpressed, it flies out of sight. Piles of snow make their last stand, resisting the sunshine warming me through the window as I relax on the couch, drinking tea and basking in the peacefulness. This is the first time in weeks I've let myself feel ease, happy to dwell in the moment. Closing my eyes and resting my head back, I consciously let out a sigh, dropping my shoulders and letting them return to their rightful place away from my ears, a place they have rarely been lately. Each breath urges the rest of my body to follow suit.

With Gregg's treatments finished, my relief is palpable. I relish the tranquility, wishing I could make it last forever. Sometimes, when I'm in a particularly joyful state of mind or in a beautiful space, I make a point of savoring the feeling or the view, so when times are tough, I can reach into my memory banks, close my eyes, and put myself back into that place, enjoying my own little pocket of bliss.

Gregg's illness has been a wake-up call, magnifying the impermanence of life. It makes me wonder about a lot of things. What have I accomplished up to this point? What is there still left to do? Am I living a purposeful life? Am I adding to the betterment of those around me or just co-existing and making myself happy? Am I missing the point altogether?

Complacency can only ever be a temporary state. There's no getting comfortable and expecting to avoid change. It is not the nature of things. You'll always find yourself on another path of learning, even though you're convinced you never wanted it and didn't ask for it in the first place. With change comes fear, fear that things will be worse than they are now, fear that you are losing something irretrievable, fear of not knowing what's next. It would be great to catch a glimpse of what the future holds, yet if you could, you wouldn't learn anything. Unfortunately, or maybe fortunately, we have to do the work. I can only pray that the learning curve doesn't become any sharper than it already is.

Gregg and I talk often about the roller coaster ride we've been on, the adjustments we've made, the low points, always tempered by the high points. Right now, the highest point is that treatment is over; we've both survived and been compelled to hunt for answers and perspective. Hopefully, we're stronger and wiser. The question is, can we maintain the new adjustments to ourselves and our thinking: Gregg to live a healthier lifestyle, no smoking, less drinking, with a renewed focus on God and spirit; me being more appreciative of each moment and not taking for granted my blessings? I know without a doubt we intend to try.

*   *   *

With some time freed up and spring already in the air, our house is calling for improvements, more major than minor, if we want to continue to live where we are. We've imagined remodeling many times, but somehow never gotten around to doing more than simple things like painting.

Our property is a good-sized corner lot within walking distance to the center of town. Neither of us ever thought we would live here for nearly twenty years. We were content to move around from rental to rental seeking new adventures in new places, but when Gregg accepted a job as a speech/language supervisor after grad school, his mom convinced us that investing in a house would be to our benefit, and, besides, the rates were fabulous. Probably she also had the ulterior motive of keeping us closer to home. Either way, the timing felt right and we relented, deciding we had to grow up sometime.

There are two additions we've wanted for a while, a fireplace for me and a sunroom for Gregg. We've even drawn up several possibilities over the years. Each time our excitement grows, but then we never take the next step. Gregg is the visionary, while I drag my feet, looking at all the practical aspects of why, where, how much, and so on. Thank God he pushes me out of my comfort zone regularly, or we'd never have changed what few things we did.

Now I delight in the idea of something to consume me other than health. We hire a local contractor and redesign the whole front of our house. It is exciting to see the possibilities on the computer screen, though dollar signs multiply with each flick of the keys. After thinking about it for a very short time, we jump in with both feet and change the front, get new windows, a new furnace, and air-conditioning, along with a new roof. It has taken us twenty years to get to this point and may take another twenty to do anything this big again.

We also have another event brewing, a trip to Cape Cod with my family, planned before Gregg got sick. When circumstances changed, we weren't sure if we'd be able to go, but now with things a bit calmer and feeling cautious optimism, we feel we deserve this vacation. My family gathers at holidays and travels individually, but we've never vacationed with all of us, including my mom. I'm personally thrilled that we all managed to clear our schedules to make it happen, and Gregg's health is allowing us to make the trip. My two nieces and Gretchen are all college age or older, and I know that this vacation will be a rare moment in time.

We have reservations about the house project continuing while we're gone, unable to supervise or answer questions, but we anticipated as many issues as possible. It's not worth giving up the vacation. Anyway, our neighbor, who watches our cats, is excited to come over and see what each day brings to the project. She loves to talk and enjoys the fun of being our stand-in.

The Cape has captivated me since I first laid eyes on it in college. A sorority sister drove a carload of us up during spring break to find jobs for the summer. I was game, though I'd never even heard of the place. I found a job at a bakery and spent the summer there with three other girls, trying not to turn into a donut myself. Gregg, Gretchen, and I have traveled here often; it's where we often rendezvous with our old pals from the couple of years Gregg and I spent teaching in England before Gretchen came along. The Norman Rockwell type quaintness always makes me feel like life is simple and uncomplicated, a feeling I'm craving now more than ever. I'm pretty sure Gregg is, too.

We fill our days with morning walks or bike rides, then wander to the beach, read, visit with each other, and play games in the evenings. Rotating the cooking chores gives the girls at least one night to show us their skills, and they do just fine. It makes me feel proud that they are so capable and happy to do it.

Gregg is in his element again, finding activities and adventures we can all partake in, such as a trip to Provincetown or Martha's Vineyard. "I was thinking it would be great to invite some of our local friends over here for dinner sometime," he announces one afternoon, grabbing a chair on the deck where he can scope out the full panorama of the sea. "It'd be fun for them to meet you guys. They don't live far. We could make it a party and have a lobster dinner. You can't come to the Cape without having a lobster dinner."

Mom and I are relaxing in the only two rocking chairs, while my niece is peacefully reading nearby. She looks up momentarily to see who is invading her space, then ignores us, and goes back to her book.

"What do you think?" he asks no one in particular.

"Sounds great!" Lila pipes up from inside in the kitchen before Mom or I can express our opinions. Apparently, she's had her ears perked up, not wanting to miss anything. "Can I get drinks while I'm up? Is it too early for wine?"

"It's never too early for wine, especially on vacation," I holler back, gently swaying in my chair, enjoying the view, and letting the smells of the ocean overtake me. "I'll have a glass. Maybe it'll help me forget about my tender, sunburned shoulders."

"I think I'd rather have a beer," Ty, my brother-in-law, responds. He's in the process of throwing wet towels over the banister to dry them. "I can get it."

Gretchen catches the end of the exchange as she comes downstairs. "I'll help carry the drinks, Lila," she offers, and sashays through the sliding door with her hands full, followed by my sister, who also carries a plate of cheese, crackers, and fruit which she lays on the table.

"We really lucked out with this house," I say, watching some distant seagulls land on the sand dune as they squawk at each other. Their noise accompanies the periodic lapping of waves hitting the shore. It's a backdrop that'll become more pronounced as the sounds of the day die down, and I imagine myself being lulled to sleep with the sliding door of our bedroom open at night. "Even though it's not directly on the ocean, the view's lovely."

"I don't mind walking over the dune. The beach is really clean and not too crowded," Gretchen replies, after taking a sip of her wine. "I think the idea of everyone coming to dinner is great, Dad," she adds.

"Do you know where we can get the lobsters?" Lila asks, looking at Gregg. "And, do you have any idea how to cook them? We don't make many lobster dinners in Georgia."

The thought of cooking lobsters gives me the willies. I made the mistake of being in the kitchen one year when the lobsters got tossed in the pot, and I've never forgotten the sound. I have a hard time even killing flies. My New England friends think I'm nuts. Besides, having my food looking back at me does nothing for my appetite. Gretchen likes the taste of lobster, but she has my penchant for not killing things and can be just as squeamish.

"Put 'em in a pot of boiling water. It can't be too hard." Gregg grins, matter-of-factly. He turns toward me with a smirk. "Deb will probably be hiding in her room," he chuckles. "We always give her something else to eat."

I turn up my nose. "Not my thing," I say, "but don't let me stop you. I'm happy for the party. There'll be one less lobster death on my conscience."

We agree on Wednesday night. The weather cooperates, with a warm breeze blowing across the water onto the shore as our guests arrive. A few distant clouds form on the horizon in an otherwise gorgeous blue sky. Gregg's sister and brother-in-law made the relatively short drive from Connecticut earlier in the day and have decided to take up residence on the living room couch for the night. Any last-minute doubts about the process of lobster cooking are allayed by our Cape Cod locals, Bella and Rob, who show up with Joe, his father. A few more friends stop by for dessert. It's a nice little group, considering we are so far from home.

When the food comes out, my sister snaps a picture or two. Gregg grabs one of the bright orange lobsters and pretends to take a bite. Everyone laughs, but I know it's all an act on his part. His appetite has been forever changed but he still tries to relish whatever aspects of his old self he can while trying to embrace the new state of his body. The lobster dinner is more for the sake of others, and he plays along as if he will be able to indulge like everyone else. I love him for always going the extra mile to make others feel comfortable and enjoy themselves in spite of his own personal situation.

The evening, with a little help from the wine, puts me in my happy place. Gregg nibbles tiny bits of the lobster; I have chicken. It warms my heart to see him so happy and hear his infectious laughter—just what the doctor ordered.

After a while, he excuses himself and walks into the house while we all continue to socialize and relax. When an inordinate amount of time passes without his return, my radar kicks into gear. Excusing myself as well, I find him hunched over on the toilet, his stomach cramping.

"What's up?" I ask, concern in my voice, but the answer is obvious. "Isn't the fish going down?" I put my hand on his back and rub his shoulder.

"Not as well as I'd like. It seems to be stuck in my throat and hurts." I've tried to imagine how this must feel, but I can't. It would probably throw me into a panic, like I was choking. Though Gregg is in pain, he seems resigned to wait it out, not that he has another option.

"Do you think maybe a sip of water might help?" I ask, wanting him to be able to finish the evening with everyone. We've been through this so often. Sometimes the food is stuck; other times air gets trapped and causes major cramping. Walking can help, accompanied by a twisting movement back and forth to move things around, but there is nothing that does the trick quickly or 100 percent of the time. The opening to his esophagus is narrow due to scar tissue, so soft food usually works best, but we never know.

It's disheartening for us both, and I'm sad that his well-planned evening is being ruined, at least for him. Others are aware something is amiss, but they are kind enough not to follow us or talk about it. I think they know we want to escape it all.

Eventually he feels relief and we return. Our local friends have departed, thanking everyone and sending Gregg their best. Lila and the girls are cleaning up the table, the rest still enjoying the night air.

My mom can see the disappointment on my face even though I carry a rather empty smile. "Are you OK?" she asks with concern. I know she's opening the door for me to share my feelings, but I don't want to go there. I sense her impotence. She worries about me and hates to see Gregg suffer.

"Yeah, fine," I say, moving past her to the kitchen, though, clearly, I am not. I've always worn my heart on my sleeve, rarely fooling anyone, yet

I try. Nothing can make it better. She wants to help, but I don't know what she or anyone can do. *I don't even know what to do.*

The week we chose to vacation happens to be same time that the August meteor showers take place. Shooting stars elude me. People say, "Oh! Did you just see that shooting star?" and it is always over by the time I look. One day it will happen, I think to myself, maybe this week.

We pick a clear night, and everyone but Mom troops out the door, laden with towels and a blanket or two. Mom says she will watch from the deck because it is too difficult for her to maneuver herself over the sand dune. I feel a fleeting melancholy that she doesn't have the wherewithal to participate in all our adventures anymore, but she is always a good sport about it, not wanting to hold us back in any way.

Once over the dune, we find a spot, spread the towels on the sand, and then the eight of us lay down on our backs next to each other like a can of sardines. Almost immediately my niece shouts, "I just saw one!"

"Where?" I ask, quickly glancing her way, knowing I missed it, even if I could actually look in the right place.

"Over there!" she says, pointing as I try and follow her direction.

"I just saw one, too!" my other niece chimes in. Soon each person is pointing to a different place in the sky. One person sees one, then another, and another, faster and faster. I decide the best method is to lie still and just look straight up hoping to catch my own, and it doesn't take long. The sky begins to light up.

My mind wanders to thoughts of the universe and the heavens. The magnificence of our world astounds me. I imagine the ancients viewed shooting stars as omens foretelling the future. It is so beautiful; I can't conceive that it could be anything but good, like God's fireworks celebrating creation.

All feels right in the world. I am surrounded by my family, in a wonderful place, snuggled next to them on the sand, looking up into a beautifully clear, midnight sky, filled with galaxies and unknown planets. As much as we know, there is still so much we don't. Gregg and Gretchen lie contentedly on either side of me, when I wasn't sure this day would even come. I realize what a special week it has been, and know it will be seared into my memory and heart forever.

*   *   *

Upon our return home, it's hard to believe we are driving up to our own house. The transformation is nearly complete and it looks fabulous. "I am so glad we took the plunge. Can you believe this is the same house?" I ask Gregg, as we check it out. "The living room seems huge!" The enormous front window adds a whole new dimension. It's one thing to see it on paper and quite another to see it in real life.

"Yeah, it looks great. The sun will definitely shine in here, just like I wanted. It really opens things up. From the looks of it, they don't have too much more to do," he says, happily, as we walk into our bedroom to see a shiny new bay window.

"Man, look at *this* window!" I exclaim. "Now you can see up and down the street, not just across it. You wanted sun; you got it everywhere! We just have to paint it and get some blinds or curtains. It's fun to see out, but everyone else can see in as well. No running around in our skivvies until then!" I laugh. "Maybe we can come up with some landscaping ideas. Won't it be great to have a walk that actually leads to the front door?"

"Everyone we know comes in the back door anyhow," Gregg jokes, as he takes a gander out the window to see how far down the street he can view. "But maybe we can change their minds and keep the garage door closed."

I nod. "We'll have to get rid of our 'Backdoor guests are best' sign," I add.

*   *   *

With fall coming, Gregg will return for his third year at the middle school. He's looking forward to it, feeling much more confident about what exactly he's teaching and how best to go about it than when he started. Teaching is often like that; once you get a rhythm going, you just tweak things as you go, depending on the particular group of students you are working with.

He's feeling great, other than the eating issues, and even there he copes better all the time. In late summer, he goes in for an endoscopy, an outpatient procedure, this time intended to stretch his esophagus to help food slide down more easily. No guarantees, but he doesn't have anything to lose either. It's helping, thank God. He asks the doctor for the pictures of his insides to aid him in visualizing what he needs to happen. They oblige, making me giggle, as I wonder how many other patients make that request.

We drive Gretchen back to Ohio University for the start of her senior year, her last one as a Bobkitten. Since both of us graduated from there and Gretchen is about to, it's a special time for us all. We encouraged her to look at other schools and opportunities, not wanting to push her into following our footsteps, but she insisted that OU was her destiny and could not be dissuaded.

It has been great to watch her mature and grow into an independent and capable young woman. She has finally found a direction for a career, teaching art, and seems happy with the choice. It was a natural path with so many teachers in the family. She is very much a leader and has discovered the self-discipline that will carry her through life. Not to say that she doesn't enjoy her extracurricular activities to the utmost, but she has a good work ethic and sets high standards for herself.

As the year draws to a close, life is back to a semblance of normal. We're finishing up the house projects. Gregg has dug and hauled what seems like a million sandstone rocks from the dirt in our front yard, depositing them to an ever-growing pile behind our shed, in preparation for the new walkway that we'll build. It feels like a new beginning.

As fall makes its official appearance, our weekends fill up, with stays at a cabin with old friends where we sit around the fire sharing stories, hikes in the nearby woods and gorges, a concert, and finally a wedding in Columbus. Of course, there are always football parties for our ill-fated Browns. The families we gather with have been close to us forever. Their kids have been Gretchen's quasi siblings as opposed to the furry, four-legged variety.

Though the endoscopy worked well in the beginning, Gregg's throat is tightening up once again. He visits a local gastroenterologist to see about further options. Gregg tells him he feels as strong as he was before the surgery, and good overall, other than when he eats. Unfortunately, we all must eat. The doctor feels that he may be able to help. Yay! He schedules Gregg for surgery in early December to remove scar tissue and eyeball the area. It goes well, and eating seems improved.

The holidays are filled with a whirlwind of activity. Out-of-towners roll in, and there are gatherings with both friends and family. My birthday is always in the mix, a few days before Christmas. All the hustle and bustle is both tiring and rejuvenating at the same time. My sister and family visit at the end of the month. Gregg has another doctor's appointment and takes Ty with him for a second set of ears in addition to some "boy" time, which lets us girls hang out together. We clearly outnumber them.

When they return, I sense a shift in mood and I'm instantly alert. With some dread, I eye Gregg, trying to read his face. The report is not good. Cancer has returned and is growing and restricting Gregg's esophagus. Everyone is crestfallen. There are no words that can make the news any lighter. It is December 31, the last day of the year just short of two years since this journey began.

* * *

Gregg's journal:

While having my last medical procedure, the doctor biopsied some suspicious- looking tissue and in fact, it is cancerous. This news was a shock but then again, not really. I have been having a great deal of difficulty swallowing for some time. I've known that something was not right. So, I anticipated further surgical work anyway. I was hopeful that it was without cancer, however. So, I will be back under the knife soon to remove any bad cancer tissue and get healthy once again.

The I Ching gave me an interesting reading: Grace. I am in a state of Grace, the name of the boat I bought. Grace can bring simplicity, pleasure to the heart, clarity to the mind, and tranquility to the soul. It changed to calculated waiting. This is what I will have to do in the weeks to come in preparation for the medical team to prepare me for surgery. "Bide your time and nourish yourself, strengthen yourself for the future. This will put your confidence to the test. It is now that you must be able to show confidence; do not show doubt."

This journal will take me through my next challenge: the preparation, operation, and recovery of the next health treatment process. I hope to write my thoughts and feelings down here as I have in past journals to keep clarity and a positive frame of mind throughout this ordeal. Please give me strength, oh Lord, to do this work, to meet this challenge and to be a positive pillar of strength for my loved ones, who are there for me always. Let them feel my love and know how much I appreciate their support.

~ 14 ~

Riding the Current

My journal:

I have been down for the past few days hearing the news about Gregg after a pretty wonderful year, but had a good meditation today. There were lanterns along my path into the woods "lighting my way" and conversations with my higher self, saying that we have been on the path and that this might be the last hurdle. All was positive and affirmative that the results would be good. I pray that I let myself trust in me (my higher self) and that I am not directing my thoughts.

Gretchen has been pretty miserable back at school. Transitions have always been hard for her as Gregg reminded me, and then this on top of things. She is very connected to Gregg and will be devastated if anything happens to him, as will I. But I feel it is human nature to let our minds wander and ask, "What if?" Sometimes I feel guilty letting my mind go there, like I don't have the faith that is needed, but I also think it is a defense mechanism, sort of a way to get a sense of what it might feel like if he wasn't here without it really being true; self-protection and preparedness, if only fleeting.

The rest of our family and friends are also feeling down, but all will rise to the occasion and have, to offer love and support. We have always been blessed in this way. Gregg is depressed but he hides it well. He has been so frustrated with eating that in some way I think he just wants it to change. I pray that we are on the right path with the new direction dealing with the clinic. I bless Gregg's doctors and all who work with him.

Medical science should be able to cure all cancers by now with as much money as has been put toward it. They have made progress albeit painstakingly slow. Cynics say it is a conspiracy and big business. I guess to me it means that there are underlying reasons, not necessarily physical, that we get sick and stay sick and we need to cure ourselves on that level first.

I am happy that I am not feeling sad at this particular moment; there will be plenty of time for that. I really feel it is out of our hands. We just have to ride it out. Easy for me to say, poor Gregg has to do the hardest work of all. It is so hard to watch your loved ones in pain.

God, grant me what I need to help my family and myself during these hard times. I continue to pray and listen for guidance.

*   *   *

I decide to pick the Runes while meditating. The Runes are a form of guidance similar to the I Ching. They originated as old Germanic alphabet characters, and each symbol carries with it a specific meaning depending on if it is right-side up or upside down. You form a question in your mind and then intuitively draw a Rune out of the bag. The one I choose this time is called *Uruz* or Strength. Two things from the reading strike me. First, "Remain mindful that the new form, the new life is always greater than the old." Since in Gregg's case, this couldn't mean that his physical body was literally going to be in a better form than it was before with all the trauma it's been through, it obviously refers to our ever-evolving spiritual selves; with each and every experience in life, we continue to learn and grow closer to knowing who we really are. Even if life takes you down the slow road with its many twists and turns, you are still always traveling the path to greater insight. We learn from both our successes and our failures.

The second bit of guidance reads, "When in deep water, become a diver." In other words, if you panic and resist, you will drown. If you go with the flow, the current will carry you forward to where you need to be. There are times in life when we clearly have no control. The only way to deal is to ride it out and see what opens up along the way. It's more apparent to me all the time that the purpose for Gregg's illness is bigger than us. Neither of us knows what lies ahead, but we will let the current sweep us along and pray that we show the courage and strength being asked of us.

The current carries us to the gastroenterology department of a well-known hospital in our area. The doctors there seem genuine and open to helping in whatever way they can. We grab on to each positive piece of information offered. They direct us on to a well-respected oncologist and say he may have some answers for us. Dare we feel that things aren't as dire as they seem? That there still might be a light at the end of the tunnel, however dim? I feel wary excitement.

The hospital is world-renowned. People from all over the globe travel here for health care, from the highest dignitaries to the homeless person on the street corner. This certainly counts for something and makes us feel that we have come to the best place.

Unfortunately, we find ourselves playing the waiting game again, waiting for direction, waiting for appointments, waiting for the doctor, waiting for results, waiting for answers. It seems interminable, and I grow to dislike it all. Nothing seems to happen in as timely a manner as it should.

The vastness of this place awes me, building after building, beautiful lobby after lobby, restaurants, artwork, people scurrying around, both healer and patient. In this environment, of multitudes seeking a cure, the importance of one ill person diminishes. Though we're overcome by our own personal crisis, perspective shifts when grasping the enormous need for healing in the world.

We deal with things by seeing where we fit along the continuum of need, knowing there are those whose problems are less than ours and those whose problems appear way worse. We only have cancer here, but that guy is blind, mute, and has no legs. I would hate to be in his situation. And yet, time and again, these are the people who inspire us and can make us feel ashamed that we looked at them with pity. Their spirit outshines what is visible. If they are blessed enough to have found that place of acceptance within themselves, they move our hearts and become an example to us all, teaching us about endurance and faith. Maybe they can't change the shape they are in, but they can offer others the gift of example. They show us that we can choose our attitude and way of perceiving our lives. You realize that *that's* what it's really all about. It's the dignity and grace with which we handle our particular circumstance that wins the day.

Our visit with the oncologist wipes away any fuzzy feelings we were having. "What are you doing here?" he opens without preamble, his manner brusque and to the point. We give him a short synopsis of Gregg's history so far, starting at the beginning with the original surgery at our local hospital. "I don't steal patients from other doctors." *What? Who is this guy?* He seems awfully rude. Maybe he is just stressed and having a bad day, so I give him the benefit of the doubt. I don't want to irritate him when he supposedly is the man who can help us.

"The doctors we saw in the gastroenterology department *here* were the ones who suggested to us that you might be able to help," Gregg explains, patiently. "They said you were very good at what you do."

Hearing this, he softens slightly and offers a mild apology, then continues with the same insensitivity as before: "The type of cancer you have is very difficult to treat. It is resistant to radiation and chemo. It is epidemic in America, especially in white Caucasian males between the ages of thirty-five and fifty-five. There is probably not much I can do."

It is immediately evident that Gregg has been tossed into the "I don't know why they sent you here" category. He's not mincing words. Surprised by his bluntness, we say nothing. Doctors up till now had never gone this far in explaining things. I suppose they all want to do the best they can to offer encouragement. They rarely come out so blatantly unfiltered; perhaps because they really don't know. People who shouldn't survive do and others who should survive don't. Even though medical science has its base level of knowledge, there is always room for God and miracles.

When I had my thyroid cancer, someone gave me the book, *Love, Medicine, and Miracles* by Bernie Siegel, M.D. In it, he relates numerous stories about miraculous healings and how one's attitude is critical to the process. He emphasizes that whenever people hear the word *cancer*, they immediately imagine it's a death sentence—including doctors who might treat you. If they hold that attitude, that you're just a disease they can either help or not based solely on statistics, how successful will they be in the long run, and how much encouragement and hope will you receive from them? You will most likely fall to their expectations. Therefore, it is vital that you only associate with people and medical professionals who believe that all things are possible and who do their very best to heal not just your physical body, but also your mind and spirit.

He looks at us both questioningly, as if wondering why we seem so shocked. Surely, we already knew all this and are taking up his valuable time by making him repeat it.

I decide to try my hand at the conversation. "We were led to believe that another surgery might be helpful."

The doctor flops the chart on the desk beside him, looks at me impatiently, and says, "Further surgery is most likely not an option."

"No one has really laid it on the line like you just did," I say, barely able to contain my anger at his total lack of empathy.

"Well, they should have. I had no idea that you didn't know."

"We did not." Awkward silence fills the room.

"So, where do we go from here?" Gregg asks, still using diplomacy, hopeful that there will at least be another step we can take in the process.

The doctor glances at his watch and tosses us a morsel, which seems more like a favor than a solution. "You can meet with the surgeon,

Dr. Riley, and see if there is anything he can do. And, also, the radiologist; he may be able to plant some radioactive seeds. I will have the secretary call down there now. They can tell you how to get there." He gets up, quickly shaking our hands, and moves out the door, not waiting for any further questions.

"What a jerk!" I say with disdain. "He must have missed the class on bedside manner."

Gregg looks dejected. I can certainly understand why. "Yeah, he was rough. I was really hoping he would have something better to tell me."

"At least we can speak with the other doctors and get their opinions. Maybe this guy doesn't know everything, even though he would like us to think so," I say encouragingly, though in truth, it felt like we just got slapped into reality, a major wake-up call—as if we needed another one.

"I sure hope that they have better news," he says, not willing to throw in the towel either.

"They will." I reach up and hug him. "Anybody is better than this guy." I hold on until the nurse comes in to hand us a slip of paper with directions to the surgeon's office. We thank her and head to the next meeting.

Maneuvering our way through the maze of hallways and down a floor, we once again land in a waiting room overflowing with people. When our turn comes, instead of the positive vibe we hoped for, we get more of the same. The surgeon spews out further unfiltered facts. We should have come to him in the first place rather than bothering with our local doctors. He would have done the surgical procedure differently in a two-part operation where he would have separated the esophagus from the stomach and put Gregg on a feeding tube for at least six weeks while healing took place and then reconnected it all at a later date. What has already been done cannot be reversed.

Is he trying to make us feel worse? He certainly succeeds. The information is tantamount to saying he might have been able to save Gregg's life, but the window of opportunity has passed, so deal with it.

We tell him Gregg has trouble swallowing saliva due to the narrow opening in his throat. He says that we swallow something like two liters of saliva a day, so of course it's not surprising that Gregg has to spit when it doesn't go down.

Apparently, we are on a roll. We leave there with our tails between our legs once again.

Finally, we see the radiologist, who is more of a gentle soul, thank God. He offers us a course of action that involves implanting radioactive pins into Gregg's tumor in an effort to kill it off from the inside out, as we were told he might. The procedure would be done in three successive visits, if Gregg is up for it. There are no guarantees, but there is a decent percentage of possible success.

Gregg agrees. At this point, I think he would have jumped at anything. It may not be a cure, but could at least prolong his life. I think about the article I read saying it's treatable. This, at least, is a treatment.

We head to my mom's to share the day's events. I'm still reeling from our encounter with the oncologist and the surgeon, who not only didn't sugarcoat the news, but who managed to make us feel like we made the biggest mistake of our lives by not seeing them first. When you're talking about life and death, it can't get much worse than that.

In my heart of hearts, I don't believe there is only one path leading you to the place you are ultimately destined to be. We all make a million decisions every day, each one affecting the next. None of us knows if they're the best decisions; they're simply the choices we make. Then along comes the next set of circumstances and we do it again. Eventually we come to the place that we were always heading toward anyhow. Maybe it's living; maybe it's not. The longer winding path with its varied twists, turns, and obstacles affords a multitude of opportunities to learn, reflect, and, hopefully, strengthen our characters, the short path, not so much. We arrive where we're meant to be bringing different perspectives. Is one way better than the other? I guess that depends on what you think life is all about.

No one knows for sure, including the doctors, whether Gregg's life will be saved. I feel we're on the path we're on, and we'll wait for the future to unfold. Still, my emotions are currently at the forefront, and I must deal with those first.

Mom's dear friend Jan is visiting; they listen intently to our story. My sadness and frustration are evident. Gregg sits rather quietly in a chair at the end of the room, letting me do most of the talking. Besides dwelling in the disappointment of his own situation, I sense he regrets putting me through all this as he listens to me rant, which of course, makes me feel worse. I don't want him to feel guilty, yet I can't stop. It seems easier to focus on the rudeness of the doctors as opposed to the message, though there is no hiding from that. I want to scream, but I know it will not change anything.

"It breaks my heart to see you have to go through this," my mom says to Gregg, her face reflecting the emotion that fills the room. "There's no reason for the doctor to be so insensitive. They're supposed to make you feel better, not worse."

"Yeah," Gregg says dryly, nodding his head slightly, staring at nothing in particular. "They sure did a shitty job of it. In their defense, I imagine there's no good way to present bad news. It probably wouldn't have mattered how nice they were. It was certainly a wake-up call, one that we didn't want to hear."

My outrage spent, I sit dejectedly. "I don't even know what more to say. The whole day just sucked." Suddenly exhausted, I look at Gregg, "Are you ready to go? We've got a long drive still before we get home." He nods in agreement, and we get up to leave. Mom goes hug him while Jan comes to me.

As she holds me, she says in my ear, "God is grand! He is always with you and always taking care of things no matter what happens in life." She is filled with excitement and conviction, no doubt in her mind. I admire her for it but feel a little less than convinced at the moment. "I will keep praying for you both. I love you, you know," she continues. "I consider you my daughter, too." With that, a floodgate of tears opens up that I can no longer hold back, nor do I want to.

Mom takes me, holding on longer than usual, silently conveying her love but too choked up to say much. She doesn't have to. I know she would do anything to change the situation, if she could.

Before we walk out the door, Jan hugs Gregg, who accepts her words of encouragement and support as well. He seems to be holding it together, not that I really expected him to be blubbering like me. That's not his style. Perhaps he's still in a state of shock.

The ride home is silent, contemplative, both of us lost in our own deliberations of the day's events. I stare out the window, watching the lights go by, but I can only think of Gregg. The news obviously affects him most of all. It's a natural inclination to protect ourselves from emotionally charged topics by only taking in what we can in small doses. I imagine he needs time to think about it and come to a perspective he can live with in the days to come.

And I know he will because it is his nature to do so. He will be himself and look to see what positive way he can spin this situation. No one knows how many days he, or any of us for that matter, has left on this earth. He will do whatever he needs to do to stay alive and live a quality existence. Knowing this brings me a small semblance of comfort and peace.

~ 15 ~

Courage

Back in 1979, I look up and watch Gregg disappear into a hole in the side of large rock face. Grabbing hold of the edges of the boulders in front of me, I climb up and follow him. The opening is about three or four feet in diameter and when I look in, I see nothing, including where I am going. Those who have gone before me encourage me, as I drop down about six feet into a small cavern. Once in, I sense the nearness of the rock walls, their damp, musty smell filling the air, which is noticeably cooler. Already inside, though nearly invisible, stand a guide, three high school students, Gregg, and now myself. One more student and a last guide drop in after me.

The only light, though dim, emanates from atop two helmets, one on the guide in the front and one on the guide in the back. The rest of us huddle sandwiched in between. I experience a moment of anxiety, wondering what exactly we're getting into. It's the darkest, quietest place I've ever been. The contrast from being outside to in here is dramatic.

We are in the Ardeche River Gorge in France, chaperoning students on an adventure trip of sorts. The gorge is magnificent. Our tents dot the riverbanks after having first climbed down 150 feet from the top to get there. Luggage was put on a pulley system and lowered down before us. There's very little around us other than huge, vertical rock cliffs on both sides, some scattered trees on small ledges here and there, along with some greenery beside the rushing river at the bottom. Lying on an overhang in the distance is a naked couple sunbathing. We're here to white-water raft and take part in some other escapades, one of which we are doing right now, caving.

We proceed forward, sometimes in a low crouch, other times on our hands and knees. To quell my feelings of claustrophobia and impending panic, I chat a little with the guide nearest me, asking him if he's come in here many times before, and how the cave was originally discovered. Gregg inches along in front of me, quiet, seemingly untroubled by being here. Perhaps he's dealing with his own anxieties, just not letting on. As adults, I think we both know we can't afford to freak out or the kids might follow our lead—and it's not like we can make a quick exit. We're literally stuck between a rock and a hard place.

As we creep further into the cave on our hands and knees, we come to the narrowest opening yet. I can barely make out the edges as the headlamp of the guide leading us intermittently lights up parts of it. What I can see looks to be a small, elongated crack in the rocks. "It gets a little tight here," he says, as he lies on his back. "The only way through is to work yourself sideways."

As he slithers out of sight, blackness overtakes us again. I'm already crouched down, mapping the irregular bottom of the cave with my shinbones and the palms of my hands, unable to lift my head without banging against the solid rock above me. The idea of lying on my back adds an unwelcome vulnerability, like offering myself up to the earth in sacrifice. A sick feeling begins to work its way up from my stomach, joining my already overactive heartbeat, and though it's chilly, sweat beads on my forehead and in my armpits. The heavy, damp air makes it hard to breathe. Suddenly, I anxiously want to turn around and get the hell out of there.

"I don't know about this," I grumble softly to Gregg, hoping the others don't hear me, though it's deathly quiet, other than the grunts of movement. No one seems to have any idle conversation to offer up.

"You can do it, Deb. We're all here together. He wouldn't lead us here if we couldn't get through."

Rather than respond, I actively work to calm my fears, and, at the same time, sense Gregg readjusting his position as he lies down and begins to move deeper into the crevice. Knowing my only choices are to enter a frozen state of inertia or forge ahead, I reluctantly choose the latter. There are still two people behind me who couldn't pass me if they tried.

The damp earth has now become mud that oozes around my whole backside and into my hair as I struggle to lie down. I can feel my heart about to jump out of my chest and wonder if I can actually do this. How much smaller can it get? The thought of getting stuck and dying in a rock in the middle of France where nobody will ever find me does not ease my growing apprehension. I tell myself that if there is a lake in this rock, we are bound to get to a larger area soon. Somebody found it in the first place; certainly it's doable!

Instead, the opening narrows considerably and gets even smaller! We are now forced to shimmy ourselves through a crack that is only about two feet tall. Seriously? Terrified thoughts fly through my head. *Maybe I can go back and meet them when they return. But there are two people behind me. I can't ask them to get out of my way. There is no place for me to get past them without going way back to the beginning and anyhow, I certainly would not want to go back alone! I might be lost in here forever.* Then, forcing myself to find a bit of resolve somewhere within me, *I will just have to deal with it. Maybe the lake is right around the corner, if I can just work my way through this part. The high school kids are doing it. I can do it too. I can't be a chicken. What will they think? That I'm a wimp? Gregg is right here beside me, but what can he do to save me? He's in here just as deep as me!* On and on. At this moment, I would fly out of body to be anywhere but where I am.

I can't see a thing. Slime gushes up my shorts, into my underwear, and around the sides of my face. My breath comes in short bursts as I wait for Gregg to move, so I can, when suddenly the thought of what it would be like to be buried alive comes unbidden. I imagine the rock above me letting loose and squishing me, locking me there forever. The blood in the vein of my neck beats loudly in my ears as if it, too, wants to escape its confines. Dread overtakes me even though I try desperately to talk myself down.

We slither along inch by inch. I'm the only female and the smallest one, so if I am sandwiched this tightly, I can only imagine what the others are experiencing. The challenge of moving brings me into the moment and distracts me, hardly aware of my panting. The line of bodies moves sideways in unison, willing ourselves to be patient, though I want to speed up and push Gregg out of my way!

Finally, I just give in, stop fighting it and let go; whatever happens will happen. It's out of my hands anyhow. I am boxed in on all sides. I have to find the courage I need and trust I will find my way out of this and back into the light.

And then, miraculously, I am taken out of my own torment with these words: "It seems to be getting a bit wider here, Deb." Gregg offers the sentiment encouragingly, his own relief evident in his voice. I anxiously maneuver my way another few feet sideways and, blessedly, feel my arms stretch higher when touching the rock above me. It seems like we've been working our way into the center of the earth, and it has taken forever. Relief washes over me ever so slightly. But we aren't there yet.

In a few more minutes, like magic, I hear Gregg as he sits up from lying in the mud and rolls back to his knees. The blackness is still blinding, my sense of hearing acute. The heaviness of the air dissipates slightly. and I take a deeper breath in an attempt to relate the message to my lungs and heart that things might be looking up. We are once again able to crouch and eventually stand upright. It feels great to be vertical. We walk on, and, finally, stop. True to the guides' word, before us, lit only by the lights on the helmets reflecting off of the damp, russet-colored walls that now rise above us, is a gigantic cavern filled with water!

"Wow!" One of the boys says. "It really *is* a lake!" The liquid casts an opaque, greenish glow, as light bounces off it in random places each time one of the guides moves his head. It is unimaginable to think that this much water could just be sitting in this huge hole inside solid rock.

"I wonder how deep it is?" another inquires.

"We haven't explored it to see," the guide answers, "but we do know it's over our heads."

"I can't imagine how it even got in here," I add, thinking that I would not want to dive in there to see anything, no matter how interesting it might be.

"Sometimes parts of caves that lie below the groundwater level become flooded. We think this might be one of them."

We stand in awe for a while longer marveling at it. Though it's beautiful in an unexpected way, I wonder to myself what inspires people to climb into holes in rocks they don't know anything about, just to see what they can see. In this case, it was quite a find, but if you were plump in the least, you would never have made it and to try would have been to take the chance of becoming stuck and not getting out. Talk about panic! I suppose if you stayed stuck long enough, you might drop enough pounds to work your way out, but you'd probably die from the wait. And, besides, what if it somehow flooded again? Ugh! I can't even think about it.

And we still have to reverse course.

Gregg takes my arm as we turn to go back toward the passage. "You feel pretty slimy, Deb. What have you been doing?" Though I can't see him, I can sense him smirking at me, pretending that the whole thing has been a piece of cake.

"Just cleaning up your muddy trail with my body!" I retort. "Seriously," I whisper, "I'm not sure my heart's come back to normal yet and we still have to return!"

"Well, we did it once, we can do it again," he offers, encouragingly.

"You might have to push me through this time. I had no idea what we were getting into. Did you?"

"No, but here we are. There's only one way out. Off you go." He gives me a little nudge.

One by one, we reenter the hole from which we had emerged a few minutes earlier and once again, I quietly steel myself for what I think lies ahead. Coming and going anywhere always affords a new experience somehow, a different perspective. I guess you can never really travel the same road twice.

Once into the warm sunshine, my personal sense of elation is acute. Talk about seeing the light at the end of the tunnel! The old adage fits this situation to a T. Each of us is solid mud from head to toe, front to back. I can see the jubilation on every face. The feeling of accomplishment and adventure is evident, but more than that, the sense of freedom! It's intense. After being cloistered in the depths of darkness, fear, and panic, the contrast of the bright, amazingly vibrant-colored world outside, where our spirits can soar unencumbered is sublime. The degree of appreciation for one would not be possible without experiencing the other.

*   *   *

About 15 years later, I'm in the kitchen making lunch when the phone rings. "Hey babe, it's me," Gregg says excitedly, as if he can hardly contain himself. "You'll never guess what I did!"

"What?" I respond, spreading mustard on a ham sandwich.

"I walked on fire!"

"You did not," I say flatly. Gregg is always pulling my leg. He's in Cincinnati attending a conference on education. As thrilling as that can sometimes be, firewalking is about as far from traditional education as one could get. The two do not go together.

"No really, I did!" he insists.

"Are your feet wrapped in bandages?" I ask snidely.

"I'm not kidding! It was so cool! I can't believe I did it!"

Hearing a note of sincerity in his voice, I ask, "You really did?"

"Yep. After the conference was over for the day, one of the ladies said that she was attending a firewalk, if anyone was interested. Of course, having seen it firsthand in England, I was curious and went with them."

"So, what happened?" I ask, a bit skeptically.

"They lit a huge bonfire, and while it burned, we all sat around and talked about our fears."

"Were there a whole bunch of you?"

"About twelve or thirteen. Many of the group turned out to be nuns who were also attending the conference."

"Nuns? They don't strike me as people who firewalk. It seems a little 'out there' for them."

"It was 'out there' for me! We went out of curiosity. None of us intended to walk."

"So, you just said what you were afraid of and then went for it?"

"We all had to come up with an affirmation to say while we walked. I decided that mine would be, 'My body will do whatever it takes to protect itself.' I said it aloud and as I walked, everyone chanted it with me."

"Did you feel the burn?"

"No, I couldn't feel anything! It was amazing!"

I picture the nuns in their habits walking on hot coals and wonder what they did with their skirts. Of course, they probably weren't actually in habits, but this picture is more interesting. "What about the nuns? Did you all watch each other go one by one?"

"Some went alone, but others held hands and went in pairs."

"And nobody got burned?"

"Nope!"

"Wow!" I say, trying to imagine it all.

"I'll tell you more about it when I get home," he says.

"OK. I'll be checking out your feet when you get here!" I joke and hang up.

Gregg is still flying high from his experience when he arrives home. He can't stop talking about it. I think that if he and the nuns could do it, maybe anyone can. But how did it work? Did it truly have something to do with mind over matter? Did a certain energy connected to his affirmation intensify when everyone focused on it? Did God give a special dispensation to Gregg because he was hanging with the nuns? I chuckle to myself. Perhaps their shield of protection swallowed him up as well. Even so, they're humans with tender skin like the rest of us. Yet, here is evidence that it was possible. Are the fears we hold in life unfounded? This experience was as important to Gregg as the caving experience was for me. He looked panic in the face and found the courage to transcend it, confirming his own survival instincts. It was a chance to delve into the well of his inner resources and move beyond the limitations he set for himself, life skills training, practiced during the down times, to be resurrected later as needed.

* * *

Sitting in the doctor's office waiting once again for Gregg to have another endoscopy procedure for his throat, I've been thinking about him and wonder what exactly goes through his mind each time he faces another procedure, another unknown. It's a slippery slope that only seems to even out for short periods of time. He must be anxious, but his options are becoming more limited all of the time. He desperately wants to live and has convinced himself that he can. I suppose a hint of doubt lingers somewhere, but he rarely lets it show. I think it surely takes courage on his part.

But how do you find the courage you need? What makes you think you can do something when the odds are against you? I stare at the giant fish tank, mesmerized by a big, blue, iridescent fish as it works its way around a plant in the corner. When the leaves rustle, a tiny yellow fish skitters out and then abruptly circles around behind the big one, giving chase. It isn't scared, even though the larger one could swallow it in one gulp. Obviously, the little fish has a sense of itself that carries him forward. Maybe he knows that even though he is small, he can outswim and outmaneuver the larger one. Or maybe, he just trusts that all will be OK, and that living in fear isn't worth the agony.

Sometimes I get lost in my own fears of what is happening in our lives, how things seem to be changing in ways that will never be the same. It makes me sad, and I wonder if I am doing everything I can to help Gregg through it. I find I have to look deeper within myself to be strong and positive for us all. So many times, I have wanted it all to go away, to be carefree and silly again.

When I get down and out, having to give myself a pep talk, I often reflect on our caving experience. It was a time when I conquered my fears and came out the other side. The fear was one that I didn't even know I had because I'd never put myself in a similar situation or even thought about it. Had I known what I was getting into in the first place, I might never have tried it, and then would never have been graced with the reward of finding resources within myself I could draw upon to survive and do what I needed to do.

When I'm in my "God space," I know God/Source energy is infinite and I am made of God, so I should always be able to rely on that connection to have my back. It can be no other way; we are one and the same. Fear in any form is unnecessary. It doesn't mean that the outcomes, whatever they may be, will always be what I want. It means that I'll find the strength and courage I need to face them if only I continue to look within, into that deep well of compassion and understanding that is always there to catch me when I fall.

Of course, my human side does have a way of complicating matters. I have found myself in a place of "knowing," (that we are all connected for example), sure that I have figured it out and riding a wave of faith. Then life pushes me into a new set of circumstances and I find myself questioning all over again. Eventually, with much reflection, I return to that place of "knowing." Round and round I go, adding dimension to my understanding, solidifying it. I suppose it's good that the dynamic flow of life won't let us linger in one place for long. Instead, it keeps sweeping us to a new spot that will once again present us with an opportunity to dig deeper and learn something new. The more we resist, the more we feel pushed. It does no good to hold on, for how else will be become better people or experience possibly even greater joy?

As I contemplate my life, I know that our current strength is a result of all that has come before. It is what gives us both a sense of assurance that we will make it through one way or another. We have also been blessed and humbled by those around us who offer their love and help in any way they can to make our lives easier. Asking for and receiving help is a lesson unto itself and teaches us even more about connection. It is something that comes much more easily to Gregg than to myself, but I am working on it.

~ 16 ~

New Pathways

In the ensuing days before Round Two, the radioactive implants, we get on with the everyday undertakings. We both mentally try to find a place for this new situation. Gregg *always* strives to carry on. He enjoys every moment that is not dominated by medical appointments or treatments and makes a point of having many. His views of himself keep readjusting to what is currently "the norm" for him.

Whenever we gather with friends, he loves to hear what's going on in their world and takes time to truly listen and offer help or support in any way he can, often without being asked. He's very aware that he's not the only guy on earth going through a tough time. I can tell it comforts and relieves him to think about someone other than himself.

I've never been able to bring myself to share the discouraging information I found on the Internet with Gregg. I never wanted to burst his bubble, sensing that he needed to believe anything is possible. He needs that freedom to hope and have a hand in creating his life and the days to come. And because of it, he continues to imagine that he will somehow conquer this. Is that why it was so hard to hear that he might not? Because they dare to rain on our parade, our very fragile mindset that we take pains to cultivate on a daily basis? It somehow makes me resentful that they presume to squash our spirits. I suppose one could argue Gregg's in denial. He could accept that his days are numbered and wait to die. But it isn't in his nature to be docile. He's a mover and a shaker. There are forces greater than us at work here, helping us both to keep our minds as open as we can. If it takes a miracle, he's still in the game. Miracles come in all forms and he's going about the business of creating his own.

Even before knowing this latest news, Gregg has continued to pursue every viable alternative method he feels might be of benefit. Besides the homeopath in central Ohio and our chiropractic/Chinese medicine friend, Jackie, he's found another naturopath who evaluates him and prescribes herbal medicines. He takes advantage of the massages and reiki offered at the cancer center, along with acupuncture, and has enjoyed learning the intricacies of it all and the effects on his body.

I don't interfere in any of it, though I sometimes think about one medicine counteracting another. Not only as his caretaker, but as an observer, I find the process instructive in ways that would not be possible otherwise, exposing me to the variety of healing options available and teaching me. I applaud any and all efforts he makes, not knowing what I would do.

Finally, he makes a point of going to the Unity Church as often as he can, where he can tap into the energy of group meditation. He tells me it's like multiplying the power of his own personal meditations exponentially. "Can you really tell the difference?" I ask when he arrives home one Sunday.

"I can, Deb. It's hard to explain, but there's just a stronger vibration in me and around me. It seems like it lifts me up and makes me feel lighter."

"You know what they say, 'Where two or more people are gathered' . . . " I respond, giving him a confirming smile. "I'm glad it makes you feel better." Little pangs of guilt that I rarely join him flash in and out of my consciousness. Why do I not allow myself to reap the same benefits? Perhaps it is my *alone* time doing my own reflection and writing that I value more at the moment.

"I just want to be in the best shape I can be, before putting more radiation into my body. I feel like, if I can be strong going into it, I can minimize whatever harmful effects it might have on the healthy parts of me."

"I'm all for that! The higher your own personal vibration, the better off you'll be, it would seem. Either way, there are bound to be some bumps ahead, and I imagine if you can keep your thoughts in a place of love and gratitude, it might be easier. At least your perspective of things will be more Zen." I watch as he hangs up his coat and follow him to the bedroom as he begins to change his clothes. The neutral look on his face belies his inner turmoil. Or perhaps he really is in that more peaceful space. I am always comparing my own feelings to his. He slips a comfortable sweatshirt on over his ever present long underwear top and torpedoes his old shirt, skimming away a few hairs on my head, toward the laundry basket as I sit on the bed.

"Nice shot. A little lower, and it would have taken me out!" I say, lightheartedly.

"Direct hit. The shortest distance between two points. A good lesson, always keep your head down," he counters.

He walks toward the door, and I get up following him down the hallway like a little puppy. When the space allows it, I hook my arm into his and say, "You know I admire you, don't you, Greggy? I don't know how I'd be in your place. You show me your strength every day, and you are certainly not one to sit around and mope. That takes courage."

"I don't always feel it." He turns toward me and leans against the wall. "God is putting me through this for some reason that I haven't figured out. It doesn't look like it's going away anytime soon, so I have to deal with it in the best way I know how."

"But many others in your place might just give up, and you keep going and living your life."

"I can't do it any other way, babe. As long as I can, I gotta keep going. Right now, I can do that. I am not going to let it ruin my life completely. It's like a necessary evil. There are people who live through worse." He looks at me tenderly, and then adds, "You have certainly helped me along, and I love you for it. You keep a positive attitude, even when I'm down."

"Funny, I think the same thing about you," I say, thoughtfully, looking into his eyes, so familiar. "One stick holding up the other. I guess life really is better in twos!" I reach up, putting my hands on either side of his face and give him a quick kiss. Gazing at him a few more seconds, I change the subject. "The sun's out and it looks warm out there. I know it's faking us out, but do you want to take a walk later?"

"Sure, but first I want to write a couple notes." We separate and go about our personal business.

Even with all of his preparation, Gregg's health these past months has moved one step forward and two steps back. The dentist finally extracted the tooth that's been bothering him for months. Then he developed a painful hernia in his groin that required surgery; he had unidentified pain in his heels that made standing on his feet teaching uncomfortable, plus hemorrhoids, caused by constantly being bound up from pain meds. And, if that wasn't enough, he developed kidney stones, which called for two trips to the ER. It seems he can't catch a break.

Six weeks after our shake-up at the hospital, we return to a different building where Gregg will receive the brachytherapy. It's an outpatient procedure that requires anesthesia, a regular event these days. I've only been waiting about an hour and a half when Gregg comes walking back out to the lobby. Not sure what I was expecting, he looks relatively unchanged. "Well, that wasn't too bad," he says, as he opens the door for me, and we walk toward the elevators.

"They must not have put you under very deeply. It didn't take too long. Is your throat sore?"

"I can tell they had something down my throat, but it doesn't really hurt."

"Maybe it will just do its work without bothering you. That would be nice." He nods in agreement, letting out a "humph" as if he isn't quite sure. We exit the elevators and head toward the door nearest the parking garage.

"The doctor says it'll be cumulative, so we'll have to wait and see. Do you want to drive over to Coventry and look around? I saw a book store there that I'd like to check out."

"Sounds good. Do you think you will be able to eat anything? Maybe some soup?"

"Let's see what we come across when we get there."

The bookstore is an interesting little shop that also sells knickknacks. We browse but leave with only a couple of boxes of blank cards. With the quantity of cards Gregg has purchased in the past few years, we could build our own card store. It's a predictable occurrence that I chalk up as another form of therapy and know that he will use every last one of them in his quest to keep up correspondence with the people in his life who mean so much to him. And there are many!

The effects of the radiation are apparent after the third and final round or radiation. There's no denying that something is happening on the inside of Gregg's body. He's experiencing a "sunburn" sensation in his throat he compares to swallowing cut glass that further compromises his ability to eat. He's down to 142 pounds from an all-time high of a little over 200. It's difficult to watch him keep losing weight because he can't get the food into his stomach.

We plead with the gastroenterologist for help. Gregg has already had a few more endoscopy procedures to stretch open his esophagus, but they have been marginally successful and only last a brief time. The space between each visit gets shorter and shorter.

"The only option before a feeding tube would be inserting a stent into the narrow part of your esophagus. It would keep the path to your stomach open so that you could get food down and gain some weight." The doctor speaks with a look of genuine concern on his face. He's darkly handsome and has an entirely different demeanor than his predecessors in the other departments. We learn he trained at our alma mater, which somehow gives him our qualified seal of approval.

A feeding tube never sounded inviting, but the choices of what to do next are becoming nonexistent. I look at Gregg. "What do you think?" His face is a mixture of hope and resignation.

"It is hard to know if I will tolerate it until it happens, I guess. Is it a difficult process to do?"

"It is not a difficult operation. We would begin with the smallest stent in diameter, and if that goes well, we will gradually replace it with another that is slightly larger. There are three to four sizes in all."

With a sigh, Gregg says, "I think we all know that eating and nutrition are issues. It's frustrating not being able to get food to go down, even soft foods. There're times that I can't even swallow water. Something has to give." He looks at me. "I think I should do it. What do you think?" He certainly doesn't need my OK, but I know he values my judgment and probably needs some moral support.

I take in all the well-known features on his face, doing my best to read the creases in his brow and the thoughts in his eyes. Another step on our journey is about to unfold. "It'd be wonderful if you could eat again," I respond, knowing that it would actually be beyond wonderful. "And Lord knows, you could use the weight," I add, sympathetically. My heart breaks each time I watch Gregg try to eat and fail. I grab hold of the back of the hand resting on his knee and look back at the doctor. "I think if Gregg's all right with it, it's worth a try."

The doctor nods and gets up. "I think we have a good shot at making this work." He smiles encouragingly and pats Gregg on the back. "I know this has been hard for you, but you're making it, and I admire your determination and your will to get better."

It's amazing to me how much more openly caring he is, and I send out a silent thank-you to the universe. He seems to have taken a liking to us and truly wants to be able to help. I am very grateful he is who he is; a little genuine TLC is worth its weight in gold.

I know the surgery will take a while, so I park myself in the waiting room, tossing my stuff on the seat next to me and begin to read my book, quickly becoming restless. Each space is different yet the same. Most are relatively comfortable with coffee or tea nearby, along with television if you care to watch. Rarely does the current program interest me, so I often tell the attendants I'm going for a walk, and they give me a beeper so they can get in touch with me if necessary. Time passes more quickly if someone is with me, but that's rarely the case, so I'm getting adept at entertaining myself.

I wander the halls, taking in the artwork and other displays, pondering again the big business of illness. I'm caught between thinking people donate money and beautiful things in gratitude in contrast to the more cynical view that perhaps medical care is overpriced. But when people feel helpless in their agony, victimized by their circumstances, so that their only road to health has to come from someone else, the price can't be too high.

Back in the waiting area after a few hours, I'm informed that Gregg is out of surgery and in recovery. They'll let me know when he's awake.

Staring out the window, I watch as dusk begins to color the sky. Rather than worry or focus on all of the challenges we have faced of late, my mind runs to more carefree moments that make me chuckle.

We like to banter and push each other's buttons to see if we can get a rise out of the other. Since we both tend to get ready for bed at the same time, the bathroom becomes a setting for this repartee. There is only one sink and a small mirror, so whoever gets there first usually lays claim to the area, making the other person wait his/her turn. More than once, I would be in the middle of my nightly ritual, and Gregg would decide to come in and floss his teeth. When he wants his chance at the sink, he will lean his hip on mine, mid-floss, and try to push me aside.

"Sto-o-o-p!" I say, pushing back without raising my head.

"Good thing you're brushing. You must have eaten a pound of garlic."

"Gee, thanks for letting me know," I respond, unenthusiastically, knowing what he is up to.

"Just trying to save you from curling the hairs on your coworkers at school tomorrow."

Not taking the bait, I continue my routine squarely in front of the sink. He leans in once again to gain access, and I give him a bigger boot with my hip, so I can guard his side of the sink as well, while I put my toothbrush in its stand and reach for the cup.

"You're so thoughtful. Maybe you better think about that brown spot on your underwear," I say, shooting a barb his way.

"Ha!" He tosses his head back with a cackle, floss in hand. "Skid marks, baby," he says, as if it is something to be proud of.

"Eeeoo!" I respond, amused, but still holding my ground and washing my face. Gregg maneuvers his way to the unguarded side of the sink as I quickly slide around, blocking the space.

"It's all thanks to your wonderful cooking."

"Nice try. If that was the case, I would have them too," I counter. Having failed with hip action, he leans over and tries to nudge me out of the way with his shoulder, flossing all the while.

"How do you know you don't?" He grabs my underwear and yanks them upward, giving me a wedgie, always the last straw that sends me over the edge. I instantly drop my washcloth, swiveling around to return the favor, and he skitters out of the bathroom laughing before I can grab him.

"You're such a brat!" I yell down the hall indignantly, secretly glad that he is out of the bathroom. Instead of chasing him, I quickly close the door and finish my business.

Gregg often has that effect on me, never letting me sink too far into self-pity or take myself too seriously. After my initial mortification that he dares make light of whatever the situation, I usually break down in laughter.

The loudspeaker catches me mid-chuckle, eyes closed. Sitting upright, more alert, I listen to them call someone else's name. With a small sigh, I relax again. Thank God for the good times; they really do make a nice distraction and help balance out the bad stuff.

Another couple of hours go by. Still no one has called for me. I'm alone in the area. Other surgeries have been completed, and each person waiting has been reconnected to his/her respective friend or family member. I check in with the nurse; surely Gregg is awake by now. She phones back to the recovery room and reports that he is still very groggy. Thanking her, I go back and sit down. I've been here since 1:00, and it is now closing in on 6:30. Why is it taking him so long to wake up, I wonder?

Another hour goes by before the sound of my name drifts through the air. Gathering my things, the need to stretch my limbs overtakes me before I can move. I follow the nurse back to where Gregg is lying in a bed. He still appears to be sleeping. We stand at the door, and she whispers softly in my ear, "The operation took a little longer than expected, and they had to use more anesthesia to put him back under as he was beginning to wake up. He is in considerable pain, and we have him on strong pain medication. Let me know if you need anything."

"Thanks," I say. She pats me on the back and walks away.

I pull up a chair next to Gregg's bed, needing to be as near him as possible. He needs to know I'm here, and somehow the proximity helps me sense what state he is in. Stirring a little when he hears my voice, he opens his eyes, but he can't even muster a comment or a facial expression other than pure misery. He turns his head away and then back again a few times, seemingly to help assuage the pain.

Reaching for his hand and shoulder, I lean over and kiss him gently on the forehead, then linger, looking at his face, so that he knows it's me. "Hey Greggy," I say again, soothingly. "I'm here now." He stares at me, affirming my presence with his eyelids, his forehead wrinkled with suffering, and tightly squeezes my hand without letting go. "The nurse said you are on some pretty potent pain meds. Are you feeling any relief?"

With a barely perceptible headshake, he moans and looks at me pleadingly.

"Let's give it a little time. You just woke up. She said they had to give you an extra dose of anesthesia, so I am sure you are under the throes of that too."

"It's awful," he manages to squeak out. I can see tears gathering in the corners of his eyes as one overflows and rolls down the side of his face onto his pillow.

"I'm sorry, Greggy," I say, helpless as he struggles with his agony. "I wish I could make you feel better. Why don't you try and sleep some more, then when you wake up again, maybe you'll be in a better place?" Reassuring him, I say, "I will be right here next to you the whole time. I'm not going anywhere."

His eyes close, but his body is still restless, fighting whatever torment he is harboring. I've never seen him look so distressed. Rubbing gently on his body, I try to relieve his discomfort the best I can, hoping maybe he'll feel like he's being rocked to sleep, distracting him from his pain. When he had his first kidney stone attack years earlier, he had grabbed onto my pants as I stood next to him lying on the gurney in the hospital and wouldn't let go, wanting me to do something. I felt as inadequate then as I do now.

In a little while, he opens his eyes again and I look anxiously at him for a better reaction. Instead he grabs my arm again and begs me for more pain medicine. The nurse sticks her head in, and I anxiously tell her what's going on. She says she'll check with the doctor and that he'll be in to talk to us shortly. I look back at Gregg. He's a mess. I fret, having never seen him in this state before, wondering if he'll survive or choose this time to leave the earth. As if reading my thoughts, he moans, his face scrunched, "I don't know if I can do this, Deb." A tear escapes my eye and rolls down my cheek, dropping onto the sheet as I witness the deep weariness of his whole being. "I don't know if it's worth it to keep fighting."

I'm shocked he's actually uttering the words. Though I certainly don't want him to go, who am I to tell him to live with it? It must be excruciating.

"I'm so sorry Greggy. I would gladly take your pain if I could. I love you dearly but if you need to leave, I will understand." My heart is about to leap out of my chest. There are just no more words. I squeeze his hand, sending him as much strength and courage as I can rally energetically, in hopes of carrying him through this moment and keeping him here with me for a while longer.

Soon the doctor walks in. I reiterate how much pain Gregg is in. The doctor says the surgery went well overall, and the stent is in place. He orders some morphine to help with the discomfort and persuades us both that Gregg should be better in the morning. Still at a loss as to how to make the situation better, I tell myself that this was to be expected, and once Gregg has had a day or so to get used to having a foreign object in his body, things will right themselves again and he'll be in a better place. I have no choice but to trust the doctor, at least for now.

Moving myself onto the bed after the doctor leaves, I talk softly to Gregg, trying my best to give him courage. I stroke his head, tell him God is with him and that he'll be all right, though I have no idea if he really will. I surround him in white light and love. I pray over him. I call in the angels, the archangels, the light beings, and anyone else I can think of. I keep checking with the nurses and the doctor to see if this reaction is normal. No one really has much to say other than that we just have to wait and see.

The surgery was a crapshoot to begin with and the doctor had been up front with us about some people tolerating it and others not. It wasn't a commonly done procedure. We were willing to try anything and now here we are. I want to scream at them to take it out right now, that I don't think Gregg can stand it, anything to give him relief, but I hold my tongue.

Gregg is in absolutely no shape to move anywhere. Instead, he'll stay for observation and more drugs, thank God. So far, my nursing skills have kept up with whatever issues he has, but this situation is beyond my capabilities.

Eventually, exhausted, frustrated, worried, and guilty, I consider going home. The staff assures me there's nothing more I can do and he's in good hands, plus, they remind me, I need the rest. Gregg's been relatively stable the last few hours, so with trepidation, I agree, but not before telling him I'm leaving and will be back as soon as I can in the morning. I pray all the way home that he will be better tomorrow.

My journal:

Today (morning after the surgery) was slightly better, but Gregg is still in much pain. He took his medicine faithfully every two hours. It is making him spacey, and he's having some hallucinations, or at least mind journeys. Yesterday he was drinking from an imaginary cup. Anyhow, he was very glad to see me this morning. He gave me a big hug and wouldn't let go, kind of like I was his safety net. Took me a bit by surprise. He told me two or three times today that the doctor said I was the biggest asset he had going for him. I thought that was nice, though I was surprised also. It seemed a personal thing to say for not knowing me well. Perhaps we sensed the loving spirits in each other. He seems like a genuine healer to me, and he has extremely good people skills. I thought a few times that I should write him a thank-you note and tell him when we get over the hump, or maybe sooner—why wait? Anyhow, Gregg seemed genuinely moved by his telling him that and now it is as if he is seeing me in a new light. I don't know how I could be any other way. I just pray that God is working through me and my hands. He is at a turning point right now, and I feel he needs as much encouragement and attention as I can give him.

Though Gregg's still extremely uncomfortable and in considerable anguish, the doctor releases him, buoying us with words of encouragement and assurances that things will only improve. We leave the hospital, begging God for each day to be better and hoping food will get through so Gregg can gain some much needed weight.

More and more, I'm using massage and my own hands to offer Gregg what comfort I can. Soon after his initial surgery, I began to massage his feet to distract him from his stomach cramps. It is one of the small pleasures we've enjoyed throughout our marriage. I make it up as I go, trying to remember how a masseuse had manipulated my own feet so well she made me practically go limp. We are both surprised when Gregg insists he can feel the massage easing and healing the discomfort in his stomach.

After winging it for a bit, I come across a wallet-sized reflexology diagram showing which parts of the foot relate to which body part. Before long, I find a book called *The Healing Energy of Your Hands* and learn a method where I use my left hand to receive energy and the right to send it, then practice this technique on Gregg's stomach in bed at night. Again, he gains comfort from it and often humbly begs me to "work" on him before going to sleep. Some doubts prevail, but as I watch his reactions, I know he isn't patronizing me just to pump me up. He actually garners relief from this form of energy work. So, I continue to hone my amateur skills and, not knowing what else to do, trust my intuition and the positive reactions that flow from him.

My journal:

Gregg has been wanting me to do healing on him every night. I am back reading my book, but I haven't finished it. I pray I am doing it correctly, although I think any effort is rewarding in some way. Last night, as I was drawing out negative energy, there was a major, audible, "thump" under my hand at the top of Gregg's stomach. We both stopped and looked at each other. Wouldn't that be great if it sucked out all of the cancer? Shoo!

Gregg's journal:

Deb can make her hands instruments of healing. She can touch my body in a way, using her focused attention that my body responds to in a very favorable way. She is learning to use her power of touch in very significant ways during this time of pain for me. She is learning how to harness their power and give me relief. Thank God!

Gregg has always managed to open doors for me. He's all about finding the experiences, but he doesn't always put the time in like I do. It's like the old saying, "You can lead a horse to water, but you can't make him drink." With us, it is the opposite. Gregg knows that if he can just get me to the water, I will most always drink. He gets the benefits without having to do so much work because he knows I will learn and digest the information, then share, and he will reap the benefits.

I feel honored to help him in any way I can beyond just being there. My efforts are opening up a whole new level of appreciation for non-traditional healing methods, and what's more, I am the one doing them. I witness the impact each time I do the work. Once again, my loving husband has been instrumental in the development of my new skills by leading me to the water.

~ 17 ~

Bittersweet

I start to have heart palpitations and anxiety. I feel like a jumping bean, always wanting to move in an effort to distract myself from my concern about Gregg's cancer. Besides being annoying, for the first time, I truly understand what my kids at school must go through when they have attention-deficit hyperactive disorder. I realize how unfair it is of us to ask them to sit still when their chemistry is off, and they just can't.

The thyroid medicine I take as a result of my own bout with cancer has usually kept things running on an even keel, but it turns out I need to wean myself off it. This is very unusual because I have no actual thyroid to take up the slack. Regardless, my body prefers to function without it for the time being.

Years later, I will realize that my body chemistry is going through a major shake-up and re-adjusting to the vibration of my more heightened emotional and spiritual awareness. What was status quo for me before Gregg got sick is no longer who I am. I am being propelled into a new mindset and spiritual knowingness in my efforts to deal with everything. A decade after Gregg's passing, I still have not returned to the higher dose of medicine that people take when they don't have a thyroid gland.

Although I might appear to outsiders to be dealing with everything, on the inside, I can never turn it off. And if I can't, what does Gregg feel like? No matter the amount of self-pity I want to wallow in, it's never as bad as actually being the one who is sick. So I don't let my thoughts travel there too often. The old kundalini yoga philosophy came in handy: when you're stuck in a headspace you don't want, transcend the situation and change your perspective.

Gregg tries to bear the pain of the stent but is miserable. The doctor gives him a narcotic patch along with morphine for breakout pain, but it befuddles his thinking and barely dents his agony. For someone who always enjoyed getting high, this is not how he wanted to do it. Ironically, I worry the drugs will be addictive but am assured that one's body uses medicine in a different way when it's used as intended, to treat a specific condition.

The doctor has implied that the pain is most likely from cancer even after all of the brachytherapy treatments, but they still cannot prove it. I think they've been trying to prepare us for the worst. Our faith is definitely being tested. My thoughts jump everywhere. I hate to think or talk about anything negative like death, but I suppose you also have to deflate the concept and keep it in perspective. If you don't face it or talk about it, it looms even larger.

Until now, we feel we've been coping pretty well. We still manage to come and go with friends on weekends, visit Gregg's parents in Florida in April, and work around the house and yard. Gregg is determined to get back to work and keeps focused on his teaching responsibilities as much as he is capable of. Sadly, he only manages to work a handful of days before the school year ends. But it keeps him in the loop.

Gretchen graduates from Ohio University in June the day after she turns twenty-two. We gather our family and all her friends along with their families and celebrate in Athens. She is moving back home for the fall to finish up her student teaching. It's bittersweet to leave her friends and the relatively carefree life she'd been leading, but given Gregg's situation, she wants the opportunity to spend quality time with her dad and me.

Though she's been in touch constantly to offer her support in many ways, she still hasn't experienced the day-to-day workings of a serious illness. Gregg and I have been reserved about sharing our pain and emotions, aware that this was a special time in her life—we didn't want to spoil it by being constantly down. She's sensitive to our moods, which hasn't always turned out well. Rather than stepping back and being objective, she often assumes our burdens, emotions at the forefront, and then we tend to bicker and press each other's buttons rather than express what our snippiness is really all about. It's become obvious we need someone to help us talk about the hard stuff.

In an attempt to help us find the balance and objectivity that seems out of reach at the moment, we meet with a counselor who has been recommended to us.

Gregg is grieving his life. He has lived through the initial shock and denial of his diagnosis, though there is a fine line between denying you have cancer and wanting only to put your energy into thinking positive and concentrating on the good. He has never really shown anger or verbalized, "Why me?" I suppose he figured, "Why not me?" If he has to face illness, he will figure it out and move on.

He's so on edge from the constant pain from the stent that he's willing to look at any solution or advice. Eventually, he concludes that he wouldn't be in this position if only he'd been more cognizant of his lifestyle and how he treated his body in the past. He vows to make himself into a "new" person with the help and support of family and friends and God's blessing. His new journal is entitled *The New Me*. He's ready to bargain.

It's true, his lifestyle most likely did contribute to his illness and push him over the tipping point, but it is also true that plenty of people do the same things or worse and don't suffer from cancer. So, what makes the difference? Why do some people have one experience and some have another? It occurs to me that something more must drive this disease and all diseases, for that matter.

Gregg feels his purpose is to be an inspiration to others in overcoming the illness by changing his thinking and the way he lives and then showing that miracles really can happen.

My counseling sessions go right to the heart of the matter. Have we discussed death? What will Gregg's funeral involve? How will we go on without him? Whew! No, we have not. We both believe that energy follows thought, and that, by talking or thinking about death, we give energy to what we don't want to happen. It already takes a great deal of energy just to stay positive and keep moving forward.

I allow myself to talk about it with the counselor, though it feels like I'm betraying a nonverbal pact that Gregg and I had made. What will I do if Gregg is gone? Find someone else? How would Gregg feel about that? If the situation were reversed, I'd want him to be happy and fulfilled in his remaining years on earth, and I hoped that he'd feel the same way. Easy for me to say; I'm not the one who might be leaving.

Later that night, sitting in the living room, I broach the subject in the gentlest way I can, sharing what I'd talked about at the counseling session. It feels awkward, like I think Gregg has one foot in the grave, like I'm losing the faith we all cling to so desperately. Our talk is excruciating. He doesn't care much about the funeral and responds favorably to my finding another mate, but I sense the difficulty it takes to say so. It's not so much about me moving on, rather about the fact that he *actually might die*. We don't delve deeply into any of it and are relieved when it's over.

As the days pass, Gregg is able to eat, and though he is still in pain and uncomfortable, we celebrate some extra nutrition and pounds. A little over a month in, the stent begins to slip and his throat becomes ulcerated. It has never really become bearable, and, eventually, after forty-four days, the doctor removes it. We're relieved but also oppressed by foreboding. Now what? We're back to square one: less food and endoscopies.

Every phase of this journey has been a testament to endurance. We build up hope with each event, only to have it slip through our fingers once again. Yet, without hope, what do we have exactly? Do we just call it quits and wait for the cancer to win? Maybe that's what we're supposed to do, let go and see where the cards fall. Trust that all happens the way it is supposed to with God's blessing. In my heart I believe that's true, but I'm not liking the outcomes. Control or let go. We humans always want to make our own decisions, but it still doesn't guarantee the favored result.

When we first contemplated how to handle the diagnosis, Gregg and I had many conversations about how his uncle, who had been living with his own cancer for twenty-one years, always referred to it as a battle to be won. Believing that what you resist persists, we agreed that perhaps, if we viewed it as a part of ourselves that lacked love, then loved it enough, thankful for giving us the opportunity to take a candid look at ourselves, the cancer would disappear, having served its intended purpose. What is more powerful than love?

At this juncture, I think we're still of that mindset. Yet, it's becoming more difficult to appreciate the reasons, whatever they might be, for Gregg's escalating pain and misery. Holding that place of gratitude teeters precariously on the brink. We still pay it lip service, but not as consistently as we did at first. The harder things get, the easier it becomes to bail. And the more difficult it is to make sense of it all.

As always, and to his infinite credit, though discouraged, Gregg rarely complains. Instead, he finds the silver lining. however small it might be, for now, that the stent has been removed. He doesn't have to endure the additional pain anymore. He turns the failure into a cause for celebration.

Gregg's journal: "What if...?"

I awoke around 3 a.m. this morning, coughing and with a headache from this cold. My nose was running and I felt hungry. I hardly ever feel hungry anymore, only pain.

So, I got up and ate some cantaloupe and a banana and thought about conversations we've had as of late with family and the many challenges that our family seems to be facing.

What if when I go back for the 'look-see' scope at the clinic, they say, not only is it still there, it has spread? I need to think about the other possibility of not getting well and what does that mean to my family. My body would deteriorate. I would not return to work, or see my daughter marry or have kids. I'd not see my loving wife grow old. It's not only what I would not see or do, because I will be happy and in heaven, but it's what life will be like for those that I leave behind. Gretchen and Deb love me dearly and I am a huge part of their lives. What a void it would create in both their lives if I were no longer here. A very sad scenario comes to mind, at least initially. I would hope that both would eventually recover and find loves in their lives to replace the loss of myself.

~ 18 ~

Celebration/Exasperation

This year, 2005, marks our thirtieth wedding anniversary. I wonder, like everyone, where time went. We have lots of living under our belts and still love each other dearly. I'm very thankful for this. It's not just luck, it took some work, but there was never a time in all the years of being together where we came even close to calling it quits. A few times we needed some space away from each other (one right before I found out I was pregnant and my hormones were raging), but other than that, it's been a fairly easy ride.

I'm plotting things we might do to celebrate and look up some flights to see what our options are. The thought of escaping to anywhere is beyond inviting, a welcome layer of normalcy in our lives. An unwanted but lingering thought intrudes in the back of my mind: we may not get many more anniversaries together. If Gregg is up for it, I'm all in. I walk to the garage where he has the hood of the car raised, with his head lost behind it somewhere.

"What're you doin'?" I ask from the doorway.

"Shoveling snow," he responds, never raising his head from whatever he's looking at.

Rolling my eyes at his predictable response, I try again. "No really, what are you doing?"

"Polishing my shoes."

I should know better than to begin a conversation this way. He rarely gives me a straight answer, especially when it's so obvious that he's working on the car. It isn't that I don't know that, it's that I'm truly interested in knowing what exactly he's doing in the car, changing the oil, checking the air filter, adjusting a hose. It always makes me walk to where he's standing to look in and then, when he sees I really am interested, he'll take the time to explain it to me. It's another of our games.

"I'm just checking the hoses and belts before I change the oil," he explains. It's something I take for granted. We rarely have to take our cars to get fixed. He always services them, so car issues aren't on my radar.

"What would you think about going back to Banff for our anniversary? We haven't been since our honeymoon. It was so beautiful, and we both loved it. It'd be like coming full circle. It is our thirtieth, so it seems like we should do something special to celebrate."

He moves the jack in place under the car and begins to pump it up off the ground. "Hand me that wrench on the workbench, would you please?" I grab it and hand it over.

"You know I would love to go. I'm feeling pretty good at the moment, knock on wood. It'd be fun to go back there."

"I know it's pretty far away, and there'd be some logistics to figure out with your medicines, et cetera, but I think we could do it. I suppose we should check with your doctors to see if there's any reason not to go."

"Or we could just do what we want," he says rebelliously, probably more than happy to thumb his nose at them all and keep control of his own life. "We'll have to check the calendar. I'm not sure July would work, but maybe around the first week of August."

"I already checked. We don't have anything planned, so it really depends on you and if you think you're up for it."

"Unh," he grunts. He lies on the creeper underneath the car, trying to loosen a screw, then takes the wrench and wraps it on the metal a few times. Tossing it down, he continues by hand and says, "Why don't you see what the plane tickets to Calgary would cost?"

"They're actually not too bad. I already looked at that, too. I figure if you don't feel like climbing around or hiking, we can be content to drive. It's beautiful, no matter how you see it."

"Sounds like you had this all figured out before you asked me, Deb." He snickers. "Let me make sure I don't have any doctor's appointments, and then we can decide exactly when to go."

I would kiss him, but only his feet are accessible and not particularly inviting. "Perfect! Do you need me to hand you anything?"

"No, I think I'm good. Thanks, babe."

I've always loved the mountains, the Canadian Rockies especially. My family had visited Banff when I was in junior high, which is why I insisted on returning with Gregg as part of our circuit out west after the wedding. Its allure is hard to resist.

In August, we pack our bags and head to Calgary. The famous Stampede has just ended, the remnants still visible. I see a giant cowboy hat in the middle of the fairgrounds from the window of our hotel room not far away. We rest the first night in town, then drive to Banff the next day.

It's as gorgeous as I remembered, with breathtaking views in every direction. We spend a week soaking in the quiet, the fresh air, the strength, the majesty of the mountains. Gregg is remarkably game for a few hikes and the exertion does him good. It nourishes our souls in ways staying home couldn't.

While sipping our tea on the outside deck of a teahouse we hiked to one day, we see a helicopter rescue of some climbers in the distance even further up the mountain. They are like dots on the landscape and lucky that they could call for help and be found, their bright-colored jackets helping to reveal their whereabouts. I wonder out loud if one of them might have broken a leg or something.

These mountains, enormous and intimidating, are nothing to mess around with. Their strength and endurance is food for our souls, our problems minute in comparison. The thrill of being here again with Gregg fills my heart; I find myself just watching him, memorizing scenes, as he moves about, unaware.

I know he wants this trip to be special for us in every way; he has probably pushed himself beyond what he really felt like doing. His spirit soared, and his body tried to keep up. It touches me so. He will definitely leave a void in my life, if and when he chooses to go.

*   *   *

Upon our return, we know something has to give with getting some food in Gregg. The endoscopies are becoming too frequent and don't hold his esophagus open for long. The scar tissue is just too much. We meet with our gastroenterologist and have a frank conversation. It seems the only option left is to insert a feeding tube that will bypass the blockage and go straight into Gregg's stomach. Neither one of us is thrilled with the thought, but there's really no other choice.

Surgery is set up and the tube inserted. Gregg now has a constant drip of food entering his stomach 24/7. At least it's portable, housed in a small backpack that goes wherever he does. It takes some training and trial and error to make sure all the tubes are adjusted properly and don't clog. Night seems to be the worst. Just as we doze off, the beeper startles us awake. I'll climb out of bed, mumbling some choice swear words, fool with it until things flow smoothly once again, then climb back in bed, and give it a few minutes with a prayer to stay quiet, before letting myself relax and trying to fall sleep once more.

I always seem to carry a little angel on my shoulder telling me to monitor myself. *Gregg doesn't want to be in this situation any more than you want him to. If he thinks he's a bother, it won't help anything.* So, I suck it up. We both do, actually, as the other option is mortality. At least I won't have to watch as Gregg slowly starves to death. I'd already been witnessing this for the past year. If this keeps him here for a while longer, I'm all for it.

As always, Gregg's fervent desire to live triumphs over the impulse to feel sorry for himself. If he has qualms about walking around with a backpack 24/7, he doesn't show it. At least backpacks are commonplace, and he doesn't look too much like a weirdo. It becomes a part of him, sort of an extra appendage.

We have a final meeting with the grumpy oncologist. Gregg has completed all of the treatment they have to offer. The cancer is still there. This same doctor, who actually had been nice the past two visits, is back to his original self, rude as ever. He enters the room in a huff and without so much as a greeting, grousing because we are late. In actuality, we were on time in the waiting room, but no one showed us back to the exam room. He lays Gregg on the table to examine him and speaks very curtly, as if we are once again taking up his precious time. It feels like we're being scolded and after the first few comments, I can contain myself no more.

"Why are you such an asshole?" I yell, getting up from my chair and moving nearer the table where Gregg lay, as he stood opposite facing me. "You're nothing but rude and nasty. We wouldn't be here if we thought there was another choice."

"I get frustrated when people don't listen to me," he stammers defensively, taken aback at my outburst.

"We heard everything you said. If you would take the time to explain things when we ask questions instead of telling us to look it up on the Internet, it would be more helpful. I'm sorry we're a bother to you."

He stands over Gregg looking at me, but I leave him no time to respond. "People come to you for help, not to be scolded. You of all people should realize how hard of a time this is for us in our lives. I pray you never have to stand in our shoes and deal with the likes of you. Or perhaps you should; then you might feel a tiny bit of empathy."

"I'm sorry you feel that way," he says quickly, as I roll right over him.

"How else should we feel? You have made absolutely no effort to assuage our fears, instead making us feel like we are a major pain in your ass. I don't know what the other doctors feel you are so good at. It certainly isn't people skills!"

I take a breath, aware that Gregg's head has been bouncing back and forth between the doctor and myself during our diatribe. He's upset that I'm upset, yet I know he agrees with me for the most part and is probably secretly cheering me on. "If you just finish what you are doing, we'll be out of your hair."

Tears stream down my cheeks and my entire body shakes as I wait for him to go through the motions. I can't remember another time in my life I have felt so angry. The doctor finishes his examination of Gregg in a more subdued manner and gives us a meager apology before leaving the room. As we walk out, I feel the eyes of the nurses surreptitiously watching us. I'm sure they could hear the entire exchange. If the doctor is that rude to us, I'm pretty sure he is no joy to work with on a regular basis. Perhaps, they, too, are cheering me on. I'll never know.

I find it hard to calm myself and stop shaking. Every helpless, hopeless feeling buried within me is finally escaping, the open air now making it easier for them to take form, spread their wings, and take flight. They exist despite my intentions to quell them.

Gregg has his arm around me, trying to comfort me as we walk to the pharmacy, telling me that it's good I let it all out. He's not patronizing me; I think he knows how impotent I feel and all I've been holding in. I take some deep breaths in the drug store as I look out the huge windows waiting for Gregg to get his prescription, then we head home.

The cancer refuses to leave even after all the agony of the treatments. We just can't catch a break. Gregg is slipping away from me, and I'm powerless to do anything about it. What's more, no one else seems able to do anything either. If a place like this hospital is done with us, is there *anyone* who can help? Have we finally come to the end of the road? And where is God in all of this?

Later, in a more productive frame of mind, I know that I have to write a letter to the doctors at the hospital in hopes that they might at least pause and rethink their bedside manner and overall patient care. It's like a huge corporation, and with its reputation, I'm sure there is far more need than they can sometimes handle. Consequently, people are quickly divided into "those we can help" and "those we can't." I get it. But to me, that's no excuse for not treating people with respect and compassion.

I write it objectively from my speech therapist self, ending with some basic suggested steps in communication style such as greeting the patient and asking how things are going. It seems pretty simple to me. I applaud those who were kind and caring and explain my criticism of those who were not, then send a copy to each of the doctors we dealt with, along with the chief of staff. Whether or not it got lost on their desks, I'll never know, but I hope it might at least start a conversation or become the impetus for a staff in-service about treating the whole person, not just the condition. We all get busy and overwhelmed at work, but no one who is dealing with a critical illness should be subjected to that.

* * *

As much as we've been through and as long as the road had been so far, once we have a little break, I'm not ready to give up completely. There might still be a few options yet undiscovered, or at least I hope so: M.D. Anderson, a well-known cancer hospital in Texas, or Sloan Kettering in New York. *Could we really go to either place for long periods of time?* It would involve money and logistics, but if they could help, how could we not go? Loving friends, who know our plight and our frustrations, are busy researching solutions on their own. They share the names of doctors in Michigan and Pittsburgh.

But even though I aspire to go to the next step, I'm emotionally spent and have difficulty finding the energy to move forward. Gregg doesn't have it either. We're somewhere between feeling numb and a state of inertia. To begin, we must gather all the information we have so far and send it off to be perused like a résumé, so the hospital can decide whether they can help him or not. I really don't know how I'll manage it. Thank God, my sister comes to rescue! After I've updated her on the phone, she offers to come up from Atlanta and give us a hand. Though I didn't ask her directly, she must have sensed the utter fatigue in my voice. But not until she arrives does she see how demoralized we are, absolutely at our wit's end. She quickly organizes the information into a huge binder. Part of the information would need to include a statement from the nasty oncologist. I'm loath to even ask him after our last encounter, but he sends a summary report and in it, in black and white, is the prognosis of two to four months of life.

I'm taken aback to see this in writing. It seems so decisive and final. Immediately, I begin to refute it in my mind. *What does he know? Does he think he is God?* I quickly mix it in with the other papers so that Gregg won't see it. He is doing the best he can every day. We contact both individual physicians and large hospitals. The overriding consensus is that the doctors we had seen were good at their jobs and knew what they were doing. All kindly regret that they cannot help. The situation has progressed beyond further surgery or any other treatment that they had to offer.

Just then, someone at Sloan Kettering calls and asks us if we have checked into a particular cancer center located in Columbus. We've never even heard of it. The referral stirs a tiny bit of hope. From the very first moment at this hospital, our experience with both staff and doctors is amazing. We find a predominant atmosphere of care and concern, which makes us both feel like people who matter. Maybe that's all any of us wants in the end. Though still a busy, bustling place, perhaps the difference is that it's a teaching hospital. One doctor tells us he gets paid the same thing, whether he spends five minutes or an hour with us. There are always medical students wandering around with the actual doctors. It is encouraging to see the physicians being good mentors in all aspects of patient care.

They tell us they have a couple of experimental programs going with Gregg's type of cancer. If he's willing, they will accept him into the program. It would involve getting a regular regime of chemo. There are no guarantees, of course. Gregg decides to go for it. At this point, what does he have to lose?

~ 19 ~

The Power of Prayer

In late fall, we decide to hold an early Thanksgiving. Feeling the weight of the year's events and the toll it's taken, Gregg wants to surround himself with his immediate family. His oldest sister, Maddie and brother-in-law, Mark, are coming anyhow, so as a surprise, he buys his sister, Nina, a plane ticket to join us as well, so she wouldn't have the added expense of another flight home from Colorado. The local bunch is here, too. The only missing piece is Gretchen, who is still at school.

After dinner, we gather in the living room. This is a family of doers. They thrive on helping others, and they want to help now too, but are at a loss as to what exactly can be done. They relate stories of friends who've encountered similar experiences with doctors or illnesses. They talk of networking to find more information that could be important or other options that might be available which have not been discussed. They speak of church and the support of those who are in need of help and hope.

Finally, the conversation turns to prayer. A few years prior to Gregg getting sick, the two of us attended a retreat at a center in upstate New York. It's a beautiful place, a transformed summer camp in the Berkshire Mountains. They offer a wide range of weekend and weeklong courses in areas such as self-help, dance, music, writing, poetry, meditation, and yoga presented by people well known in their fields.

The weekend we chose to go, I picked a class on dream interpretation while Gregg was drawn to a course called "The Power of Prayer." "This class was really interesting," he began as we drove away from the retreat.

"Guess I never really thought too much about the dynamics of prayer. You learn about it in church and take their word that it serves a purpose, if not for the other guy, at least for you in that you are taking the time to even think of others and God in the first place."

"Yeah, I suppose," I responded, watching the quaint little houses on the outskirts of town go by. "We always prayed with my grandparents, but I don't ever remember praying with my parents. It's nice that somebody gave us a little framework for how to pray, but we always said the same thing. We blessed all the little kiddies of the world," I said, smiling at the memory. "I remember being drawn in by the Lord's Prayer and the Apostle's Creed. It made me feel good when I was able to memorize it all for some reason. It was just a little goal I set for myself; I don't think anyone really drilled me on it or anything. But really, that's different from actually praying for someone in particular."

"Well, there's a lot of evidence proving that when you pray for someone, it really makes a measurable difference."

"Like what?"

He told a story about Korean women undergoing fertility treatment. The ones who were unknowingly prayed for were twice as successful at conceiving.

"Hmmm, maybe they were just lucky," I replied, playing devil's advocate.

"Apparently, there's only one-in-a-thousand possibility that it could have resulted randomly from chance. The teacher also said they've since replicated the study with other things, such as AIDS and people who have had heart attacks."

"It is pretty cool to think that the people who actually did the praying were so far away. Makes you realize that there is something to our connectedness. I always wondered how psychics could tell you about people who are nowhere near you or them physically. There's got to be a vibration that they tune into somehow. Prayer must work the same way."

"Also, it isn't so much the number of people praying or the length of time, but more the quality and sincerity with which the prayer is offered that makes the difference."

"So, you can just take a minute to send out a heartfelt, genuine desire to heal someone with love, and that's it? Maybe more people would be apt to do it if they didn't feel like they had to sit still for hours on end. I wonder if anyone let the monks know," I quipped. "It seems like that's all they do!"

"Even the smallest intention sent out for the good of another has the power to affect a change. It's pretty awesome," Gregg added as he steered the car down the quiet country lane. Thankfully, we were the only people on this part of the drive, and he could let himself get lost in thought without crashing the car. I could almost see the wheels spinning in his head as he figured out how to incorporate this into his world—not that he didn't pray already, but now he had more motivation. It seemed like such a simple thing to do, yet it had such far-reaching effects.

At the time, a friend of ours was in the throes of a ten-year battle with cancer. Gregg had written him, offering encouragement and support, along with telling him that prayer was powerful and he'd pray for him. Our friend, a psychologist, responded rather cynically, saying not to bother, that he didn't believe it would make a difference. We were a bit taken aback by his disparaging remarks, as who wouldn't want to take advantage of anything that might help? Of course, it didn't stop the prayers from going his way anyhow. Maybe the results are as subtle as feeling inexplicably less burdened or finding joy in something small that never occurred to you before. You might not make the connection of one thing affecting the other, but it doesn't mean it hasn't. No good intention goes unnoticed.

Now, in our living room surrounded by family, it's Gregg's turn.

"Since we all believe that prayer is important, why don't we ask all of our friends and families to pray for Gregg? There is nothing more powerful than love. If people send love with intention, then that loving energy becomes transformative. He has a ton of friends, and the rest of us do, too," Nina suggests. "I'm sure they'd all be willing to help!"

"People have already offered their prayers for him," I respond, "but perhaps if we organized it to happen at a certain time, there'd be a powerful rush of energy that would affect healing not only in Gregg, but in each other as well. I think people would remember better and be more apt to actually do it, if they had a specific time."

"That's an idea," his uncle says thoughtfully. "But not everyone goes to church, so making it happen at the Sunday service probably wouldn't work."

"How about if we pick a time of day, like 10:00?" I say. "It could be either a.m. or p.m. or both. That way, whenever they see the number 10, they'll think of Gregg, and it will remind them to say a quick prayer and move on with their day. I think if you just ask people to pray randomly whenever they feel like it, it might not happen as much as if you give them a time. What do you think?"

"I think it could work," Nina says. "People want to help."

It's something specific people can do to support and aid Gregg in his quest for healing—something to sink their teeth into rather than just hoping and praying as a family that things will get better. The support network will grow, which can only be a positive.

"People have their own way of praying, but if they feel pressured to say a big, long prayer, they may not tend to take the time," Maddie offers.

"Maybe we could come up with a single phrase or affirmation that would easily come to mind that they could say," I suggest, still trying to picture how it would all come together.

"I know when I pray that I try and visualize myself in good health," Gregg says. "How about something like, 'I support Gregg's radiant good health'? I could make up little cards with that statement and put 10:00 a.m. or p.m. on the card."

Suddenly my creative juices come to a screeching halt. This is where Gregg and I diverge in how we handle things in our lives. I'm on board with the belief in prayer, but handing out cards to people seems a bit out there. Granted, it's a practical application of the idea that will serve as a good reminder to people, but it strikes me as businesslike and feels both casual and awkward, when the situation is anything but.

Nonetheless, Gregg has always been more forward with people than I have. Because he takes the time every night to write to all the people who send him cards and letters, his circle of caring souls has expanded even more. He has always been a good listener and genuinely cares what others have to say. It makes them feel special, like they're the most important person in the world to him. It's a gift. Many have been drawn into this journey because of who he is.

I keep my thoughts to myself, not wanting to be openly critical of Gregg's idea. Everyone else seems OK with it and nods affirmatively. It's decided.

Gregg begins by creating a group of people he now dubs his "healers," which includes nearly everyone he has kept in touch with. He asks if they will agree to be part of the group and participate in the daily prayers. All say they will be honored. Nobody seems to think the cards are strange; rather, they are grateful for the written reminder, pleased to be able to join in.

It certainly isn't the first time I've been proven wrong, and undoubtedly won't be the last. It's food for thought. Why do I tend not to give people enough credit for offering their time and energy to help? Am I embarrassed? Would I look vulnerable and needy? I suppose, on some level, I don't personally feel I am worth it, rationalizing in my head that others are busy and have their own problems. They don't have time to be concerned with me or us.

But Gregg has shown me time and again that this isn't true, that people do respond. Many feel helpless even though their hearts are with you. They want to do something to make the situation better. When one of us hurts, we all hurt.

Something else I've been pondering is the ability to *receive* what people offer. My first response to proffers of help seems to be, "You don't have to do that." If someone asks how we are, I say, "We're doing fine," even when we're not. Accepting the kindness of others shouldn't be difficult, yet it seems to knock me off balance, often bringing tears. Once at a reading, I asked why I cry when people do nice things for me. The response was that I was feeling both love and pain and that the pain was more prominent at the moment.

What I'm realizing is that it's not just about me or Gregg accepting help, it's really about people being free to give. Others *need* to help, and when you don't let them, you're stifling their spirit and opportunity for growth, not to mention their desire to enfold you in genuine love and concern. It blocks the flow for us all.

Back in the living room, Nina suggests that we each think of a personality trait or strength we admire in Gregg that stands out for us when we think of him. If we write them down as supports or affirmations, he can refer to them during his daily meditations and lift his spirits.

I look over at Gregg to see his reaction. He doesn't appear to have any problem with receiving the love of his family or his friends. He doesn't look embarrassed or ill at ease that we're talking about him while he's in the room. Instead, he looks at everyone with love, appearing grateful that we're trying to be of service to him in some way, to ease his own personal burden. It's as if, deep down, he knows this is how people are meant to respond to each other, that when we actively work to change something with the most heartfelt intentions of good, we work from the essence of who we really are in this world, our God selves.

Before the night ends, we gather around Gregg for an impromptu "laying on of hands," a channeling of the love we feel for him and each other. It's an open declaration. The experience is powerful for us all, but especially for Gregg. He's more and more tuned in to feeling the energy flow these days. He soaks up every drop like a sponge and holds it tight. The current sweeps us forward, and we do not resist.

* * *

Gregg's journal:

The letters to all my family and friends should be arriving soon. I've sent them out over the past couple of days. That is the letter explaining my need to return to hospital to get additional health care. It was not an easy letter to write, but I feel the need to write everyone and inform them all at once. I believe in the power of prayer and I believe everyone's prayers and positive thoughts last time made a huge difference in my recovery.

It is a great comfort to get cards from loved ones. I look forward to going to the mailbox every day to see who has written. Phone calls are difficult. I have a hard time talking about all this over the phone. I can write about it though and enjoy the meditative thought that goes into the writing. I believe it is somewhat therapeutic for me to write to my friends and family. It generally brings joy to others as well, so it has two-fold benefits.

* * *

Gregg and I happen to see a report about a local doctor on the news one night. He has a reputation for faith healing beyond his usual medical practice. The story highlights two or three different individuals who feel that they've definitely been healed in his presence as he prayed over them. Naturally, our ears perk up. This did not seem hokey like the evangelists who smack you in the head and tell you that you are healed. He is an actual physician.

We make plans to attend one of his healing services, which are held in a local church and are free and open to the public. You can imagine all of the people attracted to the church in hopes of finding help. We arrive around 9 p.m. The church is filled to capacity; people are crammed in every corner—but it's still very quiet. We take a seat in the back. People sit in contemplation or prayer. A long line of people edges around the walls, softly shuffling toward the front.

There, on ground-level at the front, the doctor, a smallish, dark-haired but balding man, moves from one person to the next, murmuring prayers with them and for them, staying a few minutes with each. He sometimes touches their head or another part of their bodies. Soft music plays throughout the evening. People seem patient and peaceful as each waits their turn.

We stay until 2:00 a.m. There's no sign of things winding down. The doctor never took a break. I was amazed at his stamina and focus. We are tired, even if he seems immune, and regretfully decide to leave.

We attend another service at a different church a few weeks later. This time we come prepared with some water and a few light snacks. The church is so packed that the police actually block off the street and won't let more people in. We arrive at 7:00 p.m., and our turn finally comes just after 7:00 a.m. The entire night is spent in quiet meditation with hourly sayings of the rosary, along with beautiful music played on the piano by a woman who had been healed by the doctor and sung by his talented daughter. There are also occasional testimonials and stories from those who had their miracle, all while the doctor quietly works his way through the hordes of people.

Not being raised Catholic, I have never before experienced the saying of the rosary, though, of course, I knew it existed. But I grew up with a bias against rote prayers. I dismissed it as a shallow activity; I felt that if you are not engaged in actively having to think about what you are saying, then what's the point? It becomes a mindless repetition, an obligation that comes with going to church. Of course, I had no idea how deep in thought others actually are. I just knew that I could repeat the words while imagining what I would wear to a party or what I wanted for dinner—all sorts of things totally unrelated to the prayer. And if I was doing that, I figured others probably were as well.

But watching the people here in this church, I reconsider my earlier impressions, and see it more as a form of meditation and focus rather than a way to disengage. That's especially true of the number of repetitions in a short amount of time. It does seem to keep your head in a certain space.

As a teenager, when babysitting my neighbor's kids, I once found a child's book teaching young children the words to the Hail Mary. For some odd reason, I felt compelled to memorize it like I had the prayers earlier in my life. I have no idea what inspired me, but obviously, I felt curious and pushed enough to do it. So, in my current situation, during the reciting of the rosary, I'm able to follow along, deciding that there's no time like the present to experience what benefits it offers. And besides, why did I make myself learn the prayer in the first place? Clearly, I was sometimes naive about my own inner motivations and guidance.

As far as the healing, I can only describe my experience as feeling extremely blessed and grateful that this man can offer himself so unconditionally as a channel of God's energy to so many people in a most humble way. No one who is not authentic could sustain his efforts and give to others in that fashion for that long. If he wasn't a healer, he sure put on an amazing performance.

When Gregg's turn comes, he feels a great deal of heat and energy in his chest where the doctor lays his hands. It immediately energizes him both physically and mentally despite the fact that we've been awake all night long. It's exhilarating, and he is totally pumped as we leave.

On a subsequent visit to his actual medical office, I ask the doctor how he is able to go all night, nonstop, doing his healing work. He says he never gets tired because it is God energy that surges through him when connecting with others. It energizes him as opposed to depleting him.

Our human selves seem so finite on many levels, our thoughts and knowledge of the world based mainly on what we take in through our five senses, yet here is this human man like us, appearing to be superhuman, performing healings and miracles inexplicable to the average person. He seems to show what is possible for each of us, demonstrating what connections are already within us that we might also access.

People everywhere have been touched by praying with him. Is it just the healing energy that he brings to the table, which causes a positive change, or do we also do *our* part by tuning into that same energy source with our fervent desire to be cured of whatever ails us? Do we together then find that connection to our ultimate source enabling us to regain the perfection that we truly are? And if there is a God energy and vibration present, would it not be magnified by so many people with the common intention of being healed, thereby raising the energy level and vibration of all who are in the room? Then, of course, everybody would derive some benefit from just being there, even if you never had a direct meeting with the actual person doing the healings.

A group energy has the effect of influencing anyone in its presence. We have all experienced a time when we know we have a place to be and we don't feel like going, but once we actually get there, we find ourselves happy that we went. Our out-of-sync vibration has now meshed with the group's vibration and lifted our own.

Each time we participate in a new experience, our views of life and its possibilities expands. I am grasping the many levels of healing, not just the physical aspect. So much of what we experience is driven by perspective and emotion. Part of dealing with a physical infirmity is being able to handle it mentally, emotionally, and spiritually. It's all intertwined. Fixing just one area won't get the job done. True healing requires a change in all areas in order to be lasting and complete.

Gregg may or may not have gotten the physical healing he is looking for, but he did feel a shift, a release, a letting go of something. If we can lessen the stress and limiting beliefs and finally accept that we are not alone, that we are truly loved beyond measure and being cared for at the very deepest level, is that not also healing? We, as humans, crave that connection, for that is who we really are. And only when we realize our true nature can we then find peace.

~ 20 ~

A New Friend

"I met an interesting lady at church today," Gregg says one Sunday. He often goes alone, craving the message of the day and the boost he feels during group meditations. He would like for me to join him. I feel selfish; it doesn't seem like much to ask, especially if it makes him happy, but I would rather stay home and do yoga or write in my journal. Though Gregg may feel minor disappointment that I don't go, he knows I need my own ways of recharging and finding a way work through this, and he's willing to give me that space without fuss.

"Yeah? What was so interesting?" I ask.

"We were sitting, listening to the sermon, and right in the middle of it she got up and walked over in front of everybody to sit by Ruth, that tiny, little woman who is always dressed very properly and comes to church with a personal aide. Do you remember her?"

"Yes, I think so."

"Anyhow, she sensed that Ruth was having some heart issues even before Ruth herself knew. She sat with her for a few minutes, and then when Ruth began to have more symptoms, people realized that something was amiss, and the service was interrupted. They ended up calling 911 and taking her away in an ambulance."

"Wow! I hope she's OK. That must have been scary for her," I respond. "How do you think this lady knew?"

"I'm not sure, but it was clear she was tuned into her. Her name is Maria, and, coincidentally, she was slated to talk to the congregation about a class she's offering at the church. When all the craziness was over, she did just that."

"What's the class about?"

"It's called In Right Form. It sounds like something right up our alley. It's about our bodies, energy, diet, chakras, astrology, and lots of other things rolled into one, you know, being in the 'right form,'" he quips.

"Well, who doesn't want that?" I say.

"It just so happens, I brought home the pamphlet," he says, grinning. "The class is once a month for three months."

We sign up for the class. A registered nurse, Maria introduces herself as a medical intuitive. She discovered her abilities when patients would come in for evaluation, and she intuitively knew that even though the doctors might be looking for the problem at the site of the symptoms, the real problem stemmed from another part of the body. Because she was the nurse as opposed to the doctor, it was a sticky wicket to contradict what was happening or add her two cents. Eventually, they would come to the conclusion that the problem really did originate elsewhere, as Maria had already known.

At the time, Maria has a contract with the Sisters of St. Joseph's, doing healing work with the retired religious, combining her vast understanding of the workings of the human body and energy along with information she gathers from her guides and the extensive network of angels whom she trusts implicitly. Over the weeks, we are introduced to a variety of different experiences. She integrates talks of right eating with a visit to the local health food store, or the benefits of aromatherapy with a trip to a business where you can mix and match different smells and oils for therapeutic purposes. We learn about astrology and how the stars and planets interact with earth and how we're affected by these different energies. She brings in the components of sound and music, and explains the effects on our bodies and energies.

Though she doesn't know us personally, she certainly knows that Gregg is ill. All you have to do is look at him. He still carries himself with the bearing of a young man, but he's thin, and his healthy complexion has faded to a ghostly pallor. There is also the ever-present backpack. The group is small, lending itself to more intimate conversations. It feels safe and nonthreatening, like a therapy encounter group. At one point, we are asked to do an exercise where Gregg and I face each other, looking into each other's eyes to sense our deeper connection, a sort of window to the soul. I think I'm doing what she asked, but Maria immediately perceives a block preventing me from looking beyond what's right in front of me.

"You poor thing," she says, resting her hand on my shoulder comfortingly. "You really are stuck between a rock and a hard place." I'm not sure what she means, nor am I even aware there is a problem. "Your body is rocking side to side. You can't go back, but neither can you see your way forward."

I don't feel myself moving; it must be nearly imperceptible. Her comments catch me off guard but strike home, and I realize she's right. If I allow myself to peer into the depths of Gregg's soul, an unwanted truth might reveal itself to me. I'm scared of the knowing. It would be more than I can bear right now. I don't *want* to see because all I see is the loss, not the connection.

Confronting the truthfulness of her statement strips away the last shred of deception I had surrounded myself with. I feel exposed, like I've been uncloaked from the wrap of safety, security, and denial I have so carefully woven around myself. Lost in the day-to-day schedule of caregiving and surviving, I have refused to let myself acknowledge the next possible sequence of events. I'm stuck in idle with no forward gear. With newfound realization, Greg and I stand holding each other, overwhelmed by emotion. We must both face the music, however tragic and terrible it may be. I can no longer deny that my greatest fear is likely inevitable: Gregg may soon be leaving.

* * *

"I've been thinking I would like to invite all our friends and family to a healing service," Gregg says, as we sit with our tea in the living room one evening. He's just finished writing out a card and is addressing the envelope. "The love and energy that we all felt, me especially, when everyone surrounded me the last time was intense. Just imagine what that would be like on a larger scale!"

He never fails to surprise me. We're just two people trying to get through a tough time, not a church. What makes him think that organizing a healing service is a good idea?

"Do you really think people would come?" I respond, trying to appear open to the idea, but not feeling it. "It's a bit unorthodox and kind of weird to think of doing a church-type event with everybody. This isn't really an area we've delved into much with our friends, considering how long we've known them. Our conversations rarely go there."

"I'm pretty sure some would come. It doesn't matter how many. Whoever feels the need to be there," he says, ever his optimistic self, letting it sink in for a few minutes so I will realize he's serious, because so much of the time he isn't. Most people would be content with just handling what comes their way and leaving it at that, but not Gregg. His enthusiasm for the excitement he feels when he experiences something affirmative always leads him to want to share with others, so they can feel what he does. "I was thinking we could hold it at the depot. It wouldn't have to be long, maybe an hour or two. Maria might be willing to come and lead the service."

"Well, she at least would be able to give it some structure. Maybe we could have some light snacks and do a little meditation with everyone,"

I say. Wiley, our dog, meanders into the living room, circles around and plops down with a loud sigh, then lays his head on the carpet and closes his eyes. His world sure isn't stressful. "First prayer, now church. What next? Our friends never know what they are in for hanging out with us!" I add with a chuckle.

As usual, I feel reticent working through our story in such a public way. It's always been a struggle for me, but I force myself to ride the Gregg train along with everyone else. I know I am witness to these events for a reason I can't yet define.

We hold the service in December. A light snow falls, but the day is still bright. As we organize the facility, putting the chairs out, setting up the coffee and cookies, Gregg steps outside to sweep off the walk. A young man drives up and asks if he's in the right place for a Rotary Club meeting he's covering for a local newspaper.

The reporter's name is James; his young wife is currently in the hospital with a chronic illness. Gregg invites him to come in and be a part of the festivities, knowing he might need some healing of his own. Since he couldn't find the event that brought him to the depot, he's happy to stay. Altogether, about fifty people show up. "Deb and I are grateful that you're all here, especially in light of the fact that the Cleveland Browns are playing today," Gregg teases. "But you never know, this might turn out to be less painful!" The crowd chuckles. "All kidding aside, we really are happy to have you here with us. You all know me well enough to know what's been going on with me, and you've become part of my journey. Without you all around me, I might not be here today. I can't say it's always been easy because it hasn't, but knowing that I have you all in my corner means the world to me."

Gregg looks much like the administrator he was, except now he's bald and carries a small backpack. If you didn't know any better you might think he is opening a typical in-service he'd organized for the ranks of educators. He chats with the crowd, then introduces Maria, who takes charge.

"You all know that you're here by divine order. There are no coincidences," she begins. "We're divinely connected, and whenever something happens to one of us, it happens to all of us on a lesser scale. We feel the emotions of the event on top of what we already face in our own lives. How we deal with these emotions is important for our own well-being and our health. Whenever a thought occurs that we can't let go of, causing us to resist, we tend to rehash it over and over, and then it becomes stuck. The more we focus on it, the more stuck it becomes, blocking the easy and natural flow of energy through the body. These blocks are the result of dis-ease. They build up over time and eventually, manifest themselves as some sort of physical ailment."

I glance around the room to gauge the degree of acceptance, but all appear raptly attentive to her words, lost in their own thoughts.

"Some of these blocks are a result of happenings in our current lives, others we've carried with us over time, from past life experiences."

She coaches everyone to release their own burdens, then says, "Now, move your thoughts to Gregg. Let the feelings of sadness and helplessness go, knowing that he is living his highest and best, that what he is experiencing is his to learn." She pauses, giving us time to feel the sorrow and then imagine the heartache draining away. "That's it." Her voice is soft and velvety. "Now you're doing it. It appears as a grayish, green sludge coming out the bottoms of your feet, releasing itself harmlessly into the earth. Let it go," she encourages. One of Maria's gifts is being able to see the energy around her, her vivid descriptions helping to envision the process.

"As you feel the sadness and despair leave, imagine a shimmering, white, healing light coming into the top of your head, filling it, and then moving down through each and every part of your body, until you're totally aglow and radiating this healing energy. Feel it pulsate through you and from you." She pauses, then continues, "Now imagine Gregg standing in the center of all of you in this beautiful light that you've created, and watch as it now fills every cell in his body, surrounding him, lifting his heart and spirit. Hold him in this container of love as it permeates his being. Know that each time you lift up another, you lift yourself up as well."

Lastly, she invites Gregg to the front of the room and asks everyone to stand up, holding their hands in the air, palms forward toward him, sending love, light, and peace, as he travels this path of enlightenment. The snapshot of this scene makes the front page of the local paper, compliments of James. Not only have our friends and family been the recipients of an interesting and energy-filled afternoon, but now an even larger group of people have been brought into the possibilities of alternative healing and energy work. I overflow with gratitude that so many people have come together to honor Gregg in this unusual but profound and loving way.

~ 21 ~

Connections

I lie in bed watching Gregg sleep, listening to him breathe. When he's sleeping, he seems so peaceful. It seems he could forget all of the things that go on in his life when he's awake. I find myself yearning for his touch. I want so much for him to wrap his arms around me and tell me it'll all be OK, that he'll always take care of me and protect me as he always has. The intimacy that we once shared is fleeting now. He's said more than once how amazed he is that he has absolutely no sex drive anymore. It's a side effect of all the chemo drugs, but he's still puzzled and saddened by it. I know he'd do anything for me, pleasure me if I initiated it, but he needs every ounce of energy just to make it through the day.

Once again, I feel selfish for even thinking of my own needs and desires. I slide gently out of bed and go outside on the porch, the warm night air caressing me instead. My hand moves down to my breast as sorrow overwhelms me. How many more times will I feel his hands on my body, will we make love? As I sit holding myself and rocking, tears streaming down my face, I know that we've moved beyond our old selves, the happy-go-lucky young couple we used to be, and that those days will never come around again. I mourn each and every piece of us that no longer exists and is now just a memory. The romantics say, "Parting is such sweet sorrow." I wonder where the sweet part is. Sometimes life just sucks.

My journal:

Gregg is certainly not the man he used to be in many ways. He looks so different to me. I try and get used to it. I guess I am, as I have a hard time remembering what he looked like with hair. That's odd to think about having seen him that way for thirty years prior. I try not to think about what he's going through too much. He tries so hard to deal with it all and he does a fabulous job ninety-nine percent of the time. He was really down last night again. I don't even know what to say or do to comfort him other than hold him. I enjoy that too, as I don't know how many more times that will happen. I've been thinking how it seems like we're grieving as we live, sort of like our relationship as it once was is slowly fading away. In some ways, even though Gregg is here, it is still lonely. I miss the carefree times. And though I've been living through this with Gregg, I occasionally put myself in his shoes and I realize he's in such a different place. I guess we'll all face the transition when our time comes—back to the adage, you're born alone and you die alone. I have a hard time thinking about death. I've really come to think of it as a transition or passing to the next dimension.

The strong pain narcotics that Gregg takes are also messing with his emotions. He complains of feeling "flat," which is so unlike him. Certainly, life is more serious now. We rarely find ourselves in lighthearted moods where we can laugh and be silly. It just doesn't seem natural anymore. When they talk about emotions being heavy or the weight of the world, they aren't kidding. It's hard to leave it behind.

He also has trouble holding onto and organizing his thoughts. He's still doing his routines and keeping track of his appointments and social events, but he voices that he isn't doing so as efficiently as before, which bothers him. He continues to write to friends and family daily, but even the legibility of his letters has suffered. His thinking is spacey, and he feels depressed more frequently.

One of his main goals besides healing is to get off the drugs. In an effort to become more clear-headed, he tries to cut back as much and as often as he can, which really isn't very often, and he's careful to do it gradually. But still, narcotics are narcotics, and they mess with your head. It's a crazy balancing act. I worry about him home alone all day while I continue to go to work as much as I can. It's to the point where I'm afraid to leave him by himself. This is new and unfamiliar territory. It actually crosses my mind that he might do something to end his life, a thought that's never ever occurred to me before. I don't know who to call on to help. Most all of our friends and family work or don't live nearby.

Gregg's parents, the most likely candidates, decide to keep up with their yearly trek to Florida again for a few months. When they come over to say goodbye, Gregg and I both hint that it'd be really nice if they could stick around. I'm anxious, worrying about Gregg's state of mind, but they won't change their plans. It makes me sad and frustrated with them. Why can't they see that we need them? Perhaps we just need to be more blunt. It's not a matter of loving Gregg or me enough. I know they do. Maybe they just don't know their role or how to help. The story is being written moment to moment. I have to tell myself that they're also having a hard time dealing and need to get away, striving for normalcy like we all are, but I'm still disappointed, as is Gregg. Yet, how do you ask people to change their lives for you? If they don't do it willingly, perhaps it shouldn't happen.

And so, we do our best. One day I am particularly worried about leaving Gregg for work because he seems even more in a funk than usual. I always feel conflicted, go or stay, go or stay. My workplace has been more than forgiving with my many sick days, knowing that we're going through some extremely difficult times, but I don't feel I can keep missing so much, so I tell Gregg and myself that I'll call him at lunch to check on him, and if he needs me, I'll come home.

When I return at the end of the work day, I'm amazed to find that two of our friends, unbeknownst to each other, have each taken the day off work to hang out with Gregg. Wow! Talk about synchronicity and prayers being answered. They hear the universal call on a day we so desperately need a helping hand, and Gregg needs a morale boost. If

I entertained any thoughts we were alone in this, they are vaporized by these two angels in human form, appearing without even being asked. Many other "human angels" come to our aid by driving Gregg to his chemo appointments in Columbus three times a month. He delights in e-mailing missives to all his healers, describing the situation, and how he'd be honored if they each might take a turn being his chauffeur. Most who live locally, and a few who don't, generously take a turn. He moves right down his list, setting up the schedule a few weeks in advance. There are enough helpers that only a couple have ever been repeats.

Gregg looks forward to these days, allowing quality time and camaraderie with each and every person who joins him. I'm thrilled he has this opportunity to share his day with those dear to him and grateful for their willingness to help so I can work and keep up a somewhat normal existence while they're gone. It almost seems like a subtle little ministry that he has going. The conversations aren't solely about his own illness or his needs but also about the other person's life. It gives each the opportunity to experience Gregg's journey firsthand and adjust their own perspectives of life accordingly. It gives me a much-needed break.

~ 22 ~

Healing Holograms

The phone rattles me from a story I was reading curled up on the couch. "I got it," Gregg yells from the bedroom. "Maahk!" I hear him shout enthusiastically, mimicking the heavy New England accent of our brother-in-law, Mark. "How's everything in Connecticut?" I smile to myself, happy to hear the joyfulness in his greeting.

Eventually Gregg hangs up and tells me the gist of the conversation: Mark thought he would like to know that a well-known rocker from a 1960s rock group had been healed from pancreatic cancer by a sixteen-year-old boy in Canada named Alex. Through our own research, we learn that Alex travels to Toronto a few times a year to work with large groups of people. The next scheduled date is fast approaching, and Toronto is only a five-hour drive from our home.

"Do you want to go?" Gregg asks. "I'd love to see what he's all about."

I shrug. No reasons to dissuade him come to mind. "I wonder what he does exactly? It sounds like it might be more than the prayer of our last experience. Do you think you will feel good enough to go?"

"If I don't, hopefully, I will feel better having gone!"

"I wonder if you need a passport to get into Canada these days. If they checked us for drugs, it wouldn't take long to find some," I say, thinking of the old days. "Maybe we should get a doctor's note or something."

"I'm sure people cross the border all of the time who are sick and have medicines."

"I suppose. But I would rather be safe than sorry."

And so, we end up in an auditorium of people hoping to be helped by this young healer. An ordinary young man walks onto the stage, handsome with dark hair, dressed casually in a T-shirt and shorts. Alex explains that he'd always seen auras, not realizing early on that others couldn't, and that he'd always been filled with unharnessed energy as a child that he couldn't explain. Pencils flew out of his hands for no reason at school, things fell around him, and he'd spin in complete circles on his bike. Eventually, his mom was witness to the bike phenomenon, and his parents decided that they needed help. Remembering she'd heard about another woman in town who also saw auras, she made an appointment. The woman verified that Alex did indeed have an exceptional amount of energy, and that the reason all these things happened to him was that he was not directing it in any kind of focused way. She helped him with some techniques and suggested they look further into the practice of qigong, which means energy work or life-force discipline.

One night, Alex attempted to comfort his mother who suffered from multiple sclerosis and had trigeminal neuralgia, a stabbing pain in the face and ear. He told her to close her eyes, and placed his hand on her forehead. The pain jumped from her to him. She fell asleep comfortably and continued to feel better. He ended up with a splitting headache, though it was gone the next day. That was when he learned that he could heal people.

To explain what he does when the lights go down during the healing session, Alex plays a short video of himself standing and moving his arms, fingers, and hands sort of like he's conducting an orchestra. He says in large audiences, he works with the primary holographic images of illness that appear to him, covering the greatest amount of people. He then heals by substituting several healthy holographic images that he's found effective in replacing diseased patterns. He's given them names such as Energetic Hologram, Brain Signals Hologram, and Pattern

Energy Grid. He stresses that healing is a process, that we're all capable of healing ourselves, and that our attitude and ability to visualize are important. Our bodies don't differentiate between a real situation and an imagined one. So, the more detailed and emotionally connected visualization we can bring forth, the more likely healing will take place. We are who we think we are.

We've done our share of visualizing, but this is another level all together. I've never thought of our bodies as holograms or considered the depth and makeup of them on a subatomic level. Pictures of bodies with different healing light patterns are provided to help conjure up useful images. Adam describes how he could energetically journey into someone's physical body to see areas that weren't flowing or working as they should. He says we all have the ability to sense these areas of need within ourselves, but few of us do. Gregg and I both feel energized to try.

We go home equipped with new ideas and perspective. On the drive home, Gregg reclines in the passenger seat and falls asleep. Driving is meditative to me, a tonic of sorts, especially when I don't have to worry about directions because I know the way. Seeing Gregg lie peacefully beside me soothes my heart, and I treasure these quiet moments when all is calm. I'm glad we made the effort to go. I'd been leery of crossing the border and being in another country if anything happened, but in the end, we trusted that all would be well and it was.

As the miles fade behind us, I have plenty of time to think, not only of these new ideas, but about life in general. When you get some years under your belt, you start to see the pattern of how you evolved into your own personal philosophy of life, not only as a result of experiences, but because of people who've touched you in some way. Gregg and I are separate and unique individuals enveloped in accelerated spiritual training. We've trodden the road laid out before us and been continually shown new and expansive perspectives, our intangible but real world. The message is often the same, cloaked in different colors.

Everything is energy, energy can be manipulated, we are what we think, and we create our own reality.

My mind drifts to God, the ultimate, purest energy. I know that we're made of that same energy that God resides within each one of us. He only seems mysterious when we view him/it as separate from ourselves, like the Wizard of Oz, whom we have to beg for favors or miracles only he can grant. Now, I'm learning that it's possible to create our own miracles based on what we think, how we view the world and by acknowledging and living from that greater essence that is us.

It's exciting to know deep within my being that this is so. Yet our human selves, our egos, always manage to leave a crack open for doubt to creep in. What if it doesn't work? What if we put in all the effort, doing all of the healing and thought techniques, and we still don't heal, at least in the way that we want? Did we just not do it right? Were we not focused enough? Were our thoughts not pure enough?

No answers to the questions we face present themselves to me as I mindlessly follow the taillights of the car in front of me. And yet, the experiences we've had and the opportunities that have appeared must be teaching us something, guiding us to a new place where infinite potential hovers oh so close, waiting for us to claim it.

Gregg draws my attention, as he twists in his seat getting more comfortable, no lines of worry marking his face, just a look of ease and peace. I wonder what he's dreaming about. I've seen new sides of him these past months. He's always made things happen in his life. He's put in the effort and has reaped the rewards. But this journey has been different, even though he rarely complains. There's an underlying frustration when things don't go the way he wants or thought they would. The control he usually feels has gone tipsy. It's like being beaten down, then standing up a tiny bit less erect after each hit. To his infinite credit, he's come back with more determination than many, myself included. An intense yearning for his healing fills my heart as I rest my hand on his leg while he sleeps.

The nearly full moon makes its appearance in the sky to my left, even as the sun is setting on my right. The sky is exploding into its vivid mural of orange, magenta, and purple. I can hardly keep my eyes on the road as I marvel at its spectacular beauty. Only an essence of love could create landscapes that enrapture us so. Is it so hard to imagine that same essence inside our hearts?

~ 23 ~

Gifts

Gregg seems to be holding his own. It appears that his body is responding positively to the experimental chemo drugs he's receiving. Even though he goes through short periods of nausea after each session, he handles it well overall and enjoys the encouraging vibes that surround him from the staff at the hospital. They remain attentive to his needs and open to his ideas about improving health care. As usual, he calls many of them by their first names and has managed to ingratiate himself into their lives like he does with everyone he knows.

This is not to say that his days are easy, particularly when coming to terms with the fact that eating orally is just no longer possible. This is almost harder for him to accept than the chemo. He misses his usual menu of cereal in the morning and sandwiches for lunch. It's one thing if you are too sick to eat, but when you want to and can't, you want to all the more. It's like telling a little kid not to jump in a puddle.

Even more than the food itself, he misses the gratification of chewing, something most of us don't even think about. We tried for quite a while to work through food that might actually make it down his throat, from fish to Jell-O to soup, but less and less found its way through the passage of his esophagus. Lately, he has discovered a new love for Tootsie Roll Pops just to give him some sensation of taste and flavor, and he relies on his tube feeding to do the rest. His body accepts its new way of eating, as boring as it is, though he's definitely thin. Sadly, not only is he unable to swallow food, but with the passage through his throat mostly closed off, his saliva has nowhere to go either. As we had been told earlier, we each swallow something like two liters of saliva a day, another thing we just take of granted. This means he has to walk around with a cup to spit in. It is unpleasant but necessary, and I tell myself it is no different from what someone would do with chewing tobacco, not that that makes it any lovelier. He tries to make it as unobtrusive as possible, and it's now another part of "normal" for us both. On the up side, Gregg has often been seen at work carrying around a mug of tea as he greets people in the morning, so walking around with a cup now is not out of the ordinary.

Because we seem to be in a calmer period again, the pace of life picks up. We still get away on weekends if we can, visiting friends or going to cabins in the scenic parts of Ohio. People are constantly in and out of town for visits. Gregg still has his fun projects going on, working on various cars or puttering in the garden and around the house. He is busy organizing summer plans, including time at the Lake Erie Islands with old friends and a family vacation to Ocean City, New Jersey, to celebrate his parents' sixtieth wedding anniversary in August.

We also face the fact that keeping up with a regular work life is probably more than Gregg needs to deal with at the moment. It's more than enough just trying to stay healthy. We agree that it doesn't seem fair to the school either, even though they've never given him any grief about missing, but instead always send him good wishes and encouragement to get better.

At this point, he has used up most of the sick days he's accumulated during his teaching career. We learn that he actually could retire on disability—except that he's just shy of enough sick days to carry him to the thirty-year mark.

But word gets around at work and, lo and behold, his fellow teachers kindly donate their own sick days to help him out. Neither of us knew that you could even do that.

We're deeply touched, once again, by the generosity of others, especially since Gregg has only worked with this staff for a few years. They certainly are under no obligation to help, but they liked and supported him, taking him under their collective wing. He has been good about staying in touch and keeping tabs on what's happening there as well. The basic graciousness of human beings is healing in its own way.

*   *   *

"I ran into Barb the other day at the grocery store," I share with Gregg. We sit by the fire on our back deck. The night is chilly, but clear and starry, with the moon just peeking its face out from behind the large maple tree in our backyard. The radiant heat is warming the front of me nicely, even though the back of me is feeling the cold. "She went out of her way to tell me how much she enjoyed your healing service."

"Really? That's nice," Gregg replies, picking up the large stick he uses as a poker. "I've had some people tell me the same thing. I'm glad everyone got something out of it. I certainly did." He adjusts the logs, flames and sparks shooting up high in the air, as the wood gets tumbled around and settles into a new space. The charcoals on the bottom of the fire pit undulate a glowing, mesmerizing orange and blue.

"I actually think everyone was surprised at the impact it had on them," I say, staring at the dancing flames, enjoying the smell. "Maybe it was all of us coming together at the same time for the common purpose of helping someone we love. Not only did it energize you, it really seemed to affect all of us in a positive way, besides."

Satisfied with the fire, he sits back down. "Maria was a new twist for many of them, I imagine. She did a nice job of leading us through the meditation," he says, thoughtfully. "I could really feel the energy in the room. It was what I had hoped for on many levels."

"I'm glad. I tried to participate as much as possible, but at the same time, I was curious what everyone was thinking. Whenever I looked up, they all seemed engrossed." Taking a sip of my wine, I look over at Gregg as he ponders, rocking in the glider and watching the fire. "I'm happy you pushed to do it. It felt like a good thing all the way around." And then another thought comes: "Maybe it is all part of what you are here to do, Greggy."

He nods. As usual, my mind works constantly to find a palatable perspective on this journey for us both, but even though a part of me is soothed with the idea, a good chunk of me still feels little comfort.

"A few people have asked me when we're having another one. One was Joe. He said he'd heard about it and was sorry he missed it. He couldn't make it because he had some business out of town."

It hasn't occurred to me to think about another service. "If people want another one, they obviously gleaned something from the first one. They were there for you, but maybe their own unexpected feeling of well-being caught them by surprise."

"Maybe. I know *I* could certainly feel it. My body literally pulsated. I guess we were all lifted at the same time. A few mentioned it immediately, but others told me later, after they'd had time to think about it," he says, adding another big log to the fire. "If we do it again, I think it would be great to invite Gretchen's friends. She felt bad about not being at the first one. It would be nice to support all her supporters as well."

"It *would* be fun to involve them and see what their reactions would be. You never know what makes a difference in a person's life! Many of them have already experienced the thrill of Gretchen's birthday parties, participating in adventures they didn't know they were getting into. This might add a new wrinkle to their thought processes as well." I smile to myself.

We hold the event at Common Ground, an all-ages mind/body/spirit retreat center run by a lovely nun from the Catholic order of the Sisters of Humility and a progressive board of directors. It's a crisp winter day, the sun peeking through the trees. The room fills to capacity once again, people taking seats in chairs situated in two concentric circles, others standing around the edges. A number of people who attended the first service are here, along with friends who hadn't been able to make the first one or who had heard about it and want to be a part of it. As hoped, many of Gretchen's friends also come.

Once again, Gregg starts it off, then hands it over to Maria. Earlier we discussed with her our desire for people to have their own personal healing experiences. Maria explains the intention for the day, then creates an energetic vortex by having Gregg stand in the middle as she voices a group prayer. Within this vortex, whatever comes up for anyone, consciously or subconsciously, can be released. After the prayer, Gregg sits beside me while Maria leads us through another meditation, using her singing bowl again to lift the vibrations of the room.

I hold Gregg's hand as we sit together, feeling calm and peaceful, grateful to be a part of something like this, and reflecting on the unexpected turns that life takes. Who would have thought that we would be the key players here, the reason for this gathering? It's more than Gregg's illness this time; it's about each person called to be here, a larger and more encompassing purpose.

This service seems to have an even more profound effect on people. Later, a friend will tell me that she couldn't stop crying and didn't know why. She knows that even though she's there for Gregg, she must be releasing layers of her own unidentified emotions and thought patterns that she didn't even know she had been holding onto. One of Gretchen's male friends from college has a vision of people made of light dancing in the middle of the room. As they ascend, he sees bits of darkness coming out of them and their lights getting brighter and brighter. He tells us it was a message not to forget that on earth we deal in the physical form, but when we go to heaven, we are relieved of all our ailments and there is nothing but lightness and joy and peace. I think the darkness that was leaving the figures was the cancer and I sort of felt like at the time, this was a message that they wanted me to tell Gregg or at least know for myself, that we shouldn't worry about anything because He was going to take care of it all and to be at peace now, not to wait for peace.

~ 24 ~

Can It Be True?

When summer arrives, we both want to finish off the house remodeling by creating a new walkway to our front door, something we've never had, oddly enough. I have visions of a beautiful, winding, landscaped path working its way to the front entrance. We enlist the help of friends and family to dig a path and haul bricks. The final results perhaps aren't as fine as what a professional could accomplish, but we're happy with how it looks. As a bonus, Gregg scatters bulbs around in the new flowerbed. It will be a surprise to see where they come up.

We fill the rest of our summer with travels and the celebration for my in-laws' sixtieth wedding anniversary in Ocean City, which, sadly, includes a trip to the hospital when Gregg accidentally overdoses on his Fentanyl patches by getting overheated in a Jacuzzi, giving us all a scare. But before long we are back home, and already the school year has begun. One day as I'm changing my clothes after work, I hear the door open, and voices follow. In walks Gregg with Penny, his secretary when he was principal of the alternative school, who had driven him to Columbus that day. I greet them, giving them both a hello hug. "What's up? You guys seem in good cheer. How was the day in Columbus?"

Gregg beams at me. "Great news!" he exclaims. "I don't have to do any more chemo!"

"What do you mean you don't have to do any more chemo?" I ask, glancing from him to Penny and back again.

"The doctor felt I was doing well, and the treatment seems to be working, so they thought they would take me off the chemo treatments." He's clearly thrilled with the news.

"How do they know? They haven't really given you any official tests, have they?" I'm still incredulous and skeptical.

"They have their benchmarks," he says, obviously happy not to be questioning their decision.

I'm aware that Gregg is almost always upbeat and positive when they ask how he's doing. In his mind, the cancer is going away. I wonder if he has convinced them that it's so. I look at Penny again for verification. "Really?" I ask.

She nods and smiles. "That's what they said."

"That *is* wonderful news, Greggy!" I say, hugging him again. Gregg is animated and talkative, like he's in seventh heaven, as he tells me about the day. I still can't quite believe it. But these are doctors. They rely on science to give them direction. They must feel that Gregg really is doing well, or they wouldn't have stopped the treatment. Can it actually be true?

Even so, there are still challenges. One night Gregg comes home from walking the dog with blood dripping down his face. I am horrified. He passed out in the small crop of woods between our street and the schoolyard. When he fell, the branches must have cut him.

I don't know what to say. I can't be with him every minute, and he doesn't expect or want me to be, but this is so hard. His body is weak, even with the doctors' insistence that he's better. Yet, a short walk in the woods leads to injury. By the time he gets home, he seems to have recovered, but I picture him lying there with no one around but the dog and wondered how long it was before he woke up and came to his senses. I go into the bathroom with him and help wipe off the blood, surreptitiously checking him over at the same time, not wanting to fuss too much.

Some weeks later, Gregg has just finished washing the car and comes to sit with me on the porch where I'm just hanging up the phone with my sister. He still has a towel in his hand and is scrubbing a smudge of grease off his arm when he says, "I was thinking about gathering our friends for a celebration of fall and the fact that I'm done with chemo. They have all been here for me so often and have supported me in every way. I just want to honor them and have us all come together at one time."

"Like a party at our house?" I ask. The cat purrs and rubs her head against my outstretched fingers.

"Actually, I was thinking of Common Ground again. It's beautiful there this time of year."

"You know me, the woods always make me happy," I respond, picturing the whole place in my mind. "Maybe they would let us have a fire in their huge fire pit next to the river!" I imagine the colors of the trees, the smell of damp or burning leaves in the air, the crunching sound they make when you walk on them, the end of the heat and humidity. It's as if nature is finally revealing its true inner beauty. To me, there's nothing like a chilly, clear, blue-sky day with a gentle wind blowing the leaves around.

"I was thinking even more than that." He tosses the towel on the chair beside him and looks directly at me with a twinkle in his eye. "What if we did a firewalk?"

"Whoa! Now that would be a walk on the wild side!" I exclaim. "I know you did it, but that was years ago. Do you really think people would be eager to walk on fire? I'm not even sure that *I'm* ready to do it. I think those nuns put the whammy on you!" I tease.

"Ha!" he cackles. "If they did, it worked! It would be an opportunity, for sure. If you didn't want to walk, nobody would make you."

Amazingly, it doesn't take much convincing to persuade the folks at Common Ground to host the firewalk on a brisk Saturday night in

October. Though we had been open to having the public attend, more than three-quarters of the thirty or so people who appear are our personal friends. They arrive with generally open minds, or at least with their curiosity about what Gregg was up to now. I don't know what to expect any more than the rest of them, though I have seen it done once, and am led by the man in my life to stretch the self-imposed limitations I have placed upon myself.

We circle around a ten-foot stack of wood piled high in a meadow surrounded by trees on all sides and watch as the recently torched fire burns in the dusk of a lovely fall evening. The flames shoot high in the air, above my head, sparking and snapping. I contemplate the dichotomy of fire itself. It can be beautiful and thought-provoking, even life-giving, as when it warms us or burns dead wood in the forests, making way for new sprouts to grow—yet it can also destroy everything. The positive and the negative: Every situation we come across has at least two sides or perspectives, the good and the bad, the black and the white, the am and the am not, the love and the fear.

When Gregg described his first experience to me years ago, it seemed spiritual in nature, with the nuns and the mantras, quiet, peaceful, and contemplative. This evening is the opposite, loud and energetic, but also motivational, informative, and interactive. Not being what I'd imagined, I'm a little put off at first, but eventually, I decide that rather than trying to control what I think should happen and being disappointed, I'll let go and roll with the experience. Let the current show me the way and trust that I would get there. Release, release, release. As the fire burns down, we discuss fear. When we're asked what we are afraid of, I honestly can't think of much, yet when others list their fears, I realize I have many fears I'd been unwilling to acknowledge.

Dan, the man in charge, claims that the only fears we are born with are the fear of falling and the fear of loud noises. Everything else is learned. For example, a little baby, who is happily inspecting a spider, becomes afraid only when her mother sees it in her hand and screams.

Interesting what we pick up from those around us, often our parents. Or what fear-based thoughts we latch onto with our imaginations when talking with friends and hearing their own qualms about various things or experiences.

After a series of preparatory exercises that helped us strengthen our belief in our ability to conquer our fears, time finally arrives for the climactic walk. The wood has burned down, any large logs left raked to the edge, leaving a three- to four-inch layer of red hot, undulating coals spread along a twelve-foot long path. We quietly make our way over and encircle the area, keeping our thoughts about what we are about to experience to ourselves. Participation isn't compulsory; if it's not your time, that's perfectly OK. My heart races a little as I sense the radiant heat. Dan measures the temperature of the coals to be 1,200 degrees. I have no concept of fire temperatures, but 1,200 degrees sounds plenty hot to me! A few brave souls go for it as soon as they reach the edge, making it over without any repercussions.

Even though I have no idea what I'm in for, and even though I prefer not to tempt fate in general or with my feet in particular, I keep telling myself that this is possible. I've seen it done before in England, Gregg has done it, and I can do it too. I choose a mantra to keep my head in the best possible place: "With God, all things are possible." I repeat it over and over as I step over the threshold and glide over the coals. Incredibly, I feel absolutely nothing, no fire, no heat. I barely even feel the lumps of the coals.

Gregg waits at the other end, having gone ahead of me. I walk straight into his arms. Lost in the power of the moment, neither of us speaks. We've been through so much these past few years, trial by fire in a rhetorical sense, and now the real thing. And we have survived.

We draw apart and I wipe away a tear. "Wow. That was so cool!"

"I'm not sure that is the word I would use to describe it," Gregg laughs. We stand arm in arm in silence, watching others cross the coals. I love this beautiful night, the joyous look on the familiar faces of our friends who conquer their fear, not only of fire, but perhaps of other things as well. I'm awed by the road that each of us has traveled to get here and the love that made it all possible.

The thrill of the moment is so extraordinary to me that I have to walk the coals one more time just to prove to myself that I've actually done it and can do it again, that I can find that perspective on life, that faith, that belief in who I really am and the pregnant potential that lies in the truth of our existence. I have to be sure it wasn't a one-time fluke. It isn't; the second time is the same as the first. I place my trust in that which is the greater me, my source, God, whatever you want to call it. And it holds me, guiding me safely to the other side.

~ 25 ~

Control or Create

With the chemo drugs gradually working their way out of Gregg's system, his energy levels increase, and daily life again feels pretty good. I watch his body reverse itself and become healthier looking. His skin tone is rosy again. His head goes from bald to covered with sparse gray hair that reverts to his natural brown as it grows. I feel I'm witnessing the rebirth of all of the cells in his physical form, an old man's ravaged body turning young again. Other than being thin, he looks like the guy I married. We relish every moment and are amazed by the resilience of the human form.

It will soon be exactly a year since the first healing service; a third ceremony, born of gratitude, seems appropriate.

We decide this service will focus on affirmations. The dictionary defines affirmations as "the assertion that something exists or is true." The idea is, that if you phrase a positive statement about what you want to be true and then stay focused on it, believe and feel that it actually *is* true, you will attract it, and then it will become your reality. And if we can indeed create our own reality, then why not aim it toward the way we want our lives to be and send that good vibration out to the universe as opposed offering up a message of lack or negative thought? The tricky part seems to be in the phrasing and in taking realistic baby steps, as opposed to trying for total about-faces that don't seem authentic, no matter how much you want them to be. Little steps are easier to hang our hats on.

We send out invitations via our Christmas cards. We gather again in early December. We arrange the seating so that everyone is in a huge circle, and Maria again facilitates the events. She explains to the crowd what affirmations are, and the work of assimilating her wisdom begins.

We pass out index cards and pencils so that each person can generate a personal affirmation. I feel the energy in the room as I look at the people in the circle attempting to encapsulate a helpful phrase for their own lives and wonder what I would come up with. No sooner do I close my eyes than an affirmation just flows through me: *I am an instrument of the universe to help bring forth the energy of all that is.* I look at the words I've spontaneously written and think, "Well—OK then."

Maria discusses the use of the word "control." Someone had written an affirmation something like "I will control my outcomes at work." Maria explains how confining the word "control" is; it limits the possibilities of what the outcomes could actually be. It suggests a finite set of circumstances, whereas, just by changing the word "control" to "create" and saying, "I will create my outcomes at work," we open up a multitude of opportunities. In truth, you are actually more in charge of what's happening when you can create anything you want. Plus, you are doing what is inherent in your nature. Control seems to shout no, whereas create shouts, yes!

I think about our journey these past four years, and I wonder how control and creation have played into it. It has often felt like a runaway train that we couldn't stop. Every time we seemed to catch up to a semblance of "normal," the train would gain momentum once again; we could only hang on and pray that we didn't fall off. At least that is the way it felt to me. So, if it was about control, I wasn't doing a very good job of it.

But, what about Gregg? Did he think he was controlling the situation or creating it? He attempted to control his schedule and his doctor's appointments. He controlled his daily routines. He seemed to be in control of his emotions, and he was trying desperately to control whether he lived or died. So far, none of it was written in stone or working all the time.

Maybe attempting to establish control is just an exercise in futility anyhow, to delude us into thinking we're in charge, but are we really? Like trying to control the weeds in our yard or how people act or what others think of us. Or even whether we will live or die. There are just too many other factors in play. We think we can control our own behavior, yet even that fails us on a regular basis.

So perhaps he really was creating this experience or at least creating how it was going to go down. Creating the opportunities for his own self-evolvement. Creating a path through the darkness for others. Creating a way for me to find my own intuition and healing skills. Creating a way for others to shine their lights. Creating a way to propel Gretchen into knowing her true spirit. Creating a situation that would make a difference in the way people look at life and help them find a way to their inner truth.

We live by the moment-to-moment choices we make. With each choice, we set up the circumstances for the next moment and the next, thereby *creating* our futures. Creating seems to be the primary expression of who we are, our innate nature.

What we create with a loving intention draws forth that which is in our highest and best interest, in order to grow and to learn from. It has a purpose. If you keep creating a situation that isn't working for you, hopefully, you realize it and begin to make different choices, creating something else, as opposed to attempting to control the outcomes, until you finally see the light and feel good about it. And when you do, you will be one step closer to knowing who you really are. If what you create brings joy and goodness to you and others, doors will open up and encourage you to keep following that path, thereby multiplying your happiness.

Maria's part of the service ends, and Gregg stands to address the crowd. "Thank you all for being here," he says. "I hope you got something out of it, maybe something that you can take home with you and contemplate to live your lives in a happy place, but before you go, I want you to know that I really do feel the energy and love that you bring to these gatherings. I would like us all to do a group hug starting with Gretchen and Deb, then my family, and finally, all of you."

I'm as surprised as anyone at his words, unpredictable as ever. I rise, my heart full of emotion, as does Gretchen. We walk to Gregg, encircling each other, and forming our little triad. We're then followed by Ron and Claire and other members of the family, and, finally, the rest of the room, moving silently. Each person comes up behind another and another with arms open wide, until we are all connected, alone in our thoughts but together in body, heart, and spirit.

*   *   *

In January, our easier and more carefree existence fades as Gregg's rather continuous issues with elimination become more pronounced. The pain meds that he had been on for quite a while now cause more trouble than usual. He suffers from severe constipation. He wants things to flow in his physical body like they seem to do with his spiritual body, but nothing we try helps. I find myself rethinking how easy it is for us all to pop a pill for whatever ails us without thinking of the ramifications. The pharmaceutical companies surely love getting people hooked on medicines. For every pill you take, you have to take five more to counteract side effects and then more to counteract those. What a game they play, and how easy it is for us to fall into the trap rather than attempting to solve our own issues through diet, exercise, lifestyle, and thought changes.

But getting on my soapbox is not helping Gregg. So, back to the doctor. Eventually he's admitted into the local hospital with an impacted bowel. He stays a week while they try to work through the problem and administer another battery of tests. Eventually, we ask to go back to his team of doctors in Columbus since they know him and see the whole picture.

Gregg is transported to the cancer hospital while I make arrangement for our pets. I pack a suitcase, having no idea how long I might be gone, and ask some old friends in Columbus if I can stay with them for a few days. Gregg is in his room when I arrive at the hospital. He's already been seen by his main doctors. He's in OK spirits, considering that he just spent a week in the hospital at home, but I'm demoralized and grumpy. Doctors are everywhere, which I guess means they care. Tests are run; specialists are called in. Giving up is not an option.

At the end of the second week, a decision is made to do surgery to relieve Gregg's bowel problems. He could end up with a colostomy, they tell us, at least temporarily.

One evening I go to dinner with Gretchen and my forever friend Cayla. Though I try to be sociable, I'm overwhelmed by the circumstances, unable to quit thinking about everything. Finally, I begin to cry softly, something that has happened only a handful of times this entire journey. The reality of the situation begins to engulf me. What will I do without Gregg? What will my life be like? Will I still have the same friends, do the same things? What will Gretchen do without her dad? Cayla and Gretchen both offer whatever comfort and reassurance they can, but there are no words that can make it any better.

The day of the surgery brings more visitors. Eli and his wife, Kate, surprise me in the waiting room. Cayla returns, and Gretchen is there. There's a sense that the situation could take a turn for the worse. The operation is expected to last a few hours at least. We're in the waiting area, thinking about getting a bite to eat, when the doctor reappears. My heart nearly stops. It's not a good sign. Gregg had only been in surgery for about thirty minutes. I grab Gretchen's hand, and together we walk over to see what's going on. "He's fine," the surgeon says, pulling down his mask and letting it hang around his neck. "But I am afraid I have some bad news." Hesitating a moment, letting his words sink in, he continues. "When I opened him up, I could see that his abdomen was filled with cancer. There was no possibility of unblocking his colon, so I went ahead and performed the colostomy, then closed him back up. There is really nothing more I can do. It is beyond repair."

I cannot speak. I can barely breathe. My heart is broken. *It is beyond repair.*

"I'm sorry that I don't have better news for you. I know he's been through a lot," the surgeon adds.

"Will the colostomy take care of his elimination issues?" I ask in a daze, not really sure what to say.

"As much as is possible. He should be in recovery for a little while, then you can see him. The nurses will give you a call." When nothing else comes out of my mouth or Gretchen's, he adds regretfully, "I really am very sorry." His face is filled with such empathy, I can't help but feel bad for him in addition to the pain and despair I feel for myself and for Gregg. Who wants to give that kind of news to anybody?

"Thank you for trying." I offer my hand, and he shakes it, then disappears behind the door to the surgery area.

Suddenly, recollections flood back to me. The anxiety I've felt since the healing service was justified. The many nights we lay in bed as I massaged Gregg's stomach to give him some relief, I had felt an odd hardness where his stomach was and knew it wasn't supposed to be there, but, as usual, didn't dwell on the possibilities. I think about watching him at the New Year's Eve party that he instigated with the same people who had given me shelter in Columbus. There was a moment when everyone was laughing and dancing, and I caught sight of him sitting alone on the fireplace taking it all in, somewhat removed and pensive, perhaps sensing that this would be his last. We've never spoken about it. The giant group hug at the healing service, and finally, the quickening of the visits of family and friends. The shift had come. We were beginning the last phase of this journey.

Teary-eyed, Gretchen and I share the news with the others. *What will I say to Gregg when he wakes up?* I wonder. I don't think that he will be totally surprised, but who wants to hear that their life is about to end? He takes it as well as anyone one could, saddened and disappointed, but somewhat resigned to the circumstances. When the surgeon checks on him, reiterating what I've said, Gregg asks, "What would you do if you were in my shoes?"

The doctor's face softens and he replies, "I would live every day in the best way I could." Gregg smiles knowingly and nods. The words "terminal," "prognosis," "days left," are never spoken. They don't need to be.

~ 26 ~

I'm Going Home

As he heals from the surgery in the hospital, I'm shown how to change a colostomy. Until now, I've handled all of his care with confidence and relative efficiency. I can dole out medicine; make sure it goes in at the correct time; monitor reactions; fill and reset his feeding tube line; fix it when it doesn't work; offer massage, reflexology, and energy healing; discuss life, spirit, and the reasons for illness; and keep us both living as "normal" of lives as possible. Yet, the mastery of the colostomy seems beyond my abilities. I cringe and apologize every time I incorrectly place the seal on his skin and have to pull the adhesive off. I'm determined to figure it out, but unfortunately, Gregg must be my guinea pig. He's just grateful that I'm willing to do it and forgives me my transgressions, instead offering encouragement. Still, it's hard to be the one responsible for giving him more pain.

After three weeks in the hospital, he finally gets some relief from his bowel obstruction thanks to the colostomy, but his stomach is still upset and he has fairly frequent bouts of vomiting. Gregg is moving about his room when his doctor comes by on rounds with a group of medical students by his side. "I hear that you have been vomiting," he begins, an expression of concern on his face.

Gregg nods. "Yeah, I have been, some."

"There are a few medicines that we might be able to try," the doctor offers, but Gregg cuts him off.

"Thanks, doc. You've been great and I appreciate everything you've done to get me this far, but I'm ready to go home now."

The doctor continues as if he hadn't heard. "The meds would help soothe your stomach and make you feel less inclined to throw up, as long as you can tolerate them."

Gregg smiles, gently shaking his head. "Everyone here has done a fantastic job, and I'm grateful to have met all of you. I couldn't have asked for any better care. But I'm going home." There is a definitive tone in his voice.

I know he has made up his mind; he's done with it all. If he stays, there will always be something to fix, some procedure to have, another test to be run, or some drug to try. It is painfully clear I'm witnessing his grand finale, and I can't blame him. It's his life. He'll spend whatever days he has left calling his own shots, in the comfort of his own home, surrounded by those he loves.

The doctor hesitates, as if debating whether or not to push the issue, not yet ready to call it quits. Perhaps he's trying to set an example for the students he mentors: never stop trying to come up with an answer. But he's met with a direct and certain look, which precludes any further discussion. And so, the doctor grasps Gregg's outstretched hand. "I wish you the best of everything, Gregg. Take care and Godspeed," he says, tenderly, looking candidly into his eyes. They will not meet again on this earth. "I'll make the necessary arrangements," he says, and he strides out the door with the others in tow.

* * *

Once home in our own house, the wheels in Gregg's head churn once again. Alex is making another visit to Toronto and Gregg wants to go. "Are you *sure* you want to do this, Greggy?" I ask lovingly, sitting beside him on the edge of our bed, my hand gently rubbing his back. I'm amazed he's still considering it; he's beginning to decline. I'm not sure it's a great idea to be in Canada, another country, if anything happens.

He's still in touch with the doctors who monitor his pain medication, but they're a long way away from Toronto.

"I want to go. I'll be fine, babe," He insists. "It's not that far."

The snow is coming down hard in near blizzard conditions as dear friends drive us toward Buffalo. I can hardly see the road. I have packed several blankets along with Gregg's food and the pain meds he takes at regular intervals. I try not to focus on the fact that in an effort to save Gregg's life, we could all be killed. The conference is like the others we've attended. Though I want with all my heart for the miracle to happen, at this point, I don't think it will. We're in the home stretch. Why was Gregg so adamant about wanting to go to Toronto? Was it a last desperate effort, hoping against hope that there was still a chance it wasn't his time? Was it for his sake or was it for all of ours? Could he even voice his feelings? As deeply connected as we are, I just can't think and feel the way he does.

Whenever people ask him how he's doing, he always says something like, "As well as can be expected, but I worry about Gretchen and Deb." Sometimes, I feel it gives him a reason to keep going, and other times, I feel he's really concerned about what we'll do when he's gone. Maybe it's both.

Family and friends begin to rotate through, beginning with Lila. I wake especially early one morning to an empty bed and stumble out to the living room. Gregg is already up, sitting on the floor, leaning against a chair with his legs stretched out long before him and his journal on his lap, gazing out the large front window where the sun is just beginning to display the striking oranges, pinks, and purples of sunrise. Usually, he's in the back room where all of his talismans, family pictures, and get-well wishes are, along with our cats that enjoy their time with him on his yoga blanket. My sister is also up, kneeling beside him on the floor in her pajamas, looking intent. The air is charged and filled with change. Something has just transpired. I can feel it in my bones.

Joggled out of sleep, I'm overtaken by dread-filled expectancy as I crouch down on the other side and grasp the raw emotion in Gregg's expression. It immediately weighs heavily on my heart. "What's up?" I ask, concerned.

"I felt like getting up early to catch the sunrise and do my meditation," Gregg answers, turning tear-filled eyes toward me. "I sat here for a while, looking at the beautiful colors in the sky and praying." He moves his eyes back toward the window, still lost in thought as we both wait silently for him to go on. After a few moments, he continues. "I asked God to take me." The pain of what he's saying shrouds his face, and I know he's crossed another threshold; he has finally surrendered. I also know it had taken a great deal of courage to get to this point. He looks down at his hands lying on his journal. "Lila was just sitting here, talking with me."

I can't move. I can't speak. I'm overwhelmingly sad, but I can't blame him. What is there to say, really? That he should keep on fighting? That everything will get better and that he's just in a depressed place? It's between him and God now, as it always has been. I can only be by his side and watch it all happen.

We sit quietly together on the floor for a while longer, then Gregg speaks again. "I was wondering about saying goodbye to everyone. Do you think I need to?"

"I think you have done more for everybody than you ever imagined and that they are truly grateful," I say. "You have seen everyone we know these past few years and those closest to you several times." His deep weariness is palpable, so I add, "I'm certain they will understand if you don't say goodbye."

I think he knows with every part of his being that it's time, yet he feels like he's letting us down somehow. His demeanor is apologetic, as if asking permission, "Will you and everyone be OK if I go?"

Knowing him as well as I do, I believe he's amazed that his life was not immediately snuffed out once he finally made up his mind that it was

OK to let go, which makes his decision all the more courageous. Maybe he's even disappointed. He has worked so, so long at being positive and having hope, not allowing himself ever to have even just a moment of giving in. Though he's familiar with the words "Let Go, Let God," I am not sure he could ever do that completely, until now. No matter what the doctors told him, he always thought he could change the direction of his life, to manage the outcome somehow.

Lost in the immediacy of the moment, he doesn't see that he actually *did* change the direction of his life and that of many others as well. In the process, he has certainly become much more in tune with his own spirit and God. He prays daily, counting his blessings and sending love and healing to all the people he knows and beyond. He has reordered the priorities in his life. He has found ways to bring others aboard his journey for their own self-evolvement. He has become a true inspiration. He has weighed what was really important in life and discovered that he, too, had been searching all along for meaning and purpose, like we all do, some with full awareness, others not knowing, that we create experiences to learn from in order to help us know our own truth.

* * *

As Lila leaves for home, Gregg's sister, Nina, arrives. He is always thrilled to see whoever stayed with us, but he and Nina seem connected in a way they had not been before his illness. He values the wisdom and perspective that she offers through the cards she has continuously sent and on the phone, so having her here in person is even better. Over the course of the next days, I see his body steadily slow down. He's quieter during conversations and doesn't move around as easily or as much as he had previously. It's like watching the Duracell bunny run out of steam.

I think about hospice and realize the time has come. It has always seemed like the last step in a person's life, a way to shepherd your loved one to the door of the afterlife. What if it's more than I know how to do? I don't know what awaits us in the coming days. People connected with hospice are at least aware of the death process. The only creature I've ever seen die was my cat, and it was pretty traumatic for me and the cat. Perhaps if someone helps me understand events as they unfold, Gregg's death will be easier. Gravely dispirited, no resistance left in me, I finally offer up my own surrender and set the process in motion. There's no turning back.

The next afternoon, Gregg and I are home alone. I'm flitting about, taking care of things that need doing, when I hear him call my name. "Debbie," he calls out as he pats the couch next to him, "come sit with me." There is a subtle pleading in his voice and a longing on his face.

I'm put out that he is asking me to stop what I'm doing and sit down. I don't want to say yes, but I can't say no either. It's just inopportune. There are few chances to get things done around the house, so when I have a little time and energy, I don't want to miss it. Besides, it's a way to distract myself, a way for me not to dwell in my overwhelming sorrow.

I look at him and feel tired, exasperated, beaten down, sad, and heartbroken all at once. The feelings are unbidden, all consuming. Yet the resistance I feel takes me by surprise. After all, here is my mate and the love of my life, who just happens to be dying, asking me to sit with him, and I am being ornery? What's *wrong* with me?

Somewhere within I know I'm really feeling anger and denial, though I can't voice it. How can it be that Gregg will shortly be gone from my life? It's too soon! We were supposed to grow old together, watch Gretchen fall in love, get married, and enjoy our grandchildren someday. There were more adventures to be had and more places to see. We were supposed to be that couple who could look back at life and smile at the memories as we rocked in our chairs and gazed out at the world. I don't want this to be the last time we sit next to each other on the couch and cuddle. *If I don't participate*, I think staunchly, *then it won't be.*

If only it were that easy. Even as I unconsciously protest, I know that taking a stand at this point would be the wrong move. We both feel the drain of the hourglass. Time is precious. I don't want to build any regrets.

I tell him if he can wait a few minutes until I finish what I'm doing, then I'll join him. He says OK, and in a little while I sit down next to him. Gregg gathers me close with his arm around my shoulders. I rest my head against his chest, closing my eyes, and listen to the beat of his heart, wishing it could beat forever, knowing it won't.

I've been having a lot of these moments lately. Everything is overshadowed by a wonder if it is our last, our last hug, our last conversation, our last laugh, our last night sleeping next to one another, our last kiss. It's an anticipation I could have gladly lived without, yet I'm so drawn to savor every single thing we do. I want to burn it into the recesses of my memory because I know that it will have to hold me for the rest of my life.

A few days later, when Gretchen is home again, I walk into the living room to find her dancing with her dad to a Beatles song. I can't believe my eyes, that he's actually up dancing, even though it's a slow dance. He never stops surprising me. At that moment, the phone rings. It's Gregg's doctor checking in. "How's he doing?" he asks me.

"Well . . . he's in the living room dancing to a Beatles song as we speak!" I pronounce, a grin on my face.

The doctor laughs. "I love that guy!" he says. "What song is he dancing to?"

"Let It Be," I answer, thinking it's funny that he wants to know or that it even makes a difference to him, as if he's considering which song he, himself, might pick if it were to be the last one.

"That's great!" I can hear the smile in his voice. "Let me know if you need anything."

I hang up and stand a little longer, watching nostalgically the special bond between father and daughter, bearing witness to this special moment. Then Gregg switches his attention to me, and Gretchen moves away.

Our eyes meet and he holds out his arms, beckoning me close. I latch on, overcome with emotion, quiet tears rolling down my cheeks. I can feel the sharp angles of his bones, but still the warmth of his body manages to envelop me, surrounding my spirit with a familiar sense of comfort and belonging, right where I fit best. The song changes to "Yesterday." We move around the floor without saying a word, each of us lost in our own thoughts, knowing without a doubt that this will, indeed, be our last dance.

* * *

A few mornings later, I'm just starting to roll around in bed when I hear singing. "Pleeease release me, let me go." Still in a dreamy state, I giggle to myself thinking it's just Gregg being Gregg. He's always cheerful and noisy in the mornings. As the fog begins to clear, I open my eyes to see him sitting up in bed with his feet on the ground, his back to me. Reality swoops in like a menacing black raven. He's not being silly, but yearning once again for God to take him. He's ready.

I crawl over and wrap my arms around him from behind, resting my head on his bare back. He reaches up and covers my hands with his. "I love you, Gregg," I tell him.

"I love you, too, Deb." After a few minutes he asks, "Can you help me get to the bathroom?"

I slide around and put one of his arms over my shoulder and my arm around his waist. "On the count of three. Ready? One, two, three!" We both stand.

Afterward, we go back to the bed. He sits upright, leaning against the pillow on the back of the bed, covers pulled up to keep warm. I sit beside him on the edge. We take in the time together, lost in our own thoughts. The late February sun shines brightly into the room, though it's usually cloudy and overcast. The new bay window in the bedroom brought much more of the outdoors inside, which Gregg craved. His spirit refused to be contained.

"Well, babe," he finally says, "we fought the good fight." He holds his gaze for a moment, looking into my eyes, my soul, then withdraws, retreating into his own thoughts.

My hand rests on his leg. His face is a mixture of resignation and sadness, the side of his mouth turned up slightly. He's still handsome to me, even through the ravages of illness. There isn't an iota of his body that I haven't memorized, the smoothness of his forehead underlined by wild eyebrows, the way one ear turned a little more than the other, the line of his back, the small mass of hair on his chest that had expanded with age, the softness of his abdomen I have gently massaged so many times these past four years, the strength of his legs with their shapely calves, and the squared-off toes of his feet.

"Yeah, we did," I reluctantly agree, resignation evident in my own voice as I think back to our early conversations about cancer and how we began by attempting to "love" it away, as opposed to battling it. Now, we also have succumbed to its power and ended up viewing the experience as a confrontation. Cancer has gotten the last word.

He has come to terms with his situation, accepting his fate, and now can view more clearly the end of the road. He can look back, reflect, and see the path he has walked, knowing full well that the ensuing steps will be into the next realm and whatever awaits him there. Neither of us thinks that this is the end of him, only that he will be changing form and moving on to another dimension.

"It's certainly been a journey, hasn't it?" I comment more than inquire, as I give him a weak but loving smile, aware that I, too, have lost my fight. It's over, and we both know it.

He shakes his head, a mournfulness swirling around in his greenish eyes. Our gazes gravitate back out the window, silence filling the room once again. Our hearts are heavy. There is nothing to say. Over the course of our marriage, and especially the past four years, it feels like we've said it all. We've poured out our souls to each other in a hundred different ways.

"Pretty soon our front garden will be filled with beautiful blooms from all of those bulbs you planted last fall," I offer, still gently smiling at him, searching to find the tiniest ray of sunshine in a sea of despair. "Even though I gave you a hard time about it, I am grateful now that you did. I will always think of you when I see them." And then the thought strikes me. "I suppose you planned that on purpose!"

"Of course, I did!" he says, managing to conjure up a twinkle in his eyes. "I know how much you love your flowers, and I certainly don't want you to forget me!"

"Perhaps you should have put in some forget-me-nots!" I tease. *How could I ever forget him?*

Should I tell him about hospice? He will know soon enough anyhow. "I stopped by hospice on the way home from work and asked them to come by." Somehow it feels like I should have consulted him first, like I was already taking liberties and making unilateral decisions about his life.

Gratefully, and to my surprise, he looks right at me again and says, "I think that's a good idea, Deb." He's giving me his blessing, knowing how hard it has been for me, too. If it relieves some of my stress, that he wants that for me, a parting gift, his way of offering his support to the very end. My heart swells.

After another silence, I add, "Gretch and I will be fine. We will figure it out." He nods slightly but says nothing.

I have no idea what lies ahead or how we will fare, really, but somehow, I need to try and ease his mind. There is no way of knowing what he's thinking. He's done all he could to prepare the way for us. Whether conscious or unconscious, we have updated the entire house with a new roof, windows, furnace, and air-conditioning, besides the remodeling. We've recently purchased a new car and put it in my name. He has told everyone to look after us. What else is there, other than sticking around to be a part of it all? Interestingly, I've never felt like any of it was done because he might not be here. They're all things that we would have eventually done anyhow, but considering where we are at this juncture, it's certainly timely.

And so, I continue. "I was thinking I might use some of the life insurance money to pay for Gretchen's wedding," wondering why the words were coming out of my mouth even as I say them. Am I trying to make him feel bad? My practical nature rises up. I hope to reassure him, I guess. He loves me and understands how my mind works. There are no rules for what to say at a time like this. On some level, it seems whatever we uttered should be profound, but all we manage is the mundane.

He nods again, and we sit for a while longer, our hearts forever entwined. It's all just beyond words. Goodbye will come soon enough.

Eventually, I squeeze his hand and ask if he needed anything. He shakes his head no. Then I get up and leave the room, to begin my preparations for the day.

*   *   *

A vigil of sorts begins. Nina has to return to Denver, and our good friend Vic arrives. I'm so grateful to have those so dear to us around during these last days. It has always been about the collective experience from the very start, beginning when Gregg sent out his "all call" for prayers.

The people from hospice arrive, and we set his care up. Someone explains a little more about the death process and what signs we'll see so I won't be so anxious. I'm very relieved to learn that someone will come by daily and help me with things like hygiene. Gregg still craves the warmth of the bathtub to soothe and comfort his body, but this is becoming difficult to manage with just the two of us. His mobility becomes more compromised by the hour.

A Catholic nun appears at our door to talk and to listen. Though she offers her help to us, I felt like Gregg's parents need her more. They stop by daily, yet seem at a loss in many ways, wanting to be here and help, but not knowing how, besides dealing with their own grief at the inevitable loss of their youngest son. Even though they aren't Catholic and I'm not even sure Gregg's mom is onboard with religion at all, at a time like this, we're all on the same page, no matter what the vernacular is. It's all I can do to hold myself together. I don't have much left to comfort them or anyone else.

Gregg attempts to sit in the living room as people come and go, listening to the conversations but commenting less and less. Occasionally, he'll nod or give a thumb up with what appears to be a grin on his face. I think it's that, though later it will occur to me that it might be difficult for him to move his facial muscles and show a variety of expressions. At one point, I need him to sign a document. He grasps the pen but can only scribble illegibly. I hadn't given it a moment's thought when I handed him the pen, and I'm shocked that this thing he's done so effortlessly is now beyond his ability. I have to hide my surprise. It's a vivid example of where we were in the process. I thank him and walk away, rattled.

It quickly becomes evident that he will be more comfortable in bed. Getting up and down uses up too much of the meager energy he still possesses. He sleeps more and more. I put on music and keep a candle burning in the room, hoping it will offer some semblance of peace.

The next few days, he dozes in and out. I can see that his body is no longer accepting his tube feedings. It keeps leaking out of his stomach rather than going in. The hospice nurse assures me that it's OK to end the nourishment when I feel it appropriate, yet I still have some trepidation about it. Obviously, his organs are shutting down, and his human form no longer needs the encouragement to stay. I unhook the tube and move it all out of sight. If I can at least give Gregg the dignity of being tubeless, like the man he had been most of his life, he deserves that respect. Maybe it's more for me than him. Vanquishing whatever visible reminders I can of the tough road we have traveled these past years is important to me. I want to remember him as just Gregg, not as sick Gregg.

I can't stay in the room, constantly watching and waiting. It's just too much, but I peek at him often. When I do go in, I often lean close to him and talk softly. Knowing he can't respond verbally anymore, I kiss him and he kisses me back. It's the only way I know he is still here. I have no doubt that he is traveling in and out of this world and the next, testing the waters, so to speak.

I busy myself with whatever I can occupy my time with, usually fielding calls from friends and family. Gretchen very reluctantly left a few days earlier to go back to work in Charleston but is constantly in touch, knowing that a return trip is eminent. There is no way of knowing whether Gregg will hang on for days or weeks.

Thinking ahead, I decide it prudent to give a heads up to "Gregg's healers," the name he has given to all those whom he has kept abreast of his journey through letters and e-mails. Many live in other parts of the country, and I concluded that they might like to know the end is near in case they want to make plans to be here. I write up an e-mail and send it off.

Two days after Gretchen leaves, I call her to come home. I know she wants to be here for Gregg's passing, and we feel it's close. Every day, family will gather, say their goodbyes and go home, only to return again the next day when Gregg is still here. In some ways, it is the most difficult time of the whole ordeal, for everyone.

I lie beside him in bed each night, acutely aware of his breathing. I had been with my grandmother the day before she passed and remember vividly the rattling sound she made—the death rattle they called it. I had no idea if everyone did that or not. Either way, I am very attuned to the rhythm of Gregg's breath, listening for any changes in the pattern—or worse yet, no breath at all.

Early on Saturday morning, March 3, 2007, something is different. There is a quickening to the pattern. I quietly call Gretchen from her bedroom. She comes to sit beside Gregg on the bed. I pull up a chair on the other side of the bed, and we each hold one of his hands.

Not long after that, my mother appears from her room in the basement. She says she's just "seen" my sister (who is in Atlanta) at the end of her bed franticly waving her hands and trying to tell her something, though Mom couldn't hear what. With that, she got out of bed and came upstairs. This isn't the first time my mom has reported seeing my sister standing by her bed over the years when she wasn't physically there. They seem to have a kind of telepathic communication.

My mom positions herself at Gregg's feet so he effectively resembles a cross with us surrounding him. We speak quietly to each other as we hold vigil. I had kissed Gregg two days earlier, and he did not respond. I've tried a few more times since then with no luck. I know he is off to other dimensions while his body lies, still breathing on the bed.

"What do you want to bet he goes at 10:00 when everyone is praying for him?" Gretchen proposes.

"That would be just like your dad." I smile. "His last nod to everyone."

We stay in our respective positions for what seems like a long while. A few times it feels like Gregg is about to stop breathing—and then he starts up again. It's heart-wrenching. The anticipation begins to wear on us. Finally, I practically yell at him. "Gregg, you need to go now! This is too hard on everyone." I sound gruff, even to myself, but somewhere deep inside, I know it's time for all of us to move on. We are beyond the point of no return. Lingering helps no one.

Shortly after that, around 9:45, something draws my eyes to the candle, housed in a glass container that has been burning nonstop by the bed. It has just gone out, the plume of smoke still visible, rising into the air. There's plenty of wax left so it has not burnt out on its own. I know his spirit has left his body for the last time, extinguishing the flame on the way. A little while later, his last breath. "What time is it?" I ask Mom.

She looks at her watch, and then back at me with a knowing expression. "10:02," she says.

~ 27 ~

And So...

I haven't been sure how I will feel when it's finally over. But I've known I'll have the rest of my life to contemplate it, so until now, I've held onto each moment with Gregg instead of speculating about life without him. Now that he's gone, there's a feeling of relief that Gregg has finally escaped the jail that his body had become. And yet it's not a surprise. He has suffered for so long and taken one hit after another these past four years. His physical form gave up on him bit by bit. I always knew that he would keep going as long as he felt he could live some sort of quality life, but other than his spirit, he no longer resembled the man he once was. He made as valiant an effort as anyone could and more than most. He tried every type of healing he came across. But eventually there was nothing more to be done, except surrender.

As I look at him lying in bed, no more breath left, his eyes still open, the expression on his face is a smile. It's certainly not the easygoing smile that lit up so many rooms, but it offers some comfort, as if he is embracing what lies ahead. Earlier, he had gazed at me one last time, his eyes growing larger for a split second, perhaps seeing not only me, but also what greeted him as his spirit began to soar. One last goodbye.

I'm happy for him. I so wanted him to fly free again! I know that the part of him he left here is of no more consequence and that cremation will purify his ravaged body. Ashes to ashes, dust to dust. We would soon return it to the earth in a renewed state, no strings attached, something that we both longed for.

I reach over, close his eyes, and whisper, "Godspeed, Greggy. Until we meet again, my boy." I hug him, relishing the feel of his body touching mine. How many hugs have I delighted in during the span of our lives together? It was one of my favorite connections with him. It always gave me a feeling of being loved, grounded, and protected. I never doubted that he would look out for me no matter what happened. He understood me better than anyone. Sometimes we would just hold each other and "be." Who will hug me now, I wonder?

Mom and Gretchen have quietly left the bedroom. I stay, curled up in a ball next to him on the bed. Though I know he is no longer in his body, it's still warm, and I can imagine that he is still here with me, just sleeping. Soon even his body will be gone, and I will never lay eyes on him again. I'll have only my memories and pictures to rely on. I close my eyes, relieved to find I can scan him like a topographical map and still see every inch of his face and body. The images will have to suffice, I think sadly.

I replay his last days in my mind several times. I see him sitting on the couch and patting the seat next to him, dancing in the living room, reaching out with a smile to my friend, Karen, to hug her when she came by. I see him give a thumb up as he listened to his dear friends Vic and Eli tell stories of old times, as much a part of things as he could still be.

I try to conjure up his voice and relive our conversations, but I can't hear him. It catches me off guard and I feel my body stiffen. The harder I try, the farther away he seems. It's more difficult than I imagined, considering I have heard it so many times before. How could his voice disappear so quickly? In a panic, I wonder, *Will I ever be able to remember what he sounded like?* And then I picture him at a party with our friends, and his very loud and contagious laugh floats through the ether into my ears and into my heart. It makes me smile, as it has so many times before. Maybe his essence will stay close with me after all. Maybe he wants to remind me that he is only a laugh away and whenever I am down, I can be comforted by the memory.

It will take time to digest it all. Even though I'm used to my position on the front line, I need distance from all that's happened in order to put it in perspective. We've finally lived our last day together in our physical reality. It seems incomprehensible, yet here we are. Here *I* am. It's a lot to take in, an ending and a beginning all at once.

* * *

The evening calling hours are well attended. Cars line the streets, waiting for a parking space. Friends and family show their love in more ways than I can count. Gregg was a music buff of sorts, and so we play his favorites throughout the evening: James Taylor, Bonnie Raitt, Eric Clapton, and more. Many people comment that it feels more like a party than any sort of mourning. That's my intention. I have no doubt Gregg is there in spirit, taking it all in. It's just his style. He knew that life would go on without him, and he expected it to. But for me, the night is a blur of faces and condolences.

I ask Maria to speak at the service the next day. She graciously accepts, having been so much a part of our journey and the healing services. She knew that he had passed before even speaking with me. She told me that she had been working with a ten-year-old boy in her home. She looked up at 10:00 and "saw" Gregg standing there. She excused herself for a moment, saying that a friend was passing, and she wanted to acknowledge him and send him loving energy as he went on his way.

Others ask if they could speak at the service. I'm grateful that they want to. They each give a heartfelt interpretation not only of Gregg's journey, but of their own as well, having traveled the road beside us. Every testament is touching, funny, and stirring in different ways, but a common theme is Gregg's impact on everyone's lives, how we all thought we were helping him when, in fact, he was really teaching us.

The parting message is from Gregg, himself. In another bit of synchronicity, Maddie was cleaning her house and found a letter that he had written them. She shared it with me. It was perfect.

In spite of all the health challenges that I am presently going through, I do believe life is a magical time. I am blessed to be with loved ones, family, and friends who express so much for me. In the end, if my life should be shortened due to all this poison they put in me and treatment I endure or if the cancer should ultimately "win out," I've had a wonderful experience of learning through crisis who my friends truly are and what loved ones can and will do for you in times of need. It puts life into perspective and forces one to reflect on the things truly valuable. Challenges in life are to make us stronger and delve within to bring out our true character. I hope in the end my life will be of greater importance to not only myself, but to my loved ones after having gone through this experience.

He got his wish.

I feel strangely calm during the whole event. I shed my tears throughout our entire journey. It's not that I don't have any left; I'm just wrung out at the moment. Besides, I'm still basking in the knowledge that Gregg is in a better place now. He has left the pain behind. How could you love someone as much as I did and not feel happy about that?

*   *   *

One by one, people leave after the funeral to go back to their lives. I'm especially sad to see Gretchen leave. I don't know what the days ahead will be like for either of us. She has been so much help, organizing things, making decisions, protecting me in her own way. It will be difficult not to be able to hug her and console each other in person.

My sister Lila stays with me for the following week, helping to ease me into the quietness that will soon become my life after days, months, and years of activity, phone calls, visits, and doctors' appointments. I'm grateful for her steady presence.

The Tuesday after the funeral, I'm supposed to pick up Gregg's cremains from the funeral home. I'm not looking forward to it and don't know what to expect. After winding up some details, they hand me a rather heavy cardboard box a little less than a foot square in size. I am not sure what I envisioned, but certainly not this. Because I didn't plan to bury his ashes, I haven't bothered to purchase an urn. It just never occurred to me what they would deliver him in. I feel let down, a sense of my negligence flowing through me.

Lila drives as I sit in the passenger seat and hold it on my lap for the ride home. Without ignoring the road, she still sees me staring at the box. Finally, she asks, "What are you thinking about?"

"I'm just having a hard time comprehending that Gregg is in this box," I say sadly. "A man who was bigger than life now fills only a small box. I've never seen or touched anyone's ashes before."

"I remember my sister-in-law Sandy's. You really don't imagine the amount," she sympathized.

"It is pretty weighty." I contemplate it with a heavy heart. "I know Gregg's spirit has moved on and he is probably sitting right here between us in the car as we speak, but I'm having a hard time separating the two things."

She nods in agreement and empathy.

"It makes me feel so incredibly sad to think that his body, the body I hugged and touched, wrestled with, made love to, and nursed has been reduced to this." There is a finality to it that I'm not ready to acknowledge. "Maybe I should have bought something nicer to put him in. I'm pretty sure he wouldn't care, but I don't feel he deserves a cardboard box," I say, dejectedly.

"Why don't we go to the store and see if we can find something nicer?" she proposes. "We could make it special and decorate it just for him."

"I think I'll have to. This just doesn't seem right. I'm not sure what I'm going to do with his ashes yet, but until I do know, it would be nice to honor him and put them in a special place." At the local craft store, we purchase a nice wooden box with carvings on the top. We stain it and declare it Gregg's. It's not fancy, but it makes me feel better. I know he would be fine with whatever makes me happy. He's no longer part of the decisions I will now make solely based on what I want. But I'm not used to considering only my own wishes; I loved making decisions that made Gregg happy too. This will take some getting used to.

Soon, Lila leaves too. I've known the day would come, had to come, whether I was ready or not. She's put her own life on hold and lived through many of the last days with us both. She loved Gregg too; she must be grieving as well, though from my perspective, it seems she's here for me, her job not yet done.

At the airport, I hold on to her. How do you thank someone when there just aren't enough words? I have to trust that she knows how much her presence meant to both of us, and that I will be there for her as she has been for me. I watch as she walks through the doors with her suitcase, then get into my car and drive away to begin my new life.

* * *

Just because Gregg is no longer physically here doesn't mean that he has not left a trail of living behind. There are accounts to change, death certificates to send out, medical and funeral bills to pay, people and organizations to notify. I think I'm on top of it only later to realize that I'm moving in slow motion, the haze of grief veiling my every thought and move. Thankfully, it all gets done with the advice and help of those who have dealt with death before. Lord knows, I don't have any idea. And it keeps me busy even though I don't necessarily care to be.

I had ordered pre-written thank-you notes as part of the funeral package, but somehow, they seem inadequate. Rather than wasting them, I try to squeeze more appreciation than I could possibly express onto a very small space. There just doesn't seem to be the language to thank people for all they've done and all they've meant to us. I know that most don't even want or need thanks; they were there because of love, being part of our lives because they wanted to—for us and for themselves.

Had the situation been reversed, it would have been the same. Gregg gave as good as he got and often more.

Slowly the quietness of the house takes over, enveloping me in a space that leaves me alone with my thoughts. Much of the time I'm grateful for the silence. I can relive what has happened and begin to assimilate it, piece by piece. Each time I rehash an aspect of it, the less emotional impact it seems to have. I know it won't be simple; I've already been grieving at various stages along the way, since the very beginning when Gregg was first diagnosed. It's so fresh now that I don't even *want* to get past it. I'm still hanging on to every minute. It's all I have. I'm not ready to let go.

Everywhere I look around the house, I see Gregg. He is in the pictures. He is in the garage, in the closet, in the dog, and the cats. He is in the car and the yard. He is in the drawers, on the shelves, and most of all, he is in the back room where he spent countless hours doing yoga, praying, meditating, and writing, surrounded by all of his "stuff" that came to him through his many connections in the world. Nina has kindly asked for the return of a small singing bowl she had given him to remember him by, but I cannot oblige her. I feel selfish, but I still can't do it. It's like he has transmuted himself into everything he ever touched.

Plants and flowers fill every empty space around the house. Each is a precious gift of someone's love. They comfort me and remind me of the living, the cycle of life. Like the trees outside, dying back each year only to be reborn the next. Nature is a good teacher; the story of creation is all around, demonstrating that life is really never ending, it just changes form. I know that Gregg, too, has just changed form, but I still miss his presence, like the beautiful rose that once graced the end of the rose bush.

I make a point of getting out to walk the dog at least once daily. I love him; he's as well known to our friends and neighbors as we are, but he has always been more Gregg's than mine. They were a pair, a man and his dog. They were used to walking each other every morning and night, rain or shine, no matter how crappy Gregg felt. I think back to the night he fell and came home with blood dripping down his face. If he can walk the dog in that condition, I can walk him when I'm healthy.

Though I know I won't do two walks, I also know that Gregg would be disappointed if I don't do at least one. Besides, it gives me something to care about, a living being who demands my attention and requires more of me than the cats, keeping me from getting too self-absorbed. In return, I have his total devotion and love. We cuddle in consolation, each of us knowing something is different in our lives. The walks do me good, even though I whine to myself that it's too cold or snowy or I'm too tired. They become a part of a new routine. I feel Gregg pushing me to get on with it.

At night, I lie in bed and think. Tears come and go. I find another candle and light it on the nightstand. With it burning, I don't feel so alone, a flickering presence in the room beside me. Whenever I'm sad, one of our cats appears from out of nowhere and jumps up on the bed to rub against me. She seems like a little angel who comes to watch over me and to distract me from my thoughts.

Sometimes, I'm able to stand back and observe myself to try and assess how I'm coping. I can only compare it to what I experienced when other people I cared about had departed. The hardest one was my father. I had many nights of crying after he died. It was like a spigot that I had no control over. I was amazed at how sad I felt. We had had our differences over the years, mostly in regard to my mother, but we had rebuilt our relationship. I was grateful to be able to express it all in a letter to him in his last days, and that he was still coherent enough to read it.

When I think about Gregg, I wonder why I do not have the same steady stream of tears. He was my husband, for heaven's sake, for over thirty years. I would have thought I would be inconsolable. But it's different somehow. Maybe I'm still numb from all that has taken place. It's only been a few weeks. Or maybe I'm just continuing the mourning that I began four years prior, so it's not as intense in the short term, my sense of relief for him overshadowing the pain of his loss. Instead of crying, I seem to be spend a lot of time in contemplation, trying to come to terms with it all.

I find solace in the fact that he was not worried about what lay ahead. Our many conversations about life, where we came from and where we are going, helped both of us solidify our views of the next dimension. Though he was sad to leave, if he had to go, it didn't frighten him. He was confident in a greater consciousness, knowing that he would be fine. At the end, I have no doubt he was even looking forward to it.

Maybe how you mourn someone is a matter of where you are in life, a summation of your experiences and beliefs along with the relationship you had with that person and what has been said or unsaid. I just have to live it and not question it. How I will fare in the days ahead is any-body's guess. My expectations are nonexistent. But I seem to be putting one foot in front of the other and making it through the days with a minimum of fallout.

The phone calls slow down considerably. People seem to want to give me my space. I suppose they conclude that I will emerge when I feel like being social, yet a small part of me fears that some friendships will die along with Gregg. He brought many of our regular friends into the fold. Perhaps he was the only reason they were in our orbit. His per-sonality was so big that I often did not give myself credit for drawing people close. I will have to rise to the occasion and reach out. He was the social director for years, so long that I don't even know what of my own skills remain.

A dear friend who lost her significant other several years ago includes a comforting letter to me in a card she sends. "Someday, when the time is right, you will reinvent yourself," she advises. From my current perspec-tive, I cannot imagine that. Sure, I've been knocked around a bit, but I will still be me, won't I? Do I want to be new and improved? Perhaps I will naturally evolve as a result of continuing to exist, whether planned or not.

As I live each day, making singular decisions about my life, I am bound to rediscover and get to know myself again. It might take some serious looking to see if any of my pre-Gregg identity still lives. I used to pride myself on being independent and self-sufficient, probably as a result of telling myself I didn't need anyone back in the days when my parents were wrapped up in their problems and often emotionally unavailable. It was important to me to run my own life and make my way whether I had friends with me or not. Then Gregg showed up, and I *always* had someone to play with. Now life has brought me full circle. Only time will tell who I will be and how I will change, if indeed I do.

~ 28 ~

Feeling the Push

After a couple of weeks, it's time to return to work. Lying around the house only perpetuates the rehashing of my life. The opportunity to think of the kids I work with, along with the daily issues that concern them, will give me another place for my thoughts. I also know that my friends at work will offer me whatever grace I need as I begin to rebuild my world. They tread tenderly and make me laugh. It becomes easier for me to separate the segments of my days. At work, I think about work. At home, I think about everything else. Sometimes I catch myself in the car innocently thinking about what I would make Gregg and myself for dinner. Then I stop and remember that it will never happen again.

The more days that pass, the more compartmentalized my feelings are. If I keep my mind in the familiar mode of work or relating to my colleagues the same way I always had, I can act like nothing has changed. Yet, if someone asks me how I'm doing or if something reminds me of Gregg, my eyes start to well up and I immediately slide back into my sad place. I learn to keep the conversations light and stay away from triggers.

At home, I take solace in my journal. Rereading what I had written days or weeks before shows me the very slight progress of my healing. I'm still trying to solidify a perspective of it all. Though I have some intellectual theories about what has taken place based on my philosophy about life and death, my emotions lag seriously behind. I want it all to make sense to me, to have solid answers why Gregg lived a short life, why he got sick, why he suffered so. What does it all mean? As much as I can expound on how I feel the universe works, it's all so close to home and personal. What I consider my known "truths" are put to the test. Though I can formulate an explanation, it's not one I want to hear, at least not now.

The questionably handsome box holding Gregg's ashes now occupies a place of honor on top of the dresser in our bedroom. For some reason, in an effort at lightheartedness, my sister found the silly picture of him from our family vacation in Cape Cod. He was holding a plate with the freshly cooked lobster and pretending to take a bite with a goofy, exaggerated look on his face. She taped it to the front of the box with scotch tape, where it's been stuck for nearly a month now staring back at me. His personality shines through, but I have a hard time feeling the laughter when I look at it.

One morning on my way out of the bedroom, the picture again catches my eye and I think, "I really don't like that picture there." I gaze at it a moment longer and leave for school. Home at the end of the day, I walk back into my bedroom and am shocked to see the picture lying face down on the dresser. Somehow it detached itself from the box after being stuck there for weeks. This very day, when I conclude that it needs to go, it does. Is Gregg messing with me? Did he hear my thought and make it happen? *You don't like my picture there? I will take it down and you will know that I am here with you.* Finally, a smile makes its way across my face.

When times were more carefree, we joked about contacting whoever was still here after one of us departed. Though I always believed it when other people told their stories of communicating with loved ones on the other side, I don't know that I ever expected it to happen to me, although if anyone would make it happen, it would be Gregg. I file it away in my memory banks and wonder if there will be more. As grateful as I am, it still does not compensate for his physical absence. I long to touch him, not just know that he exists.

When I arrive to check in for an annual doctor's appointment, the secretary hands me some paperwork to fill out. It's all going as expected until I get to the section marked "Marital Status." It stops me in my tracks. What do I say? I still feel every bit of "married," but it's not technically accurate. I feel myself fall into that familiar melancholy where I dwell regularly when I'm made to deal with another repercussion of Gregg's death. The next box says, "Single." That doesn't seem right and makes me feel vulnerable. Nor does "widowed," which conjures up an image of an old woman in a black dress. That's not me either. Suddenly, I resent even being asked. What business is it of theirs anyhow? In the end, I leave it blank, but I'm reeling from having to face yet another change, no matter how minute it seemed.

My niece is getting married in Charleston, South Carolina, in April, about six weeks after Gregg's passing. I'm really looking forward to it, being with family and celebrating a decidedly happier occasion in a beautiful spot. I don't want any focus to be on me, or for my situation to overshadow the occasion in any way. But as my other niece and I dangle our feet in the pool the evening before the wedding, she catches me completely off guard when she innocently comments, "You are still wearing your wedding ring."

The air is balmy with a light breeze. The underwater pool lights reflect the blue ripples moving across the top of the water. I am happy to be away from the sadness of my life in Ohio and with all the other things that had been on my mind, I haven't thought about my ring. "Yeah," I say, looking at the diamond on my finger. It's soldered together with my wedding band, and I never take it off, even though I actually have another wedding band that matches Gregg's. *Am I supposed to remove all the remnants of my old life the moment it changes?* I wonder to myself. The observation somehow makes me feel like I'm attempting to perpetuate a falsehood by still wearing it.

At the wedding, I try to be unobtrusive and keep a low profile, but feel very single. I don't know where to sit or what to do in order to keep myself from imagining that people are feeling sorry for me. In truth, I am sure they're eagerly anticipating the actual wedding and not thinking about me, but I take a seat near the front and end up being the only one in that row, awkward like a fish out of water. I smile like it doesn't matter and tell myself I'm in a good position to take pictures. Waiting for the ceremony to begin, I read through the program in my hand. At the bottom, I see the heading "In Memory Of," and under it, along with some others, is Gregg's name. Caught by surprise, I nearly burst into tears, just as I'm trying to act cool and surreptitiously blot the corners of my eyes. The thought never crossed my mind that his name would be there, obviously added at the last moment. Each little reminder keeps him close.

The whole affair is beautiful in every way. My niece is happy, and as the day wears on, I'm able to forget myself and join in the fun and celebration. It's good to feel happy. I'm glad I've come, to celebrate love and the lives of others.

Back at home, the school year is winding down, with the typical deluge of paperwork and meetings. I barely have enough energy to wade through all of the things that need doing. Grieving is like a steady leak: you plug up one spot, thinking that you have made it past the worst of it, and then another pops open, leaving you wondering how you managed or if you even you did.

One morning I awake feeling especially lethargic and wander into the back room where I still have all of Gregg's stuff, along with pictures from the funeral, notes, and letters people had written. I casually pick up a few to reread and before long, I am sifting through the entire pile, lost in an all-consuming reverie. An intense need to relive the entire experience explodes within me. Each letter tugs my heartstrings once again, until I am totally undone with an uncontrollable surge of emotions. I release buckets of tears as one hour fades into another, my face growing into an unrecognizable, red, puffy blob. Something deep down tells me that it's time to let go, to finally begin the real process of saying goodbye.

A few days later, I'm lost in thought and scrutinizing the events of my life for the umpteenth time, while standing in the bathroom brushing my hair. The reflection staring back at me looks tired and worn out, no sparkle left. What has happened to my world? Things were great for so long. We had been blessed in so many ways. How could it all have ended like this? How will I manage alone? Gregg was by my side for so long, it just doesn't seem possible that he will never set foot in this house again. And on top of that, he had to suffer through all the miserable days of illness and treatment just to die anyhow. What was the point? Why do we even bother treating cancer? It doesn't do any good. Just makes you feel shittier than you already do!

The more I think about it, the more I feel the fury rumbling inside me. The whole idea of treatment is to live! To heal people! We worked so hard to keep going and this was our reward? What a sick joke! Some reward. "What was it all for?" I scream, hurling the brush as hard as I could at a picture collection hanging in the hallway. "Aaaaaaah!" I scream again at the top of my lungs, completely swallowed up by my anger. "Why did you have to go?" I kick the wall, and the picture crashes down, falling into several pieces and taking a giant bite out of the baseboard.

For a moment I stand, suspended in time, the sound of the crash snapping me to my senses, before I crumple to the ground, blubbering. No one cares. Nobody is listening but the walls. There is no longer anyone here to soothe me and tell me that it will all be OK, no Gregg to give me a hug, the hug I so desperately needed, the hug that will never be again.

After a while, slouched on the floor and leaning against the wall, spent from my outburst, I recover my wits slightly. I wipe the tears from my face and look at the broken frame lying in pieces on the ground beside me. *So much for my new beginning. Apparently, I'm not moving on without a fight.* But I know in my heart that life is rolling forward, whether I'm on board or not.

Though the impetus for me to begin anew is not particularly strong at this moment, I know I will do so at some point. The decision has already been made. It came to me before the funeral, as I thought of my mom, and how she let her unhappiness with my dad and the events of their marriage rule her world pretty much for the rest of her life. She could never let it go, forgive, or get past it. It seemed such a waste of all the future joy she could have reveled in, if only she could have managed to feel empowered in her relationship with my father, instead of victimized. She let her unhappiness dictate her life. It made me both sad and frustrated with her. My sister and I tried many different tactics over the years to help snap her out of it, with no success.

But I did learn a valuable lesson, one of the major ones of my life: you cannot be responsible for others' happiness or make others do what you want them. They must choose it for themselves.

Being a victim is not the existence I want. The choice I'm making is a fully conscious one. Even though Gregg is gone, I'm still here. I don't want to spend my time being miserable and unhappy, wondering, "Why me?" I thank God that my mother taught me this. Her example is proving invaluable in guiding my life and my thinking at a time when it would be easy to become bitter. Knowing what I don't want is a start down the road to knowing what I do want—in other words, choosing to be happy and finding peace in my heart at some point. Though I don't know exactly how or when it will happen, especially now when my heart is in a million pieces, I'm confident that it will.

~ 29 ~

There's More to Life

During my meditations, after prayers and gratitude, I sometimes repeat a little chant I conjured up when I had my own cancer experience in my thirties: *I am healthy, I am well, I am fine, I am healthy, I am well, I am fine*.... My mind and body respond by becoming calmer and reassured. Part of the reason it seems to work is that the repetitiveness doesn't let anything else come to mind. I can still move around and do things, but that phrase loops through my brain. It may sound obsessive, but it got me through the follow-up tests after surgery, when I was hoping and praying that the cancer was gone. It is a statement of well-being that became my reality. If it worked then, it can work now.

One day, I have the urge to continue the affirmations. I let my mind go and say whatever pops into my head. *I am healthy, I am well, I am fine, I am kind, I am peaceful, I am joy, I am love, I am knowing*.... I'm fascinated to see what came to mind. I ponder what the different words mean. *I am introspective, I am creative, I am carefree*... The phrases seem like messages sent from above and beyond. After all, I'm not taking the time to consciously choose the words to say; they're impulsive, spontaneous, and intuitive. I figured it's another tool in the search for myself among the vast realm of possibilities.

Throughout the years, I attended a number of conferences offered by places such as the Edgar Cayce Institute in a quest to become more attuned to my intuition. One conference was about showing us all that we all have the ability to "see," even though many of us think we can't. Everyone was given a piece of paper and asked to write our names on it and fold it in half. Then they were collected, mixed up, and passed back out, so that each of us got someone else's name. Without looking at the name, we were to close our eyes and see what first impressions came to mind. When we were done, we would share whatever impressions we got with the person whose name we now had.

I closed my eyes and attempted to do what was asked. The image that popped into my mind was of a little girl with blonde pigtails, about four years old, laughing, being pushed on a swing by a young man with glasses, sort of like Gregg and Gretchen might have been. *That's weird, I thought. I must have conjured that up because that's what is familiar to me. Although, I suppose the scene could actually represent something else. We aren't the only people who look like that. Maybe it's meant to represent happiness or family. I'll have to see what the other person says.*

When everyone had sufficient time to come up with something, we were told to open up the paper and see whose name we had. I did so and could hardly believe my eyes when I saw **my own** name on the page! In other words, I actually did it! I was thrilled to know I could let my intuition be my guide; the images that came to me were authentic.

I continued to make a game of testing myself by guessing numbers on the scale when weighing myself or who was calling before answering the phone, and realized how fleeting the flash of intuition really is. But practice helps and I find that the best way forward without Gregg is to trust my instincts to get me through the countless decisions that now consume my thoughts and are mine alone to make.

* * *

The multitude plants, angel statues, cards, and other items that once brought comfort begin to feel heavy, cluttered, and claustrophobic. I'm struggling to break free all while these things hold me in place. Separating from Gregg's belongings has proven to be difficult, but the urge to simplify my environment in every way slowly takes hold. Friends stop by, and I offer them plants as token of their own love for Gregg. I collect other items into piles or baskets, putting them in the back room, more out of sight. Seeing some wall space makes a major difference in my day- to-day mood, like I can finally breathe. I decide to let go of Gregg's things starting from the perimeter of his existence first, that is, stuff he hadn't used or touched for a long time. I take some old coats hanging in the basement to Goodwill and a box or two of old school papers to the garbage can. On my trips back and forth, I stumble over his work shoes and hiking boots, which are relatively new and in good condition. Someone, somewhere would be thrilled to have them. Thoughts of all the shoeless people in the world egg me on. I grab a garbage bag, fill it with every pair of his shoes I can find, and take them to the local Planet Earth drop. I've taken the first small step toward my ambivalent feelings of singleness, and much to my delight, I've survived.

My effort to stay focused in my cheery and grateful state of mind works for the most part as I make my way through the days since Gregg's passing. Lucky for me, I am generally a positive person with a good outlook, especially around other people. The weight of my loss, though immediate and tender, is different from the agony I had to manage watching Gregg go through his suffering.

Providing the sympathy he needed without being overwhelmed by his pain was a challenge. I amped up my efforts to be positive about our long-term prospects while attempting to support him. If I felt discouraged, which happened often, I tried to keep it to myself or share it only when Gregg wasn't around to hear me. On the rare occasions when I did slip in his presence, he was able to buoy me up. It was always a team effort when we were together, one doing their best to take the respective high road when the other felt low.

It's probably not a stretch to say that my happy self evolved over the course of my married life. In our early years, Gregg used to tell me what a pessimist I was. At the time, it seemed very insulting. I was certainly more optimistic than my parents, though truthfully, maybe only incrementally so. Surely, he could see that! But not growing up in the same environment, he only observed what he saw in me then. And apparently, I paled in comparison to his innate, sunny disposition. Until he mentioned it, I really didn't recognize it.

His enthusiastic nature couldn't help but rub off on me. The constant example was right before my eyes, and it was hard to deny that it worked. It made me want to change my ways. And, of course, I was in love. It is difficult to be a pessimist when you're on top of the world. Slowly, I began to catch myself and change my thinking, a conscious effort even back then, but one that would become second nature.

In my current state, however, I feel blue more often than I like. I know it's OK, and no one expects more. It is just that being sad all the time is not fun. The impetus to count my blessings is more pronounced than ever. I've just lived through the saddest time of my life and focusing on what will no longer be feels like being sucked under water with a bowling ball around my ankle.

Before Gregg passed, he kidded with our friend Maria that we should all take a trip to Amish country. Unfortunately, the timing didn't work out and it never happened. Eventually, though, I run into her at church, and she brings up the trip, saying that she would still like to go. I gather two friends from work, Thia and Karen, and the four of us make the trek down, only about an hour and a half south. The countryside is beautiful, miles and miles of rolling green hills and farm fields dotted here and there with Amish homesteads. We gab and giggle the whole time as we walk around the shops.

Not until the trip is over and we are back in the parking lot where we met this morning does Maria begin talking about Gregg, even though I've hoped all day to discuss him. "It was really amazing to watch you two and observe your relationship and the love you shared," she says, sitting in the passenger seat of my parked car, looking at me.

"Thanks," I say, not sure how to respond. Thia also commented on how comfortable our rapport was with each other. I don't know what they saw that was so special. It seemed a typical relationship to me, but perhaps our deeply felt trust and love shone through for others to see.

Maria takes a minute to find and tune into his energy and then begins to have what appears to be a conversation with him. "He's telling us to look at the leaves in the street." She is already looking as I turn to follow her gaze. In the dark, under the streetlight, an eddy of leaves spins and twirls, as the wind picks them up, dancing them in circles, before dropping them back to the ground.

"Can you see me?" Gregg says through Maria.

"I can," she responds back to him. I try to imagine him there, but cannot see him the way Maria does. "He's not *doing* anything with the leaves, he *is* the molecules of the leaves," she says. "He is part of the molecular structure, helping them to be able to breathe in the air so that they can live."

Maria tries other ways to explain what she means, but I still don't quite get it. Eventually, she says, "He had five or six exit points to leave the earth, but the first two were when Gretchen was little, and you decided that he should wait. It was all planned."

I try to remember any close calls with his life and can think of only one, when he was working on the car and had it running with the doors closed in the garage because it was cold. I happened to stick my head out to ask him something and saw that he was overcome with fumes. I helped him stumble out to the yard where he collapsed. I told him to breathe deeply in order to help clear out his lungs and ran to call Poison Control. He was OK, but thankfully, I had needed a question answered when I did, otherwise, who knows what would have happened. Another noncoincidence.

I'm too taken in with the whole situation to say much of anything in response to her conversation. If I interrupt her, he might go away, like a fragile magic bubble that can only sustain itself for a short wisp of time.

"He says you can see anyone you want as long as it isn't men." She bursts into laughter, and we all chuckle along. "He likes to see us laugh."

"Does he hear what we say?" I ask.

"He sees us as flickers of light, and, when we laugh, we collectively light up with bright colors and send it forth. It makes him happy."

It's evident that she's adept at multitasking the conversations with all of us. Her attention and focus vacillate inward and outward very quickly. "He wants you to ask Gretchen what she wants to do with her life, not her job, her life. He knows you will help her." I'm not sure Gretchen knows what she wants to do, or even if she will agree to have that dialogue. More often than not, she responds to me in short snippets, if I start the conversation. It's just the opposite if she begins it.

"In about four years," Maria says, "she'll begin to worry about her physical body and whether she'll get sick like Gregg. Tell her that she has the power to change her DNA. She needs to 'shake it loose before she gets shook up.'"

Can people really change their DNA? I thought we were pretty much stuck with what we came with, but I do believe anything is possible; I just never considered changing one's DNA.

"He wants you to honor Ron and Claire and their decisions. He's spent a lot more time with them than even you. They have created a vacuum that is keeping him close to them. He's been working with them and helping them."

The conversation moves to Thia and Karen. "He says Thia's soul is in her solar plexus and that she has a lot of love and compassion, and big brown eyes." Then after a few moments, "I knew her before you, Maria!" Maria bursts into laughter again.

She asks us to speak to Gregg directly. "You are one of the most spiritual people I know, Gregg, and I hope that I can carry on the example you set," Karen says.

"He feels the love and sends it back to you," Maria responds for him.

We've been sitting in the parking lot for a long while now, and it seems the words flow less frequently, so we end the conversation and say our goodbyes. "Thanks, Maria. It was a fun day and I am glad you came and encouraged it to happen. Gregg was probably riding along the whole time since it was his idea!" I laugh.

"I would be happy to have you come to see me. It would be my gift to you," Maria adds.

I take Maria up on her offer and make an appointment about a month after our Amish country trip. This is the first time I've gone to her for a treatment, so I don't know what to expect. She asks me to sit opposite her in a comfortable chair, both of us upright with our bare feet on the floor. We chat about everyday things, and then she directs the conversation with more specific questions about my feelings on this and that, observing me with her hyper sensory perception or HSP as she calls it. What she sees going on in my energy field, in reaction to her questions and my responses, gives her information about what direction to go with her treatment.

During our dialogue, she's also conversing with her guides, the master energies she regularly confers with. At first, she refers to them in the third person, like she did with Gregg in the car, but eventually she just repeats what she hears them say, again often finding them humorous. She said that Christ, in particular, has a great sense of humor, and the archangel Rafael has a wonderful sense of fun. She also often connects to the energies of Quan Yin, Mary Magdalene, and the archangel Michael, among others. With her extensive knowledge of the physiology of our bodies, she interprets and supplements what they say. She reiterates how our thoughts and beliefs can create blocks leading to various physical ailments.

She has me lie on her table and proceeds to manipulate my energy field, moving around the table and touching or holding various pressure points, such as the back of my neck and my ankles, feet, and toes. All the while, she probes with questions about my feelings and perspective on life, and then relates that information to how they manifest themselves in my body. "I see your energy body offset to the side of your physical body," she tells me. "You're literally 'beside yourself' in your grief." I imagine what, exactly, that looks like, when she becomes quiet. "Gregg says thank you," she says after a moment. "He knows you are sad, and he is grateful you are here with me so that I can help you." Her words, spoken tenderly, catch me by surprise, and I feel my eyes start to water, immediately overcome with emotion. "He's talking about shoes," she continues. "Did he get some new shoes or something?"

It takes me a minute to collect my thoughts, flustered that she is talking to him again. "I actually just took his shoes up to the local Planet Earth drop box," I finally say. She is at the end of the table, holding on to my feet.

"He says it is a good thing, and he is happy that others will be able to use them. He sees how much good they will do." It's very much like him to act so matter-of-fact and not dwell in the emotional entanglement of it all. There's a subtext to the message: he is allaying any doubts I have about getting rid of his stuff. He's telling me to move on.

Suddenly, Maria says, "This isn't Maria talking," surprising me once again and bringing me to attention. Then, as if she and Gregg are sharing a joke, she adds, "She's never quite sure." Maria laughs at the comment that has come out of her mouth. But it's right on. I always harbor a hint of skepticism, but so many things that she has said ring true, it's hard to deny that he is really with us.

"Hi Greggy! How's it going up there?" I say to myself in my head, as if he can hear me, too. *"I miss you."*

Maria is about tell me something else, but abruptly stops. I wait for her to continue. When she doesn't, I ask, "Why did you stop talking?"

"You were talking to Gregg and I didn't want to intrude." *She knew I was talking to Gregg? Did Gregg actually hear me? If she could, then so probably could he. I wasn't listening for any answer because I just said it on a whim. Maybe if I tried, I could!* Suddenly, I'm self-conscious and decide not to talk to him anymore.

"You know, I know Gregg better from the other side. We've worked together there in the past. I was amazed when I looked at all of the pictures of you both at the funeral and I realized that I really didn't know much about him socially in this lifetime."

Glancing at her again from my spot on the table, I see she is still immersed in what she's doing with my energy field. I close my eyes again and think about her comment. "Do you talk to him often?" I ask.

"He works with me and the archangel Raphael, whenever I have a situation or I am treating a client where he can offer help."

"Like what?"

"I told you all at the funeral that he was working to improve the air quality of the earth to ensure the survival of all who inhabit it." I remember being surprised when she said that and not able to take it in. It's still hard to grasp even after further explanation in the car. I want to believe it, but it sounds crazy. Maria continues, "If I am treating someone with asthma or breathing issues, sometimes he can help shed light on what might be causing the problem."

"So, you call in different angels or guides depending on who you are treating?"

"Yes. If I am working on someone with a heart issue, for example, there are those who have crossed over, who may have more specific knowledge than I do. They have a broader view and the expertise I might not have."

The session lasts two and a half hours, way beyond her usual hour-long appointments. When we part, she reaches for me and puts her cheek against mine, holding it there for a minute. "That's from Gregg."

I look at her, familiar tears rising again. "Thanks," I say, and hurry out the door before I lose it completely. Gregg and I had always shared the endearment of being "cheek to cheek." It was a fun little addition to our hugs, a punctuation point after our embrace. There was absolutely no way she could have known that. No one did but Gregg and me.

~ 30 ~

All Part of the Plan

Gazing around the house, I think of all the things that still need to be done, now and in the future. Sorting through more of Gregg's things, getting rid of leftover medical supplies, putting my own clothes away, doing the wash, paying the bills, taking out the garbage cans, yard chores, grocery shopping, pet care, car maintenance, and on and on. Whatever has been accomplished with the two of us will now be done solely by me. The phrase *If I don't do it, nobody will* runs through my head. There seem to be too many jobs for one person to handle. How will I do it all?

Of course, I know that many people go it alone in life, and they figure it out. I just haven't been one of them. Eventually, my motto changes: *Everything I do is something that has to be done. It doesn't matter how soon or in what order. If I can check it off my list, then it is one less thing ahead of me. What I don't do today can be done tomorrow.* I sorely miss the company of another human being. My main sounding board is missing in action. Family and friends who had recently hovered so close are now back to their own worlds. I can't impose on them any more to get me through my days. It's strange having no one to banter with, to get opinions from, to share my day with. The house seems eerily quiet.

So, I talk to myself. At first, I talk out loud for the sake of the animals. They follow me around the house and sit near me when I'm stationary. I feel them watching me often, as if waiting for me to say something. They're used to noise and more commotion than they now get. Gregg always had music going and spent many hours alone with them for company while I was at work. He often talked to them and played with them. Besides that, people were always coming and going, and the phone rang regularly. Left to my own devices, I often preferred the quiet. Now I have it ad nauseam. Looking at their fuzzy little faces, I wonder if I will be enough for them. It makes me glum, so I try to be audible in their presence, even though it feels contrived. It doesn't last long—yet another responsibility I'm not ready for.

Keeping my own counsel has its pros and cons. The good news is that I'm in charge of all the decisions. The bad news is that I'm *responsible* for all the decisions. I rely more on my intuition to guide me. Thinking had always been more my bag than feeling, so trusting my own gut, then making decisions and *living* with them is a scary prospect! No scape-goats, if things go haywire.

For years I've prayed: *Help me to know who I really am.* Perhaps it's time to pray for something else. I don't want to be tested anymore. I need a break.

*   *   *

One theory of dealing with grief is that you should not turn down invitations to do things or go places even though you might not feel like going. As a rule, I enjoy traveling and being with friends, so it's not too hard to make myself go. I am always thrilled when I have a travel buddy, but I have tried not to feel too weird if I don't. At first it seems like everywhere I look, I see only couples, an indication to me that I feel less than secure or that our society works to make single people invisible. I make an effort not to let my single self prevent me from having a good time, though it's often a struggle.

Because I'm focused on couples, I often observe relationships and interactions between the people. I note the different degrees to which husbands and wives enjoy one another, especially in the presence of company. Though some are great, it seems others just coexist. They don't talk to or touch each other. It's like a habit that they didn't know how to break. Whatever intimacy they had once shared has disappeared over time, the initial throes of love lost through the passing of years. Some seem resigned to that, others just seem unhappy.

When I'm around couples who obviously care for each other, lighter energy surrounds them and lifts us all up. I feel blessed once again that Gregg and I had enjoyed each other's company to the end. Will I ever find someone like that again? Maybe, but if I don't, I would prefer to make my way independently rather than spend time with someone I didn't enjoy.

As it turned out, there was already a plan in the works to return to the Cape for another reunion with friends from our teaching days in England. I'm thrilled that Gretchen decided to join me. Her dad is coming too. Since I've no plans to bury his ashes and don't want them to sit around my house indefinitely, I've decided to bring him along whenever we gather with old friends. He was always instrumental in making sure that we had campfires at these occasions, and I'm sure, though he's not here to do the work, this trip will be no different. Gregg and fire kind of went together. He was born under the sign of Aries, a fire sign, and being the self-designated fire builder, often hauled loads of wood from home to do so, even when the weather did not cooperate! His second great skill after starting the fire was to wing-wang some kind of wind barrier during various gales to keep the fire from overtaking the surrounding area, along with the people in it, thereby ensuring everyone would stay outdoors with him. He was not easily deterred. It was entertaining to watch him create his unusual fortresses using whatever materials he could find (sheets, blankets, sleeping bags, ropes, bungee cords, chairs) and to see if he could actually pull it off. He usually did, if you didn't mind getting lungfuls of smoke and rotating around the circle every few minutes. And as we already know, he managed to persuade people to actually *walk on* the fire.

As we arrive at the Cape and greet our friend Lisa at the front door, she says, "Look!" Turning around to where she was pointing, we see the sky behind us is a beautiful rainbow. "See! Gregg is with us. He wouldn't let us gather together without him."

The week is as fun as it can be. We laze around the house and play in the water. The pace is slow and easy, filled with good food and good company. Yet, a loneliness clings to me, though I try to push it away. No one can fill the void beside me. I'm grateful to be with everyone, but the loss is still too fresh. The day of what would have been our thirty-second wedding anniversary passes uneventfully midweek, leaving me sad and wanting to be alone with my memories. Only Gretchen is aware of its significance. Knowing I would be melancholy, she very sweetly purchases a small medallion with the word "hug" engraved on it and leaves it on my pillow.

Later in the week, on a balmy evening at dusk, all twelve of us make our way down to the fire on the beach and celebrate Gregg by returning him to the earth, as the stars sparkle high in the sky, and the waves play their sonorous melody in the background. When we drive home at the end of the week, our spirits are lighter, and Gregg's box weighs less. This had been the last official event we planned to do together before he died. I'm forlorn, knowing that he won't be a part of any future plans or adventures in either my life or Gretchen's.

Turning to look at her riding beside me in the car, I feel my heart swell. She's good kid. I've seen new sides of her these past years ,and she's probably found some in herself. She's certainly grown up, having just turned twenty-four. I'm proud of her and happy that we seem to have grown closer, managing to find the middle ground in our relationship, rather than pressing each other's buttons all of the time. We won't have Gregg to mediate our disagreements anymore, so we try harder, two comrades facing life, united, having been bound together more tightly by adversity.

On the way home, we stop in Connecticut to visit with Maddie and Mark. Maddie asks if we wanted to visit her medium friend, Rose. I've had a reading from Rose a couple times before; she's pretty good, but she doesn't know us well enough to be privy to what has transpired in our lives since the last time she saw us. Maddie has not given her any information other than setting up a mutually acceptable appointment time.

She's probably in her late seventies or early eighties, but spry with dark hair. We see her one at a time. Because Gregg's death is so recent, we're eager to see if he will come through. Beyond that, I have no expectations.

After an opening prayer, she asks if I have recently been in an accident or trauma of some kind. She feels a heaviness or sadness and wonders what it means. I tell her I recently lost Gregg. "Did he wear glasses?" She asks, but before I can reply, she adds, "Because I'm seeing someone of medium height with glasses and big smile on his face. He looks to be in his thirties."

"That sounds like him, but he definitely wasn't in his thirties!" I giggle.

"Well, you know, once people cross over to the other side, they can assume any age they want, often choosing a time when they were happiest."

"I'd say that was a good time in his life."

"Was something wrong with his stomach? I feel discomfort here?" She touches the top of her abdomen. "Like indigestion."

"He had stomach and esophageal cancer."

She nods, then opens her eyes and looks at me. "Oh. I'm sorry to hear that. It must have been hard on you both."

"It's been a rough four years. He did well until he didn't. It was almost a blessing when he passed on at the end."

She chats about her own husband who had also passed away. "He tickles my feet in the middle of the night when I'm trying to sleep. I finally had to tell him to stop and go away. I was happy to see him, but he needed to come in the daytime." She laughs. "They have no sense of time."

I chuckle, oddly comforted by her story. "Why am I seeing a big roast beef sandwich?" she asks. "A minute ago, I was smelling pizza, then I saw ice cream and now a sandwich?"

"Well," I respond, thoughtfully, "he was tube-fed for the last year and a half. Maybe that has something to do with it."

"He's nodding his head yes. He says to tell you he can have whatever he wants now." She looks at me again. "You must know I am talking to him. I never get images of this much food!"

I smile, thinking about eating on the other side. Do people actually eat there? It's not like they have human bodies to sustain. Perhaps it's all about the thought process and remembering the gratification of eating. Or maybe he was letting me know that he was whole again, in perfect form.

"Who's Eli?" She asks, throwing me a curve ball. I've had readings before, but rarely did specific names come up.

"One of Gregg's best friends."

"He says to tell Eli, that if the situation was reversed, he would do the same for him." She looks at me again. "I don't know what that means, but that is what he said." I know he's referring to asking Eli to look out for Gretchen and me. I'm still amazed that she brought him up specifically by name.

After a few more comments, she asks, "Now he's talking about Nina, Do you know who that is?"

"Gregg's sister," I answer, surprised again.

"He says to tell her that he loves her and not to fret, that everything happened as planned." I'm not sure where Nina is in her grieving process. Because she lives far away in Colorado, she's been left to manage on her own.

The reading makes me feel closer to Gregg. *Was it really Gregg?* I wonder as we drive home. It had to be. How else would she know such specific information, especially people's names? It was real enough to me.

*   *   *

The director of Common Ground, the retreat where Gregg oversaw the youth programs for several years, contacts me. Several people have been kind enough to donate money to Common Ground in Gregg's memory, and the organization wants to commemorate Gregg in some way. After tossing around ideas, we agree to erect a beautiful wind sculpture made of tiny red hearts in the gardens. When the wind spins it, it looks like one huge oscillating heart. It's an appropriate symbol to represent all that Gregg and this whole experience has stood for. The dedication is an all-day affair, on an absolutely glorious October Saturday, bright with fall foliage and sunshine. After a picnic in the woods and drumming, the dedication concludes with a firewalk, and the event is so successful it becomes a yearly event: the Annual Gregg Gilder Memorial Firewalk.

Each opportunity to remember Gregg is cathartic to me. His spirit is always present in the groups of people who gather. It helps take the sting out of his passing and encourages us to focus on the many fun adventures we've shared together, inevitably eliciting silly stories and lots of laughs. These moments are crucial in my healing, and I am grateful for everyone.

~ 31 ~

A Light in the Darkness/Full Circle

The days grow colder and nature loses its colorful leaves to the wind in preparation for the big sleep of winter. People have told me that all the first holidays are the worst. Gregg's parents inform me at the end of the summer that they will head to Florida for Christmas. It's yet another blow. We always spent at least some part of Christmas together. How could they leave, this year especially? The fact that they won't be with me or the family seems unnecessarily cruel. I plead my case, hoping they will reconsider: "Are you sure you want to be gone this year? You will be alone down there. Won't it be hard on you not being with the family? It'd really be nice if you stayed." But it's fruitless. They've made up their minds and won't be deterred, even as the tears roll down my cheeks after hearing the news.

Later, when I get over myself, I decide that being with the family and not having Gregg there will be too much for them. They're choosing to escape rather than face the pain of him being gone. I finally conclude that since things will never be the same anyhow, we may as well start new traditions right now. No time like the present! Perhaps I should just go to my sister's. It will be good to get away for me as well. But I'm still forlorn and not really looking forward to the celebrations ahead.

Gretchen makes the annual trek to the Christmas tree farm with me at Thanksgiving. The tree we cut leans against the wall in the garage in a bucket of water, trussed up in twine like a fat turkey. Unfortunately, there's no time to set it up before she leaves. I ignore it for at least a

251

week, but it can't wait forever. Psyching myself up, I lug down some Christmas boxes from the attic, thump, thump, thumping them down the steps. After clearing a spot and setting up the tree stand, I move to get the tree, not sure I can get it through the door, let alone make it stand up straight without help. But, to my surprise, I manage, getting poked endlessly with needles in the process, but still feeling pretty proud of myself.

Over the next few days, I find the boxes filled with our many outdoor decorations in the basement and set them up—though at heights that don't require me to climb high up a ladder and balance precariously while trying to attach things to hooks I can't see. Our giant wreath looks just fine much lower to the ground. Once I figure out the maze of plugs and toggle switches on the lights, I stand back to admire my handiwork. I haven't done it as efficiently as Gregg, but still everything lights up nicely. I smile with satisfaction, knowing Gregg would be proud that I still made the effort to hang them up at all.

It's anticlimactic doing it all by myself, but I make the best of it, singing along with Christmas music playing in the background. The kitties help by nosing around and batting ornaments across the room and under chairs or putting their paws into the can holding the beaded garland and trying to pull it out. The dog lies in his usual spot on the floor, feigning boredom, trying to doze off, but surreptitiously monitoring the cats, at the ready in case I need him to patrol their antics.

Later, tired after a big day of work, I trudge back through the snow and flip the switches, turning off my outside lights. It definitely looks like Christmas at the Gilder house, though it will never be as before. I undress and climb into bed with a sigh, happy to be lying prone. I reach over to the nightstand and flip off the last switch. As I take in the room before closing my eyes, I realize that it's brighter than usual. *That's weird,* I think.

I get up and peek out the window, surprised to see that my outside Christmas lights are on. *Now I know I turned them off, didn't I? I just went out about an hour ago, before getting undressed.* I grab my winter jacket, throwing it on over my nightie, then quickly step into Ron's old fire boots and go outside once again, making sure all of the lights are off and darkness prevails.

No sooner have I flipped off all the inside lights and made my way back to bed, than I look at the window and sure enough, light still floods into my bedroom. I look again, and the lights outside are ablaze.

Shaking my head and grinning, I think to myself, *Ha-ha, very funny, Gregg boy!* He's at it once more, playing with me, and probably laughing at my bewilderment. It's his way of applauding my accomplishments and letting me know his light shines on, no matter what.

There's no way I'm going out again. They'll have to shine and sparkle all night long; I'll turn them off in the morning. I climb into bed, snickering to myself, comforted by his presence.

The lights continue to play games with me the next few nights. It lightens my mood and made me smile. As I closed up shop before leaving for Georgia, I do one last circle around the house and make sure they are off. My neighbor will look after the cats while I'm gone.

Upon my return, I drive up to my house and there to greet me are the lights shining once again in broad daylight. All I can do is laugh.

*   *   *

March comes upon us that year more like a lamb than a lion, and with it, the first anniversary of Gregg's passing. Some parts of me seem to be making peace with life and circumstance while other parts are still stuck in limbo. I can enjoy the world in my own way, carrying on with whatever draws my attention without falling into tears, but it only takes a little nudge in the right direction to work through yet another aspect of loss. Moments creep up on me in a heartbeat, catching me unawares, and leave me in a heap of sorrow.

The weather on the actual day is an unseasonably warm sixty degrees. The bright sun has melted the snow enough to create puddles, water, and mud. It's difficult to feel unhappy, the respite after the long winter stirring my soul. This tempting taste of spring makes me want to jump for joy and breathe it in like fresh oxygen rejuvenating my lungs.

I take the day off from work. I deserve this day to myself, to remember, to celebrate, to simply be. I began it with yoga and meditation in front of the big living room window, the warm sun wrapping itself around me in a loving embrace. I write a letter to all the people in my life, confirming that all is well, something that Gregg would have appreciated as he enjoyed his old-fashioned snail mail, and something that I believe our friends have sorely missed in their mailboxes since he has gone.

The letter captures my spirit at the moment, not overly sad or morbid, but jubilant in the beauty of the day, the lightening of my heart, and the inevitable passage of time with its myriad of never-ending events. I want to confirm to others and to myself that though Gregg has left his indelible imprint on us all, we are still here and will continue to live the best life possible, something he would happily celebrate with each one of us.

Then Wiley and I drive to Common Ground with some of Gregg's ashes. We hike the trail beyond the buildings, dodging whatever pitfalls appear before us, and breathe in the world. The usually small creek is a rushing river with all the snow melt. I lean against a tree watching and pondering, while Wiley sticks his nose in a couple of logs to see if anything interesting hides inside. So many metaphors for life shine around us every day: the chaos, the calming, the urgent transporting of thoughts to a new place, wanted or not, the thrill of the ride, the new beginnings, and the peace of mind that comes with a fresh perspective.

I recently heard a quip from Wayne Dyer: "No one ever died from a snakebite." It's not the bite that gets you; it's the venom that travels through your body. It will take over and kill you, or you can find a way to get rid of it and turn it into medicine. I continue to turn Gregg's loss into medicine. I've made significant progress; it's easy to feel grateful surrounded by the beauty of the day and the warmth of the sun shining its love down on me, my little furry friend by my side.

Before we go, I toss some of Gregg's ashes into the woods and into the rushing waters to be deposited wherever the universe deems he should come to rest. I've always viewed the waters of the earth as the veins and bloodstream of a larger being. Gregg will forever be a part of that being, somewhere in the flow of the physical world.

Watching the water churn and roll over itself for a few minutes, I picture Gregg riding the white water, the thrill of the challenge showing in the smile on his face, off to his next big adventure. Wiley stands next to me, watching as well. Maybe he can see and sense things that are not so obvious to me. "Your dad loved it here, Wiles. It's a good place for him to be." I pat him on the head, then say, "Come on! I'll race you back!"

He wins, of course, and we hop into the car, me laughing, Wiley panting and happy to have been out exploring and hanging with me, no matter where the rest of the day takes us.

*   *   *

Ever since my visit with Maria, when she heard me silently talking to Gregg, I think about my journal writing and how it seems like I'm guided in what I say, as if I'm not the only one partaking in the thoughts in my head and what ends up written on the page. Of course, it's easy to think the obvious, that I was just talking to myself. But I often marvel at the wisdom of the words when rereading them. On the surface level, I can never quite give myself credit for what I read.

More and more often, when I meditate, I acknowledge what comes to me and write it down. Sometimes it's my interpretation of what I've just experienced, and other times, it's more direct, just writing down thoughts as soon as I they arise. Finally, I decide I may as well talk to Gregg if I want to. If he really does hear me, then perhaps I will hear him too.

My journal:

The message today is that there is a bigger picture. "I left so you could be." There is more for me to do here. Gregg was my training ground and teacher. I was his. There will be another. We are all one. Gregg and I are together in eternity. The next person won't have his sense of humor (grin), who could? (so Gregg— infusing humor). It's all part of the big plan. I have another thirty years, as long as I was with Gregg. I will continue my work with another who will lead me through the next phase of my life. We will pair up for each other, him for me and I for him. I will be at peace.

Peace—knowing the truth, seeing the larger picture, knowing that all is as it should be, questions answered.

When I wish for peace, I wish for that.

I am at a transition point between the past and the future, looking back and looking forward, not wanting to let go, knowing it is impossible to hang on. So, there is nothing left but to embrace what lies ahead with peace of mind and heart and spirit. That is the bigger picture.

Gregg is with me always. He permeates myself. He is more a part of me than ever. He is the air I breathe. We are infused together now more than in our human form. In that form, I had the obvious, now I have access to all the depths of his knowledge and connections more than ever before. By dying, I have more of him because he has more of himself. Wow! Interesting concept.

Not concept, truth. I instantly feel that I did not generate that statement, but I'm not ready to abandon my thoughts in order to figure out if it's a valid feeling. And so, I complete my reflection.

In that way, he can never leave me, ever. He is the very air I breathe. I sit for a few minutes, soaking in the gravity of what I just realized.

"Thank you for this insight," I say to no one in particular.

You are welcome. The words come to me suddenly, as if I'm having a conversation. *Is this really happening?* I wonder to myself. It doesn't feel like Gregg talking. But who?

I venture forth. *Should we continue to communicate this way?*

Why not?

Sometimes I don't feel like I hear you, like I am distracted.

You are. You will improve with time. Practice makes perfect. I talk to you all the time, you just don't write it down.

This is cool!

Yes, it is.

Who are you?

I am life itself. I am the be all, end all of time, although time is yours, not mine, on this plane.

Are you my guide?

Of sorts. There are many of us. I will speak with you anytime.

Thank you.

You are love, an angel of God. Peace be with you.

The conversation stuns me. Can I have dialogues with my guides? It thrills me to think so. Maybe somewhere deep down I've had an inkling that this is possible, but it hadn't surfaced until now. It seems to be the work of others, not me. At the same time, I'm already aware of the unclaimed wisdom in my journals. Could this have been my guides influencing my words without me being fully cognizant of what was happening? Have I just been unwilling to completely acknowledge their presence and the assistance they have unfailingly provided all along? Today's conversation seems to put it right before my eyes so that there is no denying it. Of course, Maria does it all the time, and I had read the whole series of *Conversations with God* by Neale Donald Walsh, in which he also had regular conversations with a higher intelligence. So, why *not* me? And if I am doing it, why not everybody?

I decide to take time every day to be quiet and listen, paper and pencil in hand. If I just write the words as they come to me in answer to my questions, without thought of grammar or meaning, will they make sense in the end? I'm almost hesitant to try, not wanting to risk disappointment in case it turns out to be a hodgepodge of randomness. But if I don't try again, I'll never know. I find it becomes easier each time. And, the sentences do make sense. Whenever it feels I might be leading the answers, anticipating the next string of words, a different word comes to mind and leads me another direction. There is a different energy in the answers that is not me. I recognize that I genuinely am having conversations with my guides/angels/God. The same unforeseen wisdom of my journal writing shines through in these exchanges like a beacon in the night and offers me new perspective in my reflections of life and my place within it. But even more of a blessing would be my conversations with Gregg.

I wanted to talk to you in the end, babe. There was so much going on in my head. I was withdrawing and needed my energy and strength to transition. It was beyond my control, but I knew you'd be wondering. It was like a fairytale, unreal, yet real. It is beautiful here, just like in the pictures. It forms itself instantaneously as you think. We have meshed, you are now the two of us. The same way that each experience becomes part of you, so do your connections with people. It continuously shapes and reshapes who you are. I am thankful for all of your tenderness with me. I said it many times, you made it easier and I am forever grateful. Love well, live happy. Peace in your heart always, my love.

The colloquies are informative and soothing, filling me with love, and healing my heart one dialogue at a time, completing the last arc in the full circle of our connection, from physical to spiritual. I come to know that I can always count on this communion at any moment in time, either with Gregg or my spiritual guides. It requires only that I make the time to do so.

~ 32 ~

Unexpected Grace

Prayer in my family was compartmentalized. It took place only in church or a bedroom of my paternal grandparents' house. When Lila and I were little, we would sometimes spend the night, and when it was time to go to sleep, we always knelt beside the bed sandwiched between my grandparents, hands folded and heads bowed. We looked like a scene from a Norman Rockwell picture without the dog. The Lord's Prayer always came first and we ended with, "God bless Mommy and Daddy, Grammy and Bop, and all the other little kiddies in the world." I was never quite sure if we were talking about cats or the same little children who were starving in Africa when I didn't like my food at the dinner table. It was just what we said.

My father grew up in the same household and had been a regular attendee at the Episcopalian church where my grandfather was a deacon. He sang in their rather renowned church choir from the time he could carry a tune. On Christmas Eve, I stood next to him in the pews as he loudly sang harmony to everyone else's melody. I was both proud, because I loved the music, and embarrassed that he would draw such attention to himself.

My mother, on the other hand, was the youngest of eight in a large Catholic family and had attended Catholic school until high school, when she met my dad. There was a wide gulf between Catholics and Protestants back then, even though Episcopalian was about as close to Catholicism as you could get. Their relationship began on a rough note, as neither family approved of the other. Bucking the odds, they decided to get married anyhow and met with a Catholic priest who wanted my dad to vow he would raise us Catholic. He refused, and so my parents eloped.

In the end, he didn't even raise us Episcopalian, always finding a reason not to go to church except for the occasional Christmas and Easter. My mom gave it her best shot, wanting us to have some kind of background in something, but without the support of my dad, she wasn't very successful. Lila and I dreaded being told to get ready for church and always argued because we didn't want to go.

One particular Sunday, we decided it would be a good idea to lock ourselves in the back bedroom. The little push-button locks under the doorknobs were ancient and had never been used that I knew of until that moment. Our irate parents demanded we open the door, but, of course, they were jammed tight. My dad had to pry open the window from the outside and climb in after us. We were both spanked within an inch of our lives. It was all extremely traumatic, but mission accomplished, we missed church.

I'm not sure why we found it so aversive. Maybe we could already sense the hypocrisy of it. The few times we did go, we always had to sit in the last pew of the rather large sanctuary, a ritual started by my grandparents when they brought my dad's younger brother to church. He had a form of muscular dystrophy, and with him being in a wheelchair, it was most convenient to sit there. He died at age sixteen, so by the time my sister and I were on the scene, those years were long gone. Sitting in the back was somehow a way to pay homage to his memory.

Being seated in the back seemed a way to inspect each and every person who attended church that particular day, my grandmother noting aloud who was walking in and commenting, not always graciously, on what they were wearing. We were so far from the action at the front of the church that there was little hope of me being drawn into the service, and if it wasn't for standing, sitting, and kneeling frequently, I am not sure I could have made it through. Well, that, and my grandmother's wrap, which fascinated me. It was trimmed with a dead fox body draped over her shoulders.

Mom did manage, impossibly, to get us both through confirmation classes. Her Catholic self didn't want us to be floating around in limbo. We would be official members of a church, and if we never attended another day in our lives, she could at least take comfort in knowing our souls would be saved.

In one of my confirmation classes, I asked the assistant minister where we came from. I was not looking for a lecture on reproduction, although looking back, maybe he thought so. He gave me a smile and a vague answer that did not help me in the least. It became instantly apparent to me that he didn't know the answer, and even worse, was evading the subject. Weren't clergy supposed to guide us and be our direct line to God?

My world then was relatively small, black and white. If I asked a question, I always assumed that there would be an answer. That's how the world worked, wasn't it? It was how we learned the rules, right from wrong, good from bad. It was a way to find the guideposts from which to maneuver our way through life and get to the other end with the least amount of detours and mistakes.

I knew on some level that I would not find the answers I was looking for there. Bigger questions had already begun to fill my head. Why are we here? Where are we going? It became apparent that I would have to figure things out on my own.

But perhaps he knew more than I was willing to give him credit for. He had lived longer and experienced more. He had found out for himself that there is a lot of gray in life, a lot of room for learning. Maybe he already knew that we each have to find our own way and be guided by our own decisions and experiences. That no matter what he would have told me back then, it never could have quenched my own thirst to know personally, to find out for myself, to live and experience, to make mistakes, to feel bliss and embrace the gift of life that I had been given. That the events of his life had been, and would continue to be, different from mine, leading him to his own conclusions, just as mine would for me. It is the only way it can be. There are no directions, no map, and no right or wrong answer. There is only your experience.

I have a running joke of sorts with my friends about my own description of myself over the years, versus who I really seem to be based on the course of my life, and how I have found myself doing things I had no intention of doing. For instance, I said I didn't like little kids. I hated to babysit, had no younger siblings, nor was I ever around them, but then found myself working with preschoolers for twenty-five years. When I began college, I wanted to be anything but a teacher. It seemed an easy fallback vocation for many women of my generation. I deemed it beneath me—yet I ended up working in education nearly my entire career. Apparently, the powers that be knew more about me than I did.

From my current standpoint, I suppose this was early training in my quest of knowing "who I truly am," the universe's way of demonstrating to me how my ego gets in the way and tries to lead me astray, telling me that I am one person, when I am actually somebody else. Telling me I like this, when I actually like that, or that I am good at this, when I am better at something else. Maybe it takes over in my desire to fit in, a human condition, trying to emulate something or somebody I admire, rather than acknowledging my own innate talents and abilities. I am sure there are still things about me that I am not aware of and probably never will be. It seems learning who you are really is a lifelong process and one that continually changes as you grow and experience.

What I do know is that whether we acknowledge our talents and inclinations or not, life will make sure we have a chance to think about them. We can take the short path or the long path, but we will eventually get to where we are meant to be. Intuition is always knocking at our door along with guidance in all forms. We gravitate to what captures our attention and tickles our fancy, despite what we think we should do. And what recurs, time and again, seems to be the universe's or God's way of making sure we have every opportunity to succeed at using our own unique gifts and talents, in the ways in which they were given to us and meant to be used.

For me, the draw has always been to spirituality and writing. Other interests have come and gone, but these two things have remained steadfast in my world, and I never seem to tire of them. I have often wondered about these words from Gregg: "I left so you could be." At first, I felt wronged. I certainly didn't want him to have suffered all of that for me. But then I decided he was telling me it was time to step out of his shadow and let whatever gifts I'd been blessed with in this life come forth. Since writing was becoming more an integral part of my days than it had ever been, it occurred to me that maybe I was being guided to share our story. Perhaps the message would resonate with others who are looking for their own guideposts along this road of life. However, this fact remains: I would not have had a story to write without Gregg's illness and my subsequent search for meaning and peace.

But, what is peace? How will I know when I have managed it? Is it a feeling that dwells in us constantly or is it fleeting? Does it appear in some places but not others, in my mind but not my heart, in my heart but not my body? Will a veil come down and wrap itself around me like Tinkerbell's fairy dust? Will God tap me on the shoulder and give me a high-five?

My own definition, the one I noted in my journal, of seeing the larger picture, knowing truth, knowing that everything is as it should be and having all my questions answered, seems a lot to ask in some ways. Does anyone have that other than God? We are human, after all, even if we are made in God's image. We could achieve any one of these at a given moment in time, but then things change, and we are once again in turmoil.

Maybe we each must come up with our own definition. I asked around and found that peace means something a little different to everybody. One said, "Knowing you aren't in control and adjusting your attitude accordingly." Another said, "Acceptance of all exactly as it seems and then shifting to the next moment, free of attachment." Yet another said, "An emotional feeling of utter contentment spiritually, emotionally, and physically, knowing at my core what my path is, and knowing that the reason for us, why we are in human form (for now) as spiritual beings is to remember what our souls already know, that LOVE is and always will be the answer to everything."

Maybe peace is just having a feeling of ease, knowing that it is OK if all the pieces aren't in place, accepting that we learn as we go, accepting that we have survived what has come our way and will continue to do so, and knowing that we are never alone in this world. It is appreciating the beauty and blessings in our lives, and it is being the love that we are, thereby attracting the same. It is receiving the gift of unexpected grace.

*   *   *

About two years after Gregg's passing, Gretchen and I return to Athens for a wedding shower for one of her friends. I want to let go of the rest of his ashes, as there really is no other place that it seems he needs to be. The list of locations where I've left him is already quite long. He's in Maddie's garden in Connecticut. He's made it to a fall cabin weekend with my old high school friends with whom we had had biannual visits to practically every state park in Ohio for the past thirty years. He's in the gardens at Ohio University's main gate and in his favorite bar, under the dartboard where he loved to play darts. He's gone into Lake Erie, while taking a boat ride at sunset, during a stay in a cottage with dear old friends, Vic and Eli, and their families. He's now in a glacial river in Montana, a nod to our anniversary trip to the Canadian Rockies, after I traveled with his sisters to Glacier National Park.

I'm happy to have the opportunity for just Gretchen and me to say our final goodbye, to celebrate the fact that we have made it through the past few years. The time feels right. We drive out to Hocking Hills, near to where we are staying for the weekend, and arguably the most scenic park area in Ohio, on a beautiful, blue-sky morning. The place is not yet filled with the large groups of visitors who will later be here as the day wears on. We hike along the trails, breathing in the sweet, crisp air and scenery. I feel the serenity in my surroundings that consumes me whenever I walk in the woods. It makes me smile inside. Here, there are also tall cliffs and small pools created by waterfalls calling out to the world with their roar. Birds join in the melody, while butterflies and bees flit about, enjoying the warmth of the early sun. Trees grow out of cracks in the rock walls, impossibly holding on and managing to stand upright with their roots woven into every nook and cranny.

We come to a bridge overlooking the river and gorge, stopping to take in the view. The sun streaks through the trees forming individual rays that shine down on the rocks and reflect off the moving water glittering below. It's breathtaking and peaceful. I turn to Gretchen. "What about here? It's beautiful, and we are high enough that Gregg boy can fly wherever he wants."

She nods in agreement. "I think Dad would love it."

I reach into the daypack she's wearing and pull out two containers that hold Gregg's remaining ashes, handing one to her. We lean on the railing, taking it all in once more, imprinting the moment in our hearts.

"You ready?" she asks, looking at me with a grin.

"Let's do it!"

With a giant swish, we take our ashes and throw them into the air at the same time. The breeze takes hold, and they are swept up high, lingering for a moment, suspended, shimmering in the sun's rays, and then gently lifted away, back into the arms of God.

Some say that those who have passed are not totally free to fly until the strings are severed from those still on earth. I wonder if we have held him back by hanging onto the remnants of his being for so long. I suppose I'll find out for sure when my time comes. It makes me happy that I am finally able to let him go and to know that even though it is sometimes hard for me to realize, I have, indeed, let the flow of life carry me forward. Where it eventually leads me is yet unknown. I continue to be a work in progress, as we all are.

We watch a while longer, lost in our own thoughts, conscious of yet another, but more final farewell. I feel the familiar tug of my heart, but also a wistfulness that has not been present before. Reaching over, I hug Gretchen, holding on longer than usual, then kiss her on the nose, and we walk on.

Afterword

All eyes were on me, waiting. I had been anticipating this moment for weeks now, what sage advice to pass on to my daughter, Gretchen, and her brand new husband on this most special of evenings. The night was warm and beautiful, the tent full of people dressed in their finery, sparkling lights surrounding us on the perimeter. I was aware of my heart thumping loudly as I stood alone in the spotlight, wondering if I would be able to get through my speech without falling apart. This place rightfully belonged to Gregg. He was the father of the bride and more comfortable in front of a crowd. He would have made people laugh easily with a few stories and a toast. But it was not to be, the job falling to me instead, doing my best to represent us both.

I looked at Gretchen and Mike directly across the tent from me. They smiled blissfully, whispering to each other, obviously thrilled with the occasion and happy to be the center of attention. Though the night was already filled with merriment and laughter, I felt it important to say something a bit more serious, about marriage and what makes it work. I didn't want them to take it lightly. It can be so easy to get wound up in the party and lose sight of the significance of the legal and emotional commitment a couple is making. Many thoughts had made their way through my mind, but none seemed a perfect fit. There were so many layers and nuances to consider. Should I tell them that now that they have made a commitment to each other, the world would be their oyster? That having a partner will only bring greater joy to their lives? That together, they could conquer anything? Should I mention the many challenges they will likely face: jobs, children, money, moves—and the big one I faced, illness? Should I say something about compromise and working together, knowing there's always the possibility that they may grow apart? Did I tell them to plan for the best and pray it all turned out? All of that could be right—and it still might not be what they needed to hear.

Finally, standing before my daughter and my new son-in-law and all their guests, I realized that beyond all the generalities and advice, all I really could do was share my own experience. It would be the most heartfelt and authentic wisdom I could offer. It was what I knew best.

"I think a lasting relationship is about finding your best friend," I began timidly, waiting for the words to come, hoping they would. "Someone in whose company you would rather be than anyone else's, who you can laugh with, play with, go on adventures with, cry with." Memories sprang to mind. I willed myself to focus, not wanting them to gain momentum, and instead, wrestled the quiver in my voice, measuring each phrase.

"Someone who you can talk to for hours without running out of things to say. Someone who has your back always, no matter whether you are being truly amazing or acting like an idiot." I smiled to myself as I heard Gregg's laugh in the back of my mind. "Someone with whom you share unconditional love, and at the same time, who encourages you to grow as an individual along your own path, not just as part of a couple. Finally, someone who believes in you and what you stand for— and who knows your heart." With that, I could feel my own heart swell with love, thinking of Gregg, of us, of what we had together. There was not a sound in the crowd. So many sitting around me now knew us well, had witnessed our journey, and could see my transparency. I glanced down at the makeshift, wooden dance floor, needing a minute to regain my composure.

"To me, if you're lucky enough to find this, you have found something truly extraordinary, your own little seed of paradise, and you need to cherish it, check in on it regularly, and nurture it, so that it can blossom and grow into something bigger and more beautiful with each passing year."

My eyes found the newlyweds again and I smiled, filled with emotion. Their faces were intent on mine, yet contemplative at the same time. I wondered what private thoughts were floating through their heads. They would have to find their own way, I knew. I was grateful they had good role models in each set of parents to help them see beyond any major bumps in the road.

"Gretchen and Mike, tonight, you have your little piece of paradise. Hold it close to your hearts, and it will serve you well for whatever life brings your way. And always remember what a special moment this is and how blessed you both are to be surrounded by so many friends and family who love you—for in the end, there is no greater gift they could give."

A renegade tear escaped and tumbled down my cheek. Without the tangibility of his body, Gregg's spirit was surely present in this space, with all those he loved so well in life. I knew Gretchen could feel him, too. There seemed to be nothing left to say beyond a final salute. I raised my hand in the air. "*We* wish you happiness always." I laid down the microphone vaguely aware of a standing ovation, walked over and embraced them both. The future was theirs to create.

Acknowledgements

Writing this book wasn't something I ever thought I would do, yet here it is, and I am so grateful for the wherewithal to accomplish it, especially without the immediate push, feedback, and support from Gregg, my "front man." The process of reflection along with remembering, researching, and rereading journals was at times excruciatingly sad, but also made me laugh, as if to remind me of the breadth of our connection once again. Looking back at the loss of my husband and dear partner all these years later gave me yet one more perspective, as well as the gift of healing further aspects of myself that hadn't yet seen the light of day.

Throughout my life, I have managed to produce a number of examples of my writing, usually in the form of poetry, most often inspired by people or events, from my first Mother's Day poem in second grade, through the angst of relationships, to expressing love for my family members, and, finally, to connect with myself in my journals. Recipients of my words have often commented to me that they were moved in some way, giving me courage I was unsure of. Finally, a high school friend and fellow author whose husband is dealing with his own health issues suggested that I write a book for people like her. I believe that was the turning point for me. So, thank you, Jane Davis, for offering the words I needed to hear to inspire me and to acknowledge within me that others could benefit from hearing my story.

I also want to thank the many friends and family members who were kind enough to read the various drafts of my manuscript, Marty Orcutt, Marcia Orcutt, Mat Orcutt, Alison Orcutt, Linda Mullikin, Carol Miller, Kari Foreman, Frank and Sandi Bates, Abby Mullikin, and Sherry Horton. You all patiently answered my questions and offered me your perspective along with words of encouragement when I wasn't sure anyone would manage to even make it to the end.

Gretchen Proctor, you gave me some great ideas and things to consider and think about. I love you and appreciate your common sense and all of the support that you gave and continue to give, not only with this book, but in my life. I am so blessed to have you in my world.

Thanks to Heidi Thorne, who was the first person to critique it from an outsider/editor's point of view and who gave me high praise indeed, a major boost to my confidence, giving me a new view of myself as a writer and storyteller, monikers I had never donned before.

I am grateful to Mary Maynard, Annette Hemminger, and Annita Keane for gently nudging me forward in seeing my unique gifts and what I had to offer the world and for providing me resources. Thanks to my Shamanic Reiki group for your support. Diana M. Needham was indispensable in mentoring me through the many steps of publishing and marketing. A great many thanks to my editors, Laura L. Bush, PhD, Wendy Ledger, and, especially, Holly Welker, PhD, who miraculously managed to hone my message into the work it is today. I greatly appreciate everything you ladies have taught me.

Common Ground, you will always be in my heart. Gregg would be so touched that so many now face their own fears in the yearly firewalk. And finally, thanks to all of you who were with Gregg, Gretchen, and me on this journey. Your love and support held us together more than you know.

About the Author

Image Credit: Jessica Lowman

Deborah Gilder holds B.S and M.A degrees in Speech and Language Sciences from Ohio University and Kent State University, respectively. She is a retired school speech/language pathologist. The experience of working with energy to help her husband through his illness has led her to become a shamanic reiki master. Through this work, she hopes to help others through their journeys. Her natural curiosity about the mysteries of life keeps her on an ever-evolving path of finding and expressing her own truth. She enjoys traveling, hiking, kayaking, music, reading, gardening, metaphysics, and spending time with friends and family. She lives in northern Ohio.